French Discourse Analysis

ACKNOWLEDGEMENTS

We would like to thank the following for permission to quote:

Le Monde, Le Figaro, La Croix, Libération, Marie Claire and *Télérama* (various extracts), *Le Journal du Dimanche* for 'Jeremy Irons le Chinois', 1997; Editions Gallimard for quoting from Simone de Beauvoir, *Tout compte fait*, Albert Camus, *L'Éntranger* and *L'Exile et le royaume*, J.M.G. Le Clézio, *Désert* and *La Guerre*, Annie Ernaux, *La Place* and *La Femme gelée*, Eugène Ionesco, *Tueur sans Gages*, Violette Leduc, *L'Affamée*, Francis Ponge, *Le Parti pris des choses* and Jacques Prévert, *Paroles*; Editions Bernard Grasset for Benoîte Groult, *Ainsi soit-elle* and Pascal Bruckner, *La Tentation de l'innocence* and *L'Euphorie perpétuelle*; Editions du Seuil for Azouz Begag, *Le Gone du Chaâba*, 1986, Tahar Ben Jelloun, *Les Yeux baissés*, 1991 and Jean-Pierre Richard, *Onze Etudes sur la poésie moderne*, 1964; Librairie Arthème Fayard for Julia Kristeva, *Sens et non-sens de la révolte*.

In addition, permission was obtained from Madame Brulot for the reproduction of *Le Moulin de l'Abbaye* and *Brantôme*: *La Venise du Périgord*; from *Candia*, Campagne européenne de diffusion de produits lactés; and CEDELAC S.A. for *Une Femme qui boit Silhouette ça se voit*.

Every possible effort has been made to trace and acknowledge ownership of copyright; we apologise for any omissions and would welcome these being brought to our attention.

Monique L'Huillier

Bronwen Martin

Raynalle Udris

French Discourse Analysis

PHILOMEL

French Discourse Analysis

co-authors: Monique L'Huillier, Bronwen Martin, Raynalle Udris
First edition 2000
Published by **Philomel Productions Ltd**

Philomel Productions Ltd
Contact address: 1, Queen's Gate Place Mews,
London SW7 5BG, U.K.
Tel: 020 7581 2303   Fax: 020 7589 2264
e-mail: markphilomel@productnews.co.uk

ISBN 1 898685 39 8

British Library Cataloguing in Publication Data
A catalogue record for this book is available from the British Library

TABLE OF CONTENTS

PREFACE

French Discourse Analysis is aimed primarily at final year university students of French and at teachers of French at all levels. However, the book does allow for flexibility in its usage and, approached selectively, may prove a valuable asset to younger students. Its fundamental premise, based on recent research, is that students of all ages benefit from:

a) a more explicit understanding of the linguistic devices that shape language

b) an increased awareness of the importance of social context and function in the production of meaning.

The chapters of the book can be taught consecutively as part of a twelve-week module, or they may be studied individually according to the needs of particular classes. Readers might find it useful to consult the glossary at the end of the book, where key linguistic terms are defined, and the French equivalent terminology is given, so as to facilitate reference to French grammar books.

It will become apparent that our methodological approach draws upon a variety of contemporary influences, in particular:

a) the work of M.A.K. Halliday

b) contemporary developments in discourse analysis in France, including the work of D. Maingueneau

c) contemporary developments in the Paris School of Semiotics (see Chapter 9).

The texts chosen for analysis include literary extracts, newspaper articles and advertisements.

The symbols used in the book are:

- a slash / to indicate an alternative
- square brackets [ ] to indicate an optional part of an utterance
- an asterisk * to indicate an ungrammatical or otherwise unacceptable utterance in the given context
- a question mark ? at the beginning of an utterance to indicate that it is not immediately acceptable or interpretable, or that the register is not appropriate
- round brackets ( ) to indicate an explanation
- an arrow ⟶ to indicate a possible transformation or an implication.

CHAPTER 1

NOTION OF TEXT;
INTRODUCTION TO COHESION AND COHERENCE

INTRODUCTION

The aim of this chapter is to provide a comprehensive overview of the linguistic concepts with which we shall be working in this book. You will be given the opportunity to practice your skills, principally in the assignments at the end of the chapter.

1. What is a text?

A text is a passage of any length, spoken or written, that forms a coherent whole and that makes sense. Unlike a series of random sentences, the parts of a text must fit together: phrases, clauses, sentences and paragraphs must somehow be linked.

In addition a text possesses a function, and its meanings are further determined by the broader context in which it appears and by the registers that have been chosen. For instance, a text such as the Highway Code is of an expository and didactic nature, a recipe is largely instructional, a political speech or advert is predominently persuasive, the recounting of an accident is a narrative, etc. The type or function of a text must always be identified at the beginning of an analysis, as each discourse type shares certain characteristics that distinguish it from other discourse types.

Worked example:

Decide whether each of the following short passages form a text, giving your reasons. Where possible, state the function or type of discourse and suggest a possible context.

a) *« Bonjour », m'a-t-il dit, « comment vas-tu aujourd'hui? »*
b) *Wagon-lit*
c) *Albert a acheté un chien. Les mouches ont six pattes.*
d *Perdre dans la neige.*
e) *Silence!*
f) *Demain peut-être.*
g) *Prenez un kilo de carottes. Collez les deux bords l'un sur l'autre.*
h) *Rien ne sert de courir, il faut partir à point.*
i) *Joli immeuble, mais un peu dénudé. Marie sort son journal de sa poche. Repère l'adresse. L'écrit dans son agenda.*

Suggested answers:

a) Yes, it forms a text. The phrases are linked through their use of pronouns. We recognize it as a dialogue extract, possibly from a novel written in the first person.

b) Yes, it could be a word written on a train, whose function is mainly directive and didactic. The intention is to impart information and to guide passengers towards their desired goal.

c) No, or with great difficulty. The two sentences are not linked in any way. It is therefore difficult to construct any context, and the words appear as nonsense.

d) No, the words make no grammatical sense and there is no plausible context.

e) Yes, this could be a sign: an order or an instruction.

f) Yes, it could be an answer to a question, i.e. part of a dialogue.

g) No, although it is possible to construct a context for the first five words, i.e. a recipe. The absence of any logical or referential link – explicit or implicit – between the two sentences can be seen as a source of humour.

h) Yes, the sentence is in fact a proverb. The recognition of its meaning would largely depend on cultural context and on the cultural knowledge of the receiver or addressee.

i) Yes, these sentences could well form part of the stage instructions in a play. The links between the sentences are largely implicit. In the final sentence however, these links are strengthened by the use of the pronoun *l'* referring back to the *adresse* in the third.

It is not always easy to ascertain whether a passage or sentence constitutes a text. This is because readers, in an effort to make sense of the text, invariably seek to construct links. These links may be based on their own implicit assumptions. A text in which no such links can be made is deemed to be incoherent.

What is the difference between text cohesion and text coherence?

Cohesion describes the **explicit** process whereby sentences or utterances are linked together to form a text. Cohesive devices (ties) are, therefore, those words or phrases which enable the writer/speaker to establish relationships across sentence or utterance boundaries and which help to link the different parts of the text together. Continuity of meaning is thus achieved.

Coherence, on the other hand, relates to all those links that are **implicit** such as reference to cultural and historical context or reference to underlying models or schemata. The implicit plays a key role in the construction of meaning: a text that relied solely on surface linguistic linking devices would not make sense.

PART I: COHESION

There are various types of cohesion. We will consider two types: grammatical and lexical.

Grammatical Cohesion

Here, cohesion is produced through the use of particular grammatical devices. These are listed in Sections 2 to 6.

2. Contextual reference: coreference and contrast

These relationships are expressed with the help of 'reference words'. Reference words do not have a full meaning in their own right. To work out what they mean on a particular occasion, we have to 'refer' to something else. Reference words can be: personal pronouns, demonstratives, possessives, definite articles and comparatives. Note that coreference can also be expressed lexically: see 5. Reiteration in *Lexical Cohesion*.

2.1. Personal pronouns

These are the subject personal pronouns (*je, tu, il, elle, nous, vous, ils, elles*) along with their object forms (*me, te, lui*, etc.) and 'emphatic' forms (*moi, toi*, etc.)

Whereas the first person refers directly to the speaker and the second person to the interlocutor, the third person generally points backwards to the preceding text.

Ex: *Un homme est entré. **Il** s'est dirigé vers le bar.*

Here, *il* is **anaphoric** (see Section 2.4) and points to *un homme*. There is **coreference** between *un homme* and *il*. Such an anaphoric relationship creates cohesion. The two sentences are linked into a coherent unit.

The same is true for the object form of these pronouns.

Ex: *Catherine est venue me voir. Je **lui** ai dit que...*

2.2. Demonstratives and definite articles

Demonstrative determiners (*ce, cet, cette, ces*) and pronouns (*celui, celle, ceci, cela*, etc.) can be used to point at something (see 8.1. Situational reference, in Part II, Coherence).

Ex: *Regarde **ce** chat!*
      *Donnez-moi **ceci**!*

They can also be used **anaphorically** (see section 2.4) to point backwards to the preceding text, i.e. the linguistic context.

Ex: *Hier, on m'a remis <u>un</u> rapport. **Ce** rapport précise que...*

This is called **contextual reference**.

Note that the compound forms of the demonstrative pronouns (*celui-ci, celle-là*, etc.) can be used anaphorically to express **contrast** (see also Section 2.6) rather than coreference.

Ex: <u>*Les steaks*</u> *sont prêts. Tu veux **celui-ci** ou **celui-là**?*

Definite articles (*le, la, les*) can be considered as particular types of demonstratives.

Ex: *Ouvre **la** porte!*
      <u>*Un*</u> *homme est entré. **L'** homme s'est dirigé vers moi.*

In all these cases, the referent, i.e. the object of the world referred to, is **identified**. Hence identification can be achieved either in the situation, i.e. the 'surrounding world' (see 8.1. Situational reference, in Coherence) or in the linguistic context (contextual reference). In any given text, there will normally be a mixture of both situational and contextual references.

2.3. Possessives

Possessives, like definite articles and demonstratives, belong to the class of specific determiners. They determine, i.e. **identify** a referent (see Section 2.2 above), in this case the 'thing possessed'. Possessive adjectives (*mon, ma, mes*, etc.) agree in gender and number with the 'thing possessed', and in person and number with the possessor(s).

Ex: *la fille de Paul: **sa** fille*

sa agrees in gender and number with *fille*, i.e. feminine singular, and in person and number with *Paul*, i.e. 3rd person singular.

Note that possessive pronouns can be used anaphorically to express **contrast** (see also Section 2.6. Comparatives) rather than coreference. In the following examples:

Ex: *La robe de Martine est blanche; **la mienne** est rouge.*

la mienne points anaphorically to *la robe de Martine* but it is not the same dress! Hence the gender is the same, but the number may differ.

Ex: *Tes chats sont sympathiques, mais je préfère **le mien**.*

In the following example however, the possessive pronoun is used to express coreference:

Ex: *Ce chat est **le mien**!*

2.4. Anaphora and cataphora

Note that whilst an **anaphora** is an item which refers **back** to a previously mentioned item (see examples above), a **cataphora** is an element that points **forward**. The cataphoric reference is frequently signalled in writing with a colon.

Ex: *Je **le** sais: elle ne m'aime plus.*

Here, *le* is a cataphora which cannot be understood without the knowledge of the second clause *elle ne m'aime plus*.

Ex: ***Sa voix grinçante** rendait Sylvie antipathique.*

Here, the possessive is a cataphora whose referent – *Sylvie* – can only be found later on in the sentence.

2.5. Ellipsis

Another common cohesive device in texts is to leave out a word or phrase rather than repeat it. In other words ellipsis occurs when some essential structural element is omitted from a sentence or clause and can only be recovered by referring to an element in the preceding text. It is used in conversation as a matter of course.

Ex: *Moi, je préfère **la verte***
could follow something like:
– *J'aime la robe bleue*
i.e. *Moi, je préfère la [robe] verte.*
or:

– ***Vous aussi***
could follow:
– *Vous travaillez trop*

i.e. *Vous [travaillez trop] aussi.*

– *Tout droit! (= Il faut aller tout droit!)*

– *Autre chose? (= Vous désirez autre chose?)*

Ellipsis is also to be found in coordination and comparatives.

Ex: *Dizzy attrape des oiseaux et Lizzy [attrape] des souris.*
Paul est plus grand que [qu'il ne l'était] l'année dernière.

2.6. Comparatives

Whereas personal pronouns, demonstratives, possessives and definite articles set up a relation of coreference (when used anaphorically), comparatives set up a relation of **contrast**. (See also cases when demonstrative and possessive pronouns are used to express contrast in Sections 2.2 and 2.3). Hence the same entity is no longer being referred to over again, but is being compared to another entity, which may be the same or different, equal or unequal, more or less, etc.

All the words or expressions used presume some standard of reference in the preceding text:

> *le/la/les même(s), un/une autre*
> *pareil, différent, semblable*
> *aussi/plus/moins beau que*, etc.

Ex: *Je me suis acheté une robe chez Kookai. J'ai vu que Martine avait **la même** que moi.*

la même in *J'ai vu que Martine avait la même que moi* can only be understood in relation to the preceding sentence.

Ex: *Il reste deux croissants. **En** voulez-vous **un autre**?*

en and *un autre* in *En voulez-vous un autre?* can only be understood in relation to the preceding sentence.

Note that comparative reference items can also be used cataphorically.

Ex: *Dizzy a un **plus** gros appétit que Lizzy.*

Dizzy a un plus gros appétit can only be understood in relation to what follows: *que Lizzy.*

3. Connectors and punctuation

3.1. Connectors

Some words are used to indicate a specific connection between different parts of a text. These can be conjunctions, adverbs or adverb phrases. These words are used to establish a cohesive connection between the ideas expressed in a discourse and as such can set up many different links in a text.

Connectors can for instance:

 – establish a spatial or temporal link

*La maison les avait séduits. **En haut** on trouvait une salle de bain luxueuse; **en bas** un salon confortable **où** on pouvait se reposer en toute quiétude.*

***D'abord** on a entendu des coups de feu **puis** les gens se sont mis à courir.*

 – justify or confirm an idea

*Il lui avait dit qu'il ne viendrait pas les rejoindre à la mer. Il avait **en effet** beaucoup trop de travail à faire pendant ce week-end et il avait **justement** besoin de ces quelques jours.*

 – set up an alternative

*Malheureusement, ce soir-là ils ne pouvaient offrir **ni** desserts **ni** fromages; ils se sont vus contraints d'offrir **soit** des glaces **soit** des sorbets.*

3.2. Punctuation

Although flexible in its usage, punctuation is a standard device frequently employed to reinforce other cohesive devices. Its absence, a characteristic of some contemporary writing, serves to strengthen the immediacy or emotional impact of a text.

Compare, for instance, the title of this advert (see full advertisement in Chapter 7, Section 3.1):

«*Ma tranquillité, je ne l'ai pas volée: je l'ai enfin trouvée avec l'alarme Daitem.*»
(*Télérama*, 20 September 1995)

in which the speech marks signal the direct intervention of the speaker, the comma reinforces the anaphoric link between *tranquillité* and the direct object pronoun *l'* while the colon announces the explanation for the first part of the statement, with this extract from a poem by Apollinaire, in which the lack of punctuation is used as a device to emphasize the lexical fields of the text (see Chapter 6 for details on Lexical fields) and to create the impression of an uninterrupted flow:

> *Sous le pont Mirabeau coule la Seine*
> *Et nos amours*
> *Faut-il qu'il m'en souvienne*
> *Le jour venait toujours après la peine*
>
> *Vienne la nuit sonne l'heure*
> *Les jours s'en vont je demeure*

4. Verbs and tense cohesion (tense, aspect, modality)

What is expressed or referred to by a verb when it is used in discourse is called a **process**.

Modalisation is the process by which speakers convey their attitudes towards what they say to their interlocutors. This is done through **moods** (indicative, subjunctive...), but also through parts of speech such as adverbs. Compare:

Je viendrai demain (a certainty)

and:

*Je viendrai **peut-être** demain* (a possibility)

Aspect expresses the way a process is realised. It results from an interpretation of what the speaker says. Compare for instance:

J'ai accouru

which is perfective (i.e. the process is envisaged to its completion) and accomplished (the process has been completed)

and:

Je cours

which is imperfective (i.e. the process is taking place over a period of time whose limits are not part of the meaning of the verb) and non-accomplished (i.e. the process has not been completed yet).

Through verb forms, **tenses** express temporal values (past, present, future), but also aspectual and modal ones. For instance:

– the imperfect tense can be used aspectually to express the background for events. Compare:

*Je **traversais** la rue quand une voiture **a démarré***

and:

*J'**ai traversé** la rue quand une voiture **démarrait**.*

– the future tense can have the modal value of probability.

Ex: *On sonne: ce **sera** Paul.*

equivalent to: *ce **doit être** Paul* (it probably is Paul.)

Finally, parts of speech can also situate their referents in time in relation to the moment of speaking.

Ex: *l'**ancien** président; le **futur** pape*

where the adjectives *ancien* and *futur* express respectively the past and the future in time.

Lexical Cohesion

Lexical cohesion occurs when two words or phrases in a text are semantically related in some way, i.e. they are related in terms of their meaning. The two major categories of lexical cohesion are reiteration and lexical fields.

5. Reiteration

Reiteration includes the following devices:

a) Repetition

Repeating key words or phrases can help to make a text coherent.

Ex: *L'**augmentation** des allocations familiales est nécessaire. Sans cette **augmentation**, les pauvres s'appauvriront.*

b) Synonyms and lexical anaphoras

A synonym is a word that has the same meaning or is very close in meaning to another word.

Ex: *Elle a essayé de monter **la côte** en première mais **la pente** était trop forte.*

A lexical anaphora is a word (or sequence of words) which, in the context in which it appears, has a similar or related meaning to another one and refers to the same 'object of the world' (see also Chapter 5. Reiteration, section 2).

Ex: *LES REBELLES ZAÏROIS ENTRENT DANS KINSHASA*

• *Les troupes de M. Kabila ont gagné la capitale du Zaïre au lendemain de la fuite de M. Mobutu*

• *Le «numéro deux» de l'Alliance rebelle se prononce pour une «conférence nationale» rassemblant toute l'opposition*

• *Enquête: comment le dictateur zaïrois a construit sa fortune.*

(*Le Monde*, 18-19 May 1997)

Les troupes de M. Kabila refer to *Les rebelles zaïrois* of the title, *la capitale du Zaïre* refers to *Kinshasa, Le «numéro deux» de l'Alliance rebelle* refers in turn to *M. Kabila; le dictateur zaïrois* refers to *M. Mobutu.*

c) Superordinates, hyponyms and generals

In the following examples:

*Le **Brésil** avait été touché par la Dépression et le **pays** était à deux doigts d'un complet désastre.*

*Veux-tu un **kiwi**? Merci, je n'aime pas ces **fruits**.*

Brésil is a specific instance of the more general word, *pays*, and *kiwi* is a specific instance of the more general word *fruit*. The general word is called the **superordinate** and the more specific one is called a **hyponym**.

Hence the superordinate 'animal' could have 'mammal', 'reptile', 'amphibian' as hyponyms. In turn, the superordinate 'mammal' could have 'cat', 'dog', 'monkey' as hyponyms.

Superordinates can also take the form of very **general** words like 'people', 'things', referring back to something particular.

 — *As-tu déjà mangé des **hot-dogs**?*
— *Oui, mais je n'aime pas beaucoup ce genre de **bouffe**.*

6. Lexical fields and figures of speech

A lexical field is formed by grouping together items in a text that are semantically related or that have a meaning in common.

For instance, the words 'plants', 'organic' and 'sunlight' all belong to the lexical field of 'biology'.

Lexical cohesion can be strengthened through the use of figures of speech, such as:

Metaphors

The term metaphor designates the procedure whereby a given sentential unit is substituted for another, thereby transforming its original semantic charge. In other words, a substitute name or descriptive expression is transferred to some object/person to which it is not literally applicable: 'pilgrimage' is employed, for example, instead of 'life', 'burning fire' instead of 'love', or 'lamb' to describe a child. In a particular text, the notion of death could be suggested by lexical items drawn from a wide variety of fields such as the colour black, coldness, a frozen lake, the river Lethe. It can also be said that the above items 'connote' death or are 'connotations' of death (see below).

Simile, metonymy and **hyperbole** can be examined in a similar light:

– A **simile** is an explicit comparison between two different items using words such as 'like' or 'as' (*comme* in French).

Ex: *Elle était belle **comme** le jour.*

Verbs can also introduce a simile.

Ex: *L'appartement **ressemblait à** une belle femme en haillons.*
    (Balzac, *Le curé de Tours*.)

– **Metonymy** designates the procedure whereby a given lexical unit is substituted for another with which it entertains a relationship of contiguity, i.e. cause for effect, container for contained, part for the whole, etc. For instance, we may use 'pen' to denote the notion of 'author', 'sail' for 'ship' or refer to the 'crown' to indicate the governing power in a monarchy.

Ex: *Il aime trop la bouteille.*
where *la bouteille* refers to *boissons alcoolisées*.

– **Hyperbole** is an exaggeration for the sake of emphasis. It is a figure of speech which should not be taken literally!

Ex: *Je meurs/crève de faim.*
Literally: I am dying of hunger.

Connotation refers to a procedure whereby a term, in addition to meanings allotted to it in a dictionary (**denotative** meanings), acquires additional significance resulting from the context in which it is used. In this sense, the adjective 'white', apart from **denoting** a colour, might **connote** 'absence', 'purity', 'spirituality', 'death', etc. depending on the conditions of its application.

The distinction between connotative and denotative terms is frequently blurred. It may be useful to look for **oppositions** between the lexical fields; terms connoting 'life' can be opposed to those connoting 'death' for example.

Visual representation

A similar process of grouping together under a common heading items such as objects and colours in a picture (as in advertisements and book covers) can be undertaken. These groups are termed **semantic fields**. (Although the terms 'semantic' and 'lexical' are loosely interchangeable, we may prefer to use the term 'semantic' in the context of visual/pictorial representation, reserving 'lexical' for the written word). For instance, the visual representation of a broken-down car, a tatty dress or a ramshackle house could all come under the heading of 'poverty'.

Typography

It is not unusual that a variety of character fonts as well as their size and style reinforce the cohesive devices used in a text (particularly in advertisements and press headlines or indeed textbooks) by drawing attention to the core message or some particular items of that text. The use of different titles and subtitles, sometimes up to three in newspaper articles, all using a different typography, is also often used as a cohesive device. Its emphasis on the core message of the text contributes to the newspaper's saleable value.

PART II: COHERENCE

The things we know about the world assist us in our interpretation of a text. Coherence, then, relates to background knowledge and particular situations. It includes those implicit assumptions and presuppositions without which a text would be meaningless (however many explicit cohesive devices were brought into play). Briefly, the notion of coherence covers the following areas:

7. Presence of the speaker

The principal focus here will be on some strategies of enunciation. By enunciation is meant the process of communication between a speaker and an interlocutor. One must therefore begin by examining the **explicit** traces which reveal the presence of the speaker.

These can be detected in the following linguistic items:

7.1. Deictics

– The first and second person personal pronouns: *je, tu, nous, vous*. These pronouns are a means of involving the reader and of breaking down the boundaries between text and the 'real'.

– The demonstrative determiners: *ce(t), cette, ces*.

– Adverbs that only make sense in relation to the speaker (enunciative instance) such as *ici, maintenant, aujourd'hui, hier*.

Ex. **Aujourd'hui** *maman est morte, ou peut-être* **hier**, *je ne sais pas.*

(Albert Camus, *L'Étranger*)

*Je suis seul ici, **maintenant**, bien à l'abri. **Dehors**, il pleut, **dehors** on marche sous la pluie en courbant la tête…; **Dehors** il y a du soleil; il n'y a pas un arbre, ni un arbuste.*

(Alain Robbe-Grillet, *Dans le labyrinthe*)

7.2. Use of tenses

The verb tenses are organised around the present of the speaker.

Ex: *Tout mon être s'est tendu et j'ai crispé ma main sur le révolver. La gâchette a cédé, j'ai touché le ventre poli de la crosse et c'est là, dans le bruit à la fois sec et assourdissant que tout a commencé.*
(Albert Camus, *L'Étranger*)

Here for instance, the use of the perfect tense draws attention to the subjective experience of time which is presented explicitly in relationship to a speaker. A spoken, conversational register is also evoked: as with deictics, the reader is more directly involved, the boundaries between the 'text' and the 'real' are blurred.

7.3. Evaluative and modalizing terms

Evaluative and emotive terms imply a judgement or a particular attitude on the part of the speaker.

Ex: *La nouvelle baisse des prix vers l'international, c'est **vraiment bien**; les prix sont encore plus bas aux moments qui m'intéressent **le plus**.*
(from a Telecom advert)

Modalizing adverbs such as *peut-être, sans doute, sûrement,* or adjectives such as *possible, probable, certain,* likewise draw our attention to the narrator's viewpoint.

7.4. Quotations

There could be more than one speaker in the text. These voices could strengthen or conflict with that of the narrator. In newspaper articles, quotations are often used to support the argument of the narrator.

Ex: *'C'est un camp de concentration', a estimé le député social-démocrate Pavel Dostal, en rappelant que 'c'est ainsi que les nazis avaient commencé leur «solution» de la question juive.'*
(Martin Plichta)

The use of quotations can also sometimes be a means of dissociating oneself from a statement (lack of familiarity with a particular neologism, plain disagreement with the choice of word(s) used, etc.). The presence of the speaker can thus be felt in the distancing effect produced.

Ex: *Le gouvernement a fixé ses conditions à un dialogue avec les rebelles «Zapatistes», qui consistent à cesser le feu et à une remise de leurs armes.* (*Le Monde,* 7 January 1994)

(The quotation marks around *solution* in our first example have a similar distancing effect.)

7.5. Other traces of the speaker

You should also look for other, **implicit**, traces of the speaker in the text. For example, its hidden presence can be detected through the image of the reader that is constructed. In its particular choice of vocabulary, a tabloid newspaper like *The Sun* might create the image of a working class reader in possession of a stereotyped set of social attitudes (towards women, race, etc). For instance, references to women frequently construct the semantic field of 'sex object'. The following were all found in *The Sun,* 5 May 1998: 'a blonde model', 'former Wonderbra girl', 'the US beauty', 'the World's Hottest Blonde', 'Winning Cups', 'ex-Girlie show hostess', 'a romp with the supermodel. . .'

It must not be forgotten that the choice of pronouns in a text is a conscious decision adopted by the author in order to produce a particular persuasive effect. There may, for instance, be little resemblance between the *je* used in a text (the fictive stance) and the true historical *je* outside the text. Each speaker seeks through language to construct an image of herself/himself. Indeed, many texts are characterised by a process of mystification, that is of hiding from the reader the true enunciative source. This is true, for example, of adverts, where the choice of a *nous* can produce a familiar, chatty tone (register) involving the addressee in an immediate, personal experience. The true source of the advert, the company, remains hidden behind this stance. The use of personal pronouns here is one of the many means by which the reader is being seduced into carrying out a specific action, i.e. making a particular purchase.

8. Situational reference and cultural assumptions

8.1. Situational reference

Items do not necessarily need a linguistic context to be identified. A special mention should be made of elements which can only be identified **in relation to**

the speaker: *je, ici, maintenant, hier, demain*, etc. (also called **deictics**: see Section 7.1).

Ex: **Demain, je** *vais à Paris.*

- *Demain* can only be understood in relation to the moment when the speaker says *demain*.

- *je* is whoever says *Demain, je vais à Paris.*

Other 'objects' which can be identified in the situation include:
- proper nouns, e.g. 'Paris', 'Winston Churchill' (but see also Chapter 2, Section 1, NB(2), where an explanatory apposition may be needed)
- unique objects in our world, e.g. *le soleil, la lune*
- abstract words, e.g. *l'amour, la beauté*
- concrete words taken in their abstract sense, e.g. *l'or, le marbre, le sang*, or in their generic sense, e.g. *l'homme, le singe* (as in *l'homme descend du singe*)
- complete dates, e.g. *le 14 juillet 1989* (See also Section 8.2).

Finally, objects pointed to by the speaker (**exophora**) or unambiguously identified by the interlocutor:

Ex: *Où sont **les chats**?* (for instance the speaker's own or his/her interlocutor's cats)
*Regarde **ce chat**!* (the speaker points at a particular cat)
*Passe-moi **le vin** s'il te plaît!* (the one which is on the dining table)
*Fermez **la porte**!* (the only one to be open in the room where both speaker and interlocutor are).

8.2. Cultural knowledge and assumptions

This could include references to individual people or places as well as implicit assumptions concerning human behaviour.

Ex: 'I've never been out with anyone even though Mum says I'm quite pretty.' (quoted from a girl of 14 in the problem page, *Blue Jean*, No 488, 24 May 1986).

This statement could only make sense within a particular society (Western and contemporary). It takes for granted a set of assumptions concerning human behaviour, assumptions which might be quite different in, for example, an Asian community.

Newspapers often resort to cultural puns in their headlines. For instance, when Ken Livingstone was elected Mayor of London in May 2000, some newspapers wrote headlines like: 'They've elected Kenny! The bastards!', a direct reference to 'Kenny', one of the characters in the popular cartoon 'South Park', who meets a sticky end at the end of most episodes, when his friends then cry out: 'They've killed Kenny! The bastards!'

9. Textual schemata

Coherence also relates to structures of meaning that pre-exist a particular text and that account for underlying patterns of organisation. These structures function as mental models or mind-sets. The most general of these is what is known as story grammar or a fundamental logic of human behaviour. Without the assumption of this logic (expressed in narrative models) no text can make sense. For example, in the sentence 'He took careful aim and shot the man dead', we assume that:

a) the man has acquired a gun ('he')

b) he knows how to shoot

c) he has a motive for the shooting.

The most fundamental narrative model is that of the quest where a subject (person or animal) goes in pursuit of an object of desire.

10. Register and genre

Our interpretation of a given text is strongly influenced by the genre (type or category) into which it falls and by its overall function within society. We read a poem differently from a recipe: the assumptions we bring to the text are different. For instance, we expect to get some information about how to carry out a task from a recipe but not from a poem.

Together with cohesive devices, register is what helps define a passage of discourse as a text and what gives it its coherence. Register can vary at the lexical (use of vocabulary) as well as at the syntactic (sentence formation) level, with a greater or lesser degree of formality depending on the situational context.

The reader's expectation of a given text is itself determined by factors such as:

• the identification of the purpose of the text: a political speech will for instance try to convince, while a political press correspondent will mostly comment, inform or evaluate;

• the degree of lexical specificity of the text: a report about a war will require a different vocabulary from an article about the economic state of the country;

• the coherence of the text register or the degree of language formality between narrator and reader: the adolescent writing to his best friend about appreciating the latest prized film is likely to use more informal lexical and

31

grammatical forms than the critical report about the same film in a film magazine.

These features – purpose of the text, lexical specificity and register – are some of the aspects which contribute to the appreciation of textual genres. The journalistic piece about the latest cars on the market will, for instance, differ significantly from an advert for one of these cars. Similarly, within the literary field, an autobiographical text uses rather different narrative devices from those used by the thriller or poetical genres.

PART III: PUTTING IT ALL TOGETHER

It is clear that there is a large measure of overlap in the elements which have been listed in relation to coherence and cohesion. You will only be expected to focus on those elements you feel are most significant in a given text. Moreover it is not the intention of this book to give a comprehensive account of textual coherence. Our aim is simply to draw your attention to the notion of the implicit and to the role that **background knowledge** must always play in the construction of meaning.

11. Titles

Titles too can play a role in establishing patterns of coherence and cohesion (see Typography in Section 6).

12. Texts

Full texts with their titles can be analysed in a comprehensive fashion, using all the relevant cohesive devices and the various aspects linked to coherence mentioned in this book. Through the full analysis of a given text (which may be as diverse as an article, a letter, a literary extract, an advert, etc.), interrelations between cohesion and coherence can be shown. You can thus become aware of the specificity of the text in question and of the particular way in which the message has been constructed.

ASSIGNMENTS

The following exercises are designed to help raise your awareness of some of the main notions of coherence and cohesion presented in this chapter. You may practise first with the questions and check your answers with the suggested answers at the end of each chapter, or you may work with the questions and suggested answers at the same time, if more appropriate.

Text 1: *Europe plurilingue* (leaflet advertising magazine)

Study the cohesion and coherence of the following text; the accompanying questions will help you in this task.

> * *EUROPE PLURILINGUE* * *MEHRSPRACHIGES EUROPA* *
> * *PLURILINGUAL EUROPE* * *EUROPA PLURILINGUE* *
>
> *Créée en 1991 par l'Association pour le Rayonnement des Langues Européennes (ARLE), la revue EUROPE PLURILINGUE est à ce jour la seule publication européenne réellement multilingue. Elle se veut un carrefour d'idées dans lequel vous êtes invités à vous exprimer et à répondre à ceux qui s'y expriment dans les 11 langues officielles de l'Union Européenne.*
>
> *En manifestant votre intérêt ou votre engagement pour la défense et l'illustration de ces langues et de ces cultures, vous nous aiderez à répondre à une attente, à agir de façon concrète pour que l'Europe offre une alternative à l'uniformisation, dans un esprit de complémentarité et non de concurrence. Vous contribuerez à rendre possible notre objectif, qui est de satisfaire, sur le plan culturel, le besoin d'information et la liberté d'expression de chacun.*
>
> *Nous vous proposons donc un lieu de réflexion, d'échanges d'idées et de projets sur la communication interculturelle avec nos partenaires européens. Nous sommes persuadés que cette communication doit être fondée sur la reconnaissance de ses composantes linguistiques et sur la promesse de leur enrichissement réciproque.*
>
> *Participez à notre dialogue. Abonnez-vous afin de recevoir dès maintenant le dernier numéro paru dont nous vous invitons à découvrir le sommaire.*
>
> *La Rédaction*

COHESION

Grammatical Cohesion

1) Find examples of the following and say what they refer to:
   a) demonstrative determiners and pronouns.
   b) third person personal pronouns and possessive determiners.

Lexical Cohesion

2) Make a list of all those words that relate:
   a) to language (i.e. the lexical field of language). Begin with the word *plurilingue* in the title.
   b) to communication. Begin with *un carrefour d'idées* in the first paragraph.

COHERENCE

Presence of the speaker

3) List the 1st and 2nd person personal pronouns and possessive determiners in the text and comment on their use.

Specific cultural knowledge

4) What background cultural knowledge is assumed by the text?

Schemata

5) Most texts are structured around the opposition hero vs villain, good vs bad or true vs false. Who do you think are the heroes in this passage and who are the (implicit) villains? What is the quest of the hero(es)? What is the quest of the villain(s)?

Text 2: *Les monstres de Manhattan*

Study the cohesion and coherence of the following text; the accompanying questions will help you in this task.

Histoires sombres, climats crépusculaires…, le jeune public accroche! La preuve? Le récent succès de la série animée Batman. Les Gargoyles *s'inscrivent dans cette lignée. Tout y est pour créer un climat mystérieux et inquiétant. Les héros de cette série? Des créatures tout droit échappées de l'imaginaire médiéval: les gargouilles, des monstres au faciès patibulaire qui d'ordinaire ornent les gouttières des cathédrales ou des forteresses médiévales. Transportés dans l'univers hostile d'une mégapole contemporaine, ces héros de pierre reprennent vie à la tombée du jour et mènent leur combat jusqu'aux premières lueurs de l'aube. Dégradés de noirs et de gris, lumières crues des néons, agressivité de l'environnement urbain…, les réalisateurs de cette série plongent leurs jeunes téléspectateurs dans un inquiétant climat nocturne. Avis aux amateurs de frissons!*

Canal +, Magazine des abonnés, No 95, 1995

COHESION

1) How many examples of ellipsis can you find? Rewrite the sentences giving the words that are missing.

2) Justify the use of the definite article in *Le récent succès de la série animée* Batman (line 2).

3) Give examples of how demonstratives are used to strengthen cohesion.

COHERENCE

Presence of the speaker

4) Make a list of those items that suggest the emotive (emotions, feelings) and/or the evaluative (good, bad).

Specific cultural knowledge

5) What cultural knowledge does this passage assume? Would it be as meaningful, for example, to untravelled African tribespeople?

Schemata

6) Look carefully at lines 1-2 and 3-4. What conventional rhetorical device is being employed here?

7) In what way does this passage enact traditional story patterns? Does it remind you of fairy-tale or myth? If so, why?

Text 3: *Richard Outcault*, Atlas, Air-France

Study the cohesion and coherence of the following text; the accompanying questions will help you in this task.

> *Il s'appelait Richard Outcault. Il était américain et dessinateur. Le grand public peut-être a oublié son nom. Il est pourtant à l'origine d'une aventure extraordinaire. Il y a cent ans, il inventait la bande dessinée.*
>
> *Bien sûr, il y avait eu des précurseurs. De tout temps l'homme s'est plu à raconter des histoires en images. Que sont les vitraux du Moyen Age ou la «tapisserie» de Bayeux sinon des bandes dessinées avant la lettre? Et, au fond, ne peut-on pas voir dans les peintures rupestres de la préhistoire la première forme de la BD?*
>
> *Mais, avec Richard Outcault, une mutation se produit. Jusque là, le dessin ne faisait qu'illustrer un texte placé sous l'image. C'est encore en employant cette formule que le Français Christophe, son contemporain, produira ses chefs-d'œuvre, le Sapeur Camember, la Famille Fenouillard… Mais cela manque de vie. Outcault a l'idée d'introduire le texte dans le dessin grâce à des bulles, des phylactères, corrigeront les puristes. Du coup tout change. Les personnages «parlent». Les cases défilent comme les images d'un film. Le lecteur est rendu spectateur.*
>
> *Atlas, Air-France*, April 1996

COHESION

Coreference and contrast

1) Does the pronoun *il* in the first sentence function in an anaphoric or a cataphoric way? Justify your answer.

2) What is the function of the personal pronouns and of possessive determiners in the rest of the first paragraph? What do they refer to?

3) Can you find an example of simile in the passage?

Connectors

4) How many examples of the following can you find? Make a list:
   a) concessive/adversative connectors
   b) temporal connectors.

COHERENCE

Presence of the speaker

5) What indications are there of the presence of the speaker in the first paragraph?

Schemata

6) How is the passage structured like a story? Are there any conventional story-telling patterns\?

Text 4: Extract from *La Fée carabine* by Daniel Pennac

Which elements of cohesion and coherence can you identify in this text?

> *Avant l'arrivée du vieux Risson parmi nous, c'était moi, Benjamin Mallaussène, l'indispensable frère aîné, qui servais aux mômes leur tranche de fiction pré-nocturne. Tous les soirs depuis toujours: «Benjamin, raconte-nous une histoire.» Je me croyais le meilleur dans le rôle. J'étais plus fort que la téloche à une époque où la téloche était déjà plus forte que tout. Et puis Risson survint. (Il se pointe toujours tôt ou tard, le caïd tombeur du caïd...). Il ne lui a pas fallu plus d'une séance pour me ravaler au rang de lanterne magique et s'octroyer la dimension cinémascope-panavision-sun-surrounding et tout le tremblement.*

Text 5: *Maudite et Oscar à la fois. Certaines ont vraiment tout pour plaire!*
(*Libération*, no 4620, 28 March 1996)

Study the role of cultural knowledge and assumptions as well as of visual representation in the title of this film advert. Explain how the understanding of the message is made possible.

Production exercise:

Extract from ***Pour faire le portrait d'un oiseau*** by Jacques Prévert

The following words have become part of a text in the first half of a poem by Jacques Prévert, *Pour faire le portrait d'une oiseau,* also reproduced below:

cage	*oiseau*	*peindre*	*toile*
forêt	*porte ouverte*	*jardin*	*se cacher*

Peindre d'abord une cage
avec une porte ouverte
peindre ensuite
quelque chose de joli
quelque chose de simple
quelque chose de beau
quelque chose d'utile
pour l'oiseau
placer ensuite la toile contre un arbre
dans un jardin
dans un bois
ou dans une forêt
se cacher derrière l'arbre
sans rien dire
sans bouger (…)
Quand l'oiseau arrive
s'il arrive
observer le plus profond silence
attendre que l'oiseau entre dans la cage
et quand il est entré
fermer doucement la porte avec le pinceau

Create a new text, this time in prose, by re-using the same list of words (not necessarily in the same order).

SUGGESTED ANSWERS TO ASSIGNMENTS

Text **1:** *Europe plurilingue*

COHESION

Grammatical Cohesion

1) Examples of:

    a) demonstrative determiners and pronouns and what they refer to:

- *à ce jour* = *aujourd'hui* (para. 1)
- *ces langues* and *ces cultures* (para.2): the *ces* points backwards to *de l'union européenne.*
- *cette communication* (para.3): the *cette* refers back to *la communication* in the first sentence of the paragraph.
- *ceux (qui s'y expriment)* (para. 1): the demonstrative pronoun *ceux* does not point anaphorically to anything here. It is identified by its complement, the relative clause *qui s'y expriment,* in which the pronoun *y* refers back to *la revue Europe Plurilingue.*

    b) third person personal pronouns and possessive determiners:

- *elle* of the second sentence (para.1) refers back to *la revue Europe Plurilingue.*
- *ses composantes* (para.3): the *ses* refers back to *cette communication* in the same sentence.
- *leur enrichissement* (para.3): the *leur* refers back to *ses composantes linguistiques.*

Lexical Cohesion

2) Words that relate to:

    a) The lexical field of language: *plurilingue* (para.1), *langues européennes* (para.1), *multilingue* (para.1), *langues officielles* (para.1), *ces langues* (para.2), *composantes linguistiques* (para.3)

    b) The lexical field of communication: *un carrefour d'idées* (para.1), *vous êtes invités à vous exprimer* (para.1), *à répondre à ceux qui s'y expriment* (para.1), *satisfaire... le besoin d'information* (para.2), *un lieu... d'échanges d'idées et de projets sur la communication interculturelle* (para.3), *nos partenaires européens* (para.3), *dialogue* (para.4).

COHERENCE

Presence of the speaker

3) 1st and 2nd person personal pronouns and possessive determiners:
  - *vous êtes invités à*
  - *votre intérêt, votre engagement*
  - *vous nous aiderez*
  - *vous contribuerez*
  - *notre objectif*
  - *nous vous proposons*
  - *nos partenaires européens*
  - *nous sommes persuadés*
  - *participez* (2nd person plural imperative form)
  - *notre dialogue*
  - *abonnez-vous* (2nd person plural imperative form)
  - *nous vous invitons à*

The *nous, notre,* etc. point to the presence of the speaker/addresser (i.e. *la Rédaction de la revue Plurilingue*) in the text. Likewise, the *vous, votre,* etc. point to the presence of the reader/addressee. The barrier between text and reader (addresser and addressee) is thus being broken and a sense of immediacy is being established: the reader is personally and repeatedly addressed and hence personally involved in the experience.

Specific cultural knowledge

4) The text assumes that the existence of a multilingual Europe is under threat (*défense... de ces langues et de ces cultures,* para.2). It takes for granted that the reader is familiar with debates about the proposal for a standard language for communication and the threat it represents (*offre une alternative à l'uniformisation,* para.2).

Schemata

5) The 'heroes' are those who strive for a multilingual Europe. The 'villains' are those who seek to impose a uniform language. The quest of the heroes, therefore, is to promote linguistic diversity among the member states of Europe.

Text 2: *Les monstres de Manhattan*

COHESION

1) Examples of ellipsis are:

a) *La preuve? Le récent succès de la série animée* Batman (lines 1-2)

Rewritten: *Où est/quelle est la preuve? C'est le récent succès...*

or:

La preuve, c'est le récent succès...

b) *Les héros de cette série? Des créatures tout droit échappées de l'imaginaire médiéval: les gargouilles...* (lines 3-4)

Rewritten: *Qui sont les héros de cette série? Ce sont des créatures...*

or:

Les héros de cette série sont des créatures...

2) *succès* is identified by the noun complement *de la série animée* Batman; the adjective *récent* is not sufficient here to provide identification; *série* is itself identified by its name, the proper noun 'Batman'.

3) Examples of demonstratives are:

cette lignée referring back to *la série animée* Batman

cette série referring back to Les Gargoyles

ces héros de pierre referring back to *les gargouilles, des monstres au faciès patibulaire*

cette série referring back to *cette série* (Les Gargoyles) of sentence 6.

COHERENCE

Presence of the speaker

4) Examples of emotive and/or evaluative items:

histoires sombres, un climat mystérieux et inquiétant, l'univers hostile, lumières crues des néons, agressivité de l'environnement urbain, inquiétant climat nocturne, avis aux amateurs de frissons.

Specific cultural knowledge

5) The passage assumes the appreciation of, for example, references to Batman and to aspects of Western medieval civilisation: the gargoyles on the cathedrals. It would recall the tradition of Western horror stories, with the association, for instance, of darkness with evil. The reference to *une mégapole contemporaine*, with its *lumières crues des néons*, would also probably not be fully appreciated by an untravelled tribesperson.

Schemata

6) The question and answer format is being applied (pattern for argumentation). The speaker answers his or her own question, a conventional rhetorical device. This is a type of rhetorical question.

7) The use of the monster image reminds one of the traditional fairy story and myth as does the motif of a struggle *(mènent leur combat)* between good (the heroes) and evil *(l'univers hostile d'une mégapole contemporaine)*. The association of the monster with good, however, marks a subversion of conventional story patterns.

Text 3 *Richard Outcault*

COHESION

Coreference and contrast

1) We can say that the pronoun *il* in the first sentence functions in a cataphoric way because it refers forward to the name *Richard Outcault*.

2) The pronoun *il* at the beginning of the second sentence is an anaphora referring back to *Richard Outcault*. The noun phrase *son nom* in the third sentence also refers to *Richard Outcault* as does the pronoun *il* in the middle of the last sentence; *il* at the beginning of the fourth sentence refers to *son nom*.

3) An example of simile can be seen towards the end of the text:
   Les cases défilent **comme** *les images d'un film.*

Connectors

4) Examples of:
   a) concessive/adversative connectors are: *pourtant* (para.1), *bien sûr* (para.2), *au fond* (para.2), *mais* (para.3), *mais* (para.3)
   b) temporal connectors are: *de tout temps* (para.2), *jusque là* (para.3).

COHERENCE

Presence of the speaker

5) In the first paragraph the evaluative adjective *extraordinaire* and the modalising adverb *peut-être* indicate the presence of the speaker.

Schemata

6) The text is structured like a story because it dramatizes the information by highlighting the process of transformation or change. As with all stories, a sharp contrast is made between the initial situation *(le dessin ne faisait*

45

qu'*illustrer un texte placé sous l'image*) and the final situation (*Outcault a l'idée d'introduire le texte dans le dessin grâce à des bulles*). This contrast is presented in the text in the following oppositions:

life	vs	death (*mais cela manque de vie*)
silence	vs	sound (*les personnages «parlent»*)
static	vs	moving (*les cases défilent*)

Text 4: *La Fée carabine*

The answer may include the following:

COHESION

a) **Coreference and contrast:**

*Il se pointe… **le caïd** tombeur du caïd…*: there is a cataphoric relationship between *il* and *le caïd*.

*J'étais **plus fort** que la téloche à une époque où la téloche était déjà **plus forte** que tout*: a contrast is established by the double comparison.

*c'était moi, **Benjamin Mallaussène, l'indispensable frère aîné,** qui servais…:* note the double apposition, for the purpose of emphasis and identification.

Presence of anaphoric *lui*, identified in the text: *il ne **lui** a pas fallu plus d'une séance pour me ravaler au rang de lanterne magique,* (refers to 'Risson' mentioned earlier). Note that *il* in ***il** ne lui a pas fallu* is the impersonal pronoun.

b) **Tense cohesion:** the use of the imperfect (*c'était, servais, croyais, étais…*) as a background tense to insist on the ongoing process, is contrasted with the past historic and the perfect tense (*Risson survint, il ne lui a pas fallu…*) for punctual and/or completed, events.

c) **Use of connectors:** *Avant* (temporal), *tous les soirs* (temporal) are contrasted with *Et puis* (additive and consequential/temporal link), which reinforce the expression of the punctual event, followed by the two additive *et* of the following sentence.

COHERENCE

a) **Presence of the speaker:**

– Use of *je* and its related elements : *moi, nous, me.*

– The opinion of the speaker is given between brackets: *Il se pointe toujours tôt ou tard, le caïd tombeur du caïd...*

– The contrastive use of the present in the quotation « *Benjamin, raconte-nous une histoire.* »

b) **Register and genre**

This short extract, which is part of a novel written by the contemporary writer Daniel Pennac, shows signs of a traditional novel genre with its tense cohesion and the alternation of imperfect and perfect tenses. However its register, characterised by the repeated use of familiar/slang words and expressions – *mômes, téloche, il se pointe, ravaler au rang de lanterne magique, et tout le tremblement* – contrasts strikingly with the traditional expectations of the classical novel genre. Through the regular use of spoken/familiar features, the text reveals a more contemporary mode of writing and, with the emphasis on colloquialism, constitutes one of the most distinctive traits of Daniel Pennac's style.

Text 5: *Maudite et Oscar à la fois...*

The feminine form of the adjective, *maudite,* and of the indefinite pronoun, *certaines,* leads the reader to assume that the heading of the advert refers to a woman, probably the woman pictured below. In this advert the visual representation contributes to the partial clarification of the message.

Indeed the title read in isolation represents an enigma: one wonders who is *maudite?* What does the reference to *Oscar* mean and what does the indefinite *certaines* refer to? The picture, with its accompanying label: *Mira Sorvino Oscar du meilleur second rôle féminin*, acts as a spatial hinge in the advert and clarifies further the title. The coreferential link established between *maudite* and *Mira Sorvino* on the one hand, and between *Mira Sorvino* and the Oscar actress on the other, provides some necessary background knowledge.

However, even if we recognise the role played by the visual design with its label in the clarification of the title, we still cannot make full sense of this title if we do not share with the text producer a common and specific Western cultural knowledge or background, i.e. the knowledge that *Mira Sorvino* is the *second rôle féminin* of the famous Oscar winning film *Maudite Aphrodite* made by the even more famous American film maker, Woody Allen.

CHAPTER 2
COREFERENCE AND CONTRAST:
CONTEXTUAL REFERENCE

INTRODUCTION

When we speak or write, the 'objects of the world' we mention are either:

a) presented as existing but **not immediately identifiable** by one of the interlocutors, or even both (i.e. the reference has **not** been constructed) if preceded by:
   – an indefinite article: *un, une, des*
   – a numeral adjective: *un, deux, trois…*
   – an indefinite adjective: *quelques, peu de…*

Ex: *Une étudiante est venue me voir hier. Elle m'a dit avoir **quelques** problèmes avec la construction de la référence.*

or:

b) presented as **immediately identifiable** by both speaker and interlocutor (i.e. the reference has been constructed) if preceded by:
   – a definite article: *le, la, les*
   – a demonstrative adjective: *ce(t), cette, ces*
   – a possessive adjective: *mon, ton, son…*

Identification can be achieved either in the situation, i.e. the 'surrounding world' (see Chapter 8, Situational reference) or in the linguistic context (contextual reference). In any given text, there will normally be a mixture of both situational and contextual references.

1. Contextual reference: coreference

Whereas *je* and *tu* constitute the persons **in the linguistic exchange**, the third person refers to something **outside this linguistic exchange**. It corresponds to noun phrases (NP) and their pronominal substitutes, and any other element with the same syntactic status as the NP: they are the 'objects' talked about by *je* and *tu*. Hence only *il* (*ils, elle, elles*) is a real 'pro-noun', i.e. an anaphoric element which replaces a NP which has already been introduced in the discourse. Whilst *je* and *tu* derive their reference from the situational context in which they appear, *il* derives its reference (as any other anaphoric element) from the **linguistic context** (contextual reference): *je* and *tu* are completely identified by the situation, whereas the third person may or may not be identified.

Ex: *Je connais **la sœur** de Marie:* identified (by the expansion of the NP, see below)

*Certains chats** ne sont pas très aimables:* not identified.

Finally, there should be a special mention of the pronoun *on*, which not only can stand for any other personal pronoun:

Ex: *Ce soir, **on** va au cinéma.*
Here, *on* is likely to stand for *nous*.

***On** est aimable avec eux et ils vous insultent.*

Here, *on* is likely to stand for a generic *vous*, equivalent to *Même si vous* (i.e. people in general) *êtes aimable avec eux, ils vous insultent.*

but can also be used as an indefinite pronoun (as an alternative for the passive for instance):

Ex: *Le député du Maine et Loire vient d'être élu.*
→ ***On** vient d'élire le député du Maine et Loire.*

We have **contextual reference** in the following cases:
a) The object has already been mentioned in the discourse.

Ex: *Tu n'as pas vu <u>Médor</u>? **Ce chien** va me rendre fou!*
(*ce chien* refers back to *Médor*)

*<u>Une étudiante</u> est venue me voir hier. **Elle** m'a demandé de lui expliquer les adjectifs et pronoms indéfinis...*
(*elle* refers back to *une étudiante*)

*<u>Un chat</u> est arrivé chez moi un beau matin. Dans la cuisine, **le matou** s'est assis devant le réfrigérateur.*

In the last example, *le matou* refers to the previously introduced *un chat*, hence the referent is identifiable because it has already been introduced in the **linguistic context.** This is called the **anaphoric** use of the definite article, and brings the function of the definite article close to that of the pronoun (personal and demonstrative). Indeed, we could have instead:

Ex: <u>*Un chat*</u>...   **Il** *s'est assis...*
                              Celui-ci *s'est assis...*
                              Ce dernier *s'est assis...*

In all the above examples, we have coreferential anaphoras: an element is referred to by another, coreferential, element.

Whilst elements that refer backwards have an **anaphoric** function, elements that refer forwards are said to have a **cataphoric** function, as in the following examples:

Je <u>les</u> ai trouvées, **tes chaussures.** (which is an example of dislocated structure).

Paris ne sera plus le même sans <u>elles</u>: **les publicités** *vont disparaître des murs de la capitale.*

'En <u>la</u> contenant dans des phrases, mon récit fait de **mon histoire** *une réalité finie'*

(Simone de Beauvoir, *Tout compte fait*)

b) The object is identified in the context immediately after being mentioned, by an expansion of the NP. These expansions can be:
   – a noun complement (*le chat* **de la voisine**)
   – a relative clause (*le chat* **que j'ai recueilli ce matin**)
   – an apposition (*le chat,* **celui de la voisine,**...)
   – a qualifying adjective (*le chat* **noir**)

NB(1): **not all expansions of the NP provide identification!**

Ex: **Le** *formidable* **succès** *de Frédéric Dard (alias San Antonio) n'étonne plus personne aujourd'hui.*

Here, the adjective *formidable* is not sufficient to identify the NP *le succès* (*Le formidable succès n'étonne plus personne aujourd'hui* leaves one to wonder 'Whose?' or 'Which?'). The prepositional phrase (noun complement) *de Frédéric Dard* is needed to justify the presence of the definite article.

Ex: *Avez-vous vu* **le** *dernier* **film** *de Woody Allen?*

The adjective *dernier* is not sufficient to identify the noun *film*. It is the noun complement *de Woody Allen* which provides this identification (*Avez-vous vu le dernier film?* would merely refer to the last one in a sequence).

Ex: **Les étudiants,** *une majorité de garçons, avaient décidé de faire grève.*

Here, *une majorité de garçons* is merely descriptive: the purpose of this apposition is to bring a supplement of information. The justification for the use of the definite article *les* has to be found in the context or the situation (see also identifying appositions below).

NB(2): Identifying appositions are often used after proper nouns which are little known, be they placenames or names of people. Compare:

Je vais **à Paris** *la semaine prochaine.*

J'ai fait la connaissance de **François Mitterrand** *il y a dix ans.*

(neither needs any further introduction, at least for a Western European interlocutor)

and:

J'ai rencontré M. Dupont, **charcutier à Nemours**, *à la soirée des Martin.*

Je passe mes vacances à Novéant, **petit village de la Moselle.**

Worked example:

Look at the following passage: what do the words in bold refer to?

> *La connaissance de la société a d'abord dû dépasser la recherche de principes ou de facteurs placés en dehors du champ social.* **Elle** *a appris à reconnaître des situations sociales et à* **les** *analyser; puis s'éloignant d'une définition de* **ses objets** *dans le temps et dans l'espace,* **elle** *a cherché à isoler des fonctions ou des mécanismes.* **Ce progrès** *conduit vers une spécialisation croissante des études...*
>
> Alain Touraine, *Pour la sociologie*

Suggested answers:

line 2: the pronoun *elle* refers back to the NP *la connaissance de la société.*

line 3: the pronoun *les* refers to *des situations sociales.*

line 4: the NP *ses objets* also refers to its 'possessor' *la connaissance.*

line 5: the pronoun *elle* has a similar function to that of line 2.

line 6: the NP *ce progrès* refers back to the whole of the preceding text and not to any individual word or item.

2. Contextual reference: comparison, contrast and ellipsis

Comparison and **contrast** are expressed with comparative forms but also with words such as *même, autre* or *tel.* The use of definite articles, pronouns, etc. in this type of construction follows similar rules to those expounded above. Although there is no **co**reference, anaphoric reference makes it possible to use pronouns and therefore avoid tedious repetition of nouns or noun phrases. Consider the following examples:

Ex: • *même*
> – *J'ai la même robe que toi.*

where *la même robe* is identified by its expansion, the comparative *que toi.*

> – *Regarde ma robe!*
> – *J'ai la même!*

where *la même* is identified by reference to the previous sentence (avoids *j'ai la même robe*).

> *Quant au nombre de jours de congé, nous avons le même.*

where *le même* refers back to *le nombre de jours de congé* (avoids *nous avons le même nombre de jours de congé*).

Ex: • *autre*
> *Catherine et Marie sont parties mais les autres étudiants sont restés.*

where *les autres étudiants* refers to students other than *Catherine* and *Marie.*

> *Catherine et Marie sont parties mais les autres sont restés.*

where *les autres* refers to people other than *Catherine* and *Marie* (we do not know anything else about them).

> *Prenez ce crayon, j'en ai un autre.*

where *un autre* refers back to *ce crayon.* Note that in this particular example, we have existence of another pencil, but not identification.

Ex: • *tel*

tel can be used as an equivalent to *comme celui-ci/là, celle-ci/là,* etc.
> *Je ne veux plus entendre de telles histoires* (or: *des histoires comme celles-là*).

Examples of **ellipsis** can already be observed in the above examples, where article + adjective *même/autre* + noun can be replaced by article + *même/autre*, the latter now functioning as pronouns.

> *la même robe* → *la même*
> *le même nombre de jours de congé* → *le même*
> *un autre crayon* → *un autre*

Other examples of ellipsis of the verb can be found:
   – in comparisons.

Ex: *Marie est plus gentille que vous [ne l'êtes].*

   – in coordinations.

Ex: *Au restaurant, Marie a choisi le gigot et Paul [a choisi] le tournedos.*

   Mon chat attrape des souris et celui de la voisine [attrape des souris/en attrape] aussi.

Finally, ellipsis of the verb, or even of the subject and the verb, is used in conversation as a matter of course.

Ex: *Derrière toi! (= C'est/Ça se trouve/Regarde derrière toi)*
   Un peu de vin? (= Voulez-vous un peu de vin?)

ASSIGNMENTS

1. *L'HYDRATATION: L'ATOUT JEUNESSE DE VOTRE PEAU*

   a) Read the extract (on opposite page) from an advertisement for a beauty product and identify the following elements:
- 3rd person personal pronouns: state to what word or phrase/clause, etc. they refer in the text.
- 3rd person possessive determiners: who are the 'owners' of the items 'possessed'?

   b) You will also find 1st and 2nd person personal pronouns and possessive determiners which do not refer to anybody in the text. Who do they refer to?

   c) What effect is produced in this advert by the frequent use of personal pronouns and possessive determiners?

L'HYDRATATION: L'ATOUT JEUNESSE DE VOTRE PEAU

Votre peau a soif… de jeunesse et de beauté. Faites-lui plaisir, ressourcez-la intensément avec le tout nouveau Soin Hydratation Optimale des Laboratoires Diadermine. Votre visage paraîtra tout de suite plus jeune, plus lisse.

L'eau, c'est simple, c'est la meilleure amie de notre peau. Et lorsqu'elle n'est pas au rendez-vous, notre beauté tombe aussitôt en panne sèche. L'hydratation est donc un geste essentiel et les Laboratoires Diadermine ont décidé de le rendre encore plus efficace et agréable, avec le Soin Hydratation Optimale.

L'efficacité: Jusqu'à 60% d'hydratation en plus

Spécialement conçue pour limiter les pertes en eau de l'épiderme et lui assurer un taux d'hydratation optimal tout au long de la journée, cette crème est une véritable bénédiction pour la peau. Vous allez vous en rendre compte tout de suite car son action est instantanée. Grâce à ses agents hydratants à effet immédiat, la peau retrouve sur le champ souplesse et confort et son taux d'hydratation augmente jusqu'à 60% dès la première heure qui suit l'application. Incroyable mais vrai! Mais le Soin Hydratation Optimale ne s'arrête pas là; il contient aussi des actifs hydratants à fort pouvoir rétenteur qui prolongent leurs effets pendant 24 heures. Ainsi, ce soin haute performance utilisé quotidiennement empêche la peau de se déshydrater et fixe l'eau durablement au cœur de l'épiderme. Et comme sa formule contient aussi des fibres solaires et de la vitamine E, c'est une crème de jour idéale!

Le plaisir: La caresse d'un soin ultra-féminin

Avec le Soin Hydratation Optimale, vous allez aussi découvrir un véritable geste-plaisir: vous aimerez sa texture légère et veloutée, son parfum délicat, son joli conditionnement rose, blanc et or, tout doux et très féminin. Mais vous aimerez surtout l'effet qu'il vous fait: grâce à cette crème-douceur, vous allez retrouver une peau douce, confortable, bien hydratée, et tout cela sans avoir d'effort à faire: ce soin s'applique aussi bien le matin en base de maquillage que le soir pour adoucir ou ressourcer la peau. Et toutes les peaux y ont droit puisque, comme toutes les crèmes DIADERMINE, le Soin Hydratation Optimale est garanti hypoallergénique et testé dermatologiquement. On connaissait l'efficacité, le sérieux des produits DIADERMINE, aujourd'hui, on découvre qu'ils n'ont jamais été aussi proches de nous! 39F env. En grandes surfaces.

Marie-Claire, October 1995

2. *La Place*

Read the following text:

J'ai passé les épreuves pratiques du Capes dans un lycée de Lyon, à la Croix-Rousse. Un lycée neuf, avec des plantes vertes dans la partie réservée à l'administration et au corps enseignant, une bibliothèque au sol en moquette sable. J'ai attendu là qu'on vienne me chercher pour faire mon cours, objet de l'épreuve, devant l'inspecteur et deux assesseurs, des profs de lettres très confirmés. Une femme corrigeait des copies avec hauteur, sans hésiter. Il suffisait de franchir correctement l'heure suivante pour être autorisée à faire comme elle toute ma vie. Devant une classe de première, des matheux, j'ai expliqué vingt-cinq lignes - il fallait les numéroter - du Père Goriot de Balzac. «Vous les avez traînés, vos élèves», m'a reproché l'inspecteur ensuite, dans le bureau du proviseur. Il était assis entre les deux assesseurs, un homme et une femme myope avec des chaussures roses. Moi en face. Pendant un quart d'heure, il a mélangé critiques, éloges, conseils, et j'écoutais à peine, me demandant si tout cela signifiait que j'étais reçue. D'un seul coup, d'un même élan, ils se sont levés tous trois, l'air grave. Je me suis levée aussi, précipitamment. L'inspecteur m'a tendu la main. Puis, en me regardant bien en face: «Madame, je vous félicite.» Les autres ont répété «je vous félicite» et m'ont serré la main, mais la femme avec un sourire.

Annie Ernaux, *La Place*

a) Find examples of identifying:
   – noun complements
   – adjectives
   (i.e. justify the use of the definite article before the noun).

b) Find examples of appositions. Say whether they are identifying or merely descriptive.

c) Find examples of the use of:
   – third person pronouns
   – the definite article
   referring back to previously introduced elements.

d) Find an example of contrast.

e) Find an example of cataphor.

f) Find an example of ellipsis.

3. *L'Affamée*

Read the following text, which constitutes the very beginning of Violette Leduc's *L'Affamée*:

> *Elle a levé la tête. Elle a suivi son idée sur mon pauvre visage. Elle ne le voyait pas. Alors, du fond des siècles, l'événement est arrivé. Elle lisait. Je suis revenue dans le café. Elle suivait d'autres idées sur d'autres visages. J'ai commandé une fine. Elle ne m'a pas remarquée. Elle s'occupait de ses lectures. Quand elle arrive on nettoie le café ou bien on finit de le nettoyer. Le carrelage sèche. On le voit sécher: un carreau trop pâle, un carreau trop rouge. Plus il est fade, plus il sèche. Les chaises sont sur les tables, deux par deux, renversées l'une sur l'autre. Les tables dégraissées supportent ces enlacements obscènes. On passe la main sur le marbre humide. On a un frisson. Cette propreté qui s'envole me calme. Le patron a déposé sa gueule de patron à la caisse. Il astique. Il a travesti la moitié de son corps avec un tablier. Son sexe, auquel on ne pensait pas, est derrière un paravent de toile bleue. Les garçons l'aident. Ils ont ressuscité des mouvements non automatiques. La porte du café est ouverte. L'odeur du tabac vadrouille. La rue a l'exclusivité des bruits.*
>
> Violette Leduc, *L'Affamée*

a) What is the referent of the pronoun *elle*, repeated eight times in the first five lines? What is the effect produced on the reader? Are we likely to find something similar in a newspaper article?

b) What are the referents of the other personal pronouns?

c) What does *cette propreté* refer to?

SUGGESTED ANSWERS TO ASSIGNMENTS

1. *L'HYDRATATION: L'ATOUT JEUNESSE DE VOTRE PEAU*

a) – 3rd person personal pronouns:

*faites-**lui** plaisir: votre peau*

*ressourcez-**la**: votre peau*

*lorsqu'**elle**: l'eau* in the previous sentence.

*de **le** rendre: un geste essentiel*

*et **lui** assurer: l'épiderme*

***il** contient: le Soin Hydratation Optimale*

*qu'**il** vous fait: le Soin Hydratation Optimale*

***on** connaissait:* although classified as a 3rd person pronoun, *on* here represents *nous,* i.e. all the potential readers who use hydrating creams.

***on** découvre:* ditto

*qu'**ils** n'ont: les produits DIADERMINE (des = de les)*

– 3rd person possessive determiners:

***son** action:* refers to *cette crème*

***ses** agents hydratants:* ditto

***son** taux d'hydratation:* refers to *la peau*

***leurs** effets:* refers to *des actifs hydratants*

***sa** formule:* refers to *ce soin*

***sa** texture:* refers to *le Soin Hydratation Optimale*

***son** parfum:* ditto

***son** joli conditionnement:* ditto

b) 1st and 2nd person personal pronouns and possessive determiners:

***vous** allez vous en rendre compte:* the reader

***vous** allez aussi:* ditto

***vous** aimerez sa texture:* ditto

***vous** allez retrouver:* ditto

***vous** aimerez surtout l'effet:* ditto

*qu'il **vous** fait:* ditto

***on** connaissait: nous* (i.e. all the potential readers who use hydrating creams)

***on** découvre:* ditto

*proches de **nous**:* see *on* above.

***votre** peau:* the reader's

***votre** visage:* ditto

> **notre** *peau:* the community of readers using hydrating creams
> **notre** *beauté:* ditto

c) – 3rd person:

The reader's attention is being constantly drawn to the numerous qualities that the product possesses. The accumulation of these possessives suggests a state of perfection.

– 1st and 2nd persons:

A dialogue effect is produced by the alternation between 1st and 2nd persons (i.e. between the manufacturer of the product and the potential customer), the aim of which is to convince the latter. Although *vous* is obviously the reader, *on/nous* is in fact the whole community of such cream users and possibly includes the speaker/advertiser, hopefully also a cream user.
(See also Chapter 7, Presence of the speaker).

2. *La Place*

a) Identification with:

– noun complements:
> *les épreuves **du Capes***
> *la partie **réservée à l'administration et au corps enseignant***
> *le bureau **du proviseur***

– adjectives:
> *l'heure **suivante***

b) Appositions:

– identifying:
> *mon cours, **objet de l'épreuve*** (equivalent to *l'objet de l'épreuve*)

– descriptive:
> *l'inspecteur et deux assesseurs, **des profs de lettres très confirmés***
> *une classe de première, **des matheux***
> *les deux assesseurs, **un homme et une femme myope avec des chaussures roses***

c) – third person pronouns:
> ***il*** *était assis,* ***il*** *a mélangé...* (referring to *l'inspecteur*)
> ***ils*** *se sont levés tous trois* (referring to *l'inspecteur et les deux assesseurs*)
> *comme **elle*** (referring to *une femme*)
> *il fallait **les** numéroter* (referring to *vingt-cinq lignes*)

– definite article
> ***les*** *deux assesseurs* (referring to *deux assesseurs*)

d) Example of contrast:

   les autres (i.e. the people there other than *l'inspecteur*)

e) Example of cataphor:

   « *Vous **les** avez traînés, **vos élèves**.* » (which is a dislocated structure).

f) Example of ellipsis:

   *Mais la femme [a **répété je vous félicite et m'a serré la main**] avec un sourire* (i.e. *l'a fait*).

3. *L'Affamée*

a) The pronoun *elle* has no referent. We, the readers, are supposed to know who *elle* refers to but we don't. The effect is to hook our attention firmly from the start and exacerbate our curiosity: who is this *elle*?

   It is unlikely that this device would be used in a newspaper article or any other information giving medium.

b) Referents of the other personal pronouns:

   — *Elle ne **le** voyait pas: mon pauvre visage*

   — ***on** nettoie le café;* ***on** finit de le nettoyer:* the use of *on* here is equivalent to a passive: whoever is cleaning the *café* is not important. What is important is how the effect of the cleaning is perceived by the observer: ***on** le voit sécher.*

   — *on finit de **le** nettoyer: le café*

   — *on **le** voit sécher: le carrelage*

   — *plus **il** est fade, plus **il** sèche: le carrelage*

   — ***on** passe la main, **on** a un frisson, auquel **on** ne pensait pas:* the observer (see above)

   — ***il** astique, **il** a travesti, les garçons **l'**aident: le patron*

   — ***ils** ont resssuscité: les garçons*

c) *cette propreté* refers to everything that has just been said about the cleaning of the floor (*le carrelage*) and tables.

CHAPTER 3
CONNECTORS AND PUNCTUATION

INTRODUCTION

Important devices in establishing textual cohesion are the use of link words, known as connectors, and of punctuation.

1. Connectors

Some words or phrases are used to indicate a specific connection between different parts of a text. These words can be conjunctions, or adverbial expressions. They can express different types of connections such as:

a) **A temporal link:**

Temporal relationships exist when the events in a text are related in terms of the timing of their occurence. The connectors used can be: *puis, ensuite, après, maintenant, d'abord, avant, enfin…*

Ex: *La recette est extrêmement simple. **D'abord** vous prenez 250 grammes de farine. **Puis** vous ajoutez 150 grammes de sucre.*

b) **A causal link:**

Causal connectors indicate that two pieces of a text are related as cause and effect or cause and consequence. The connectors used can be:
donc, ainsi, comme, parce que, car, il s'ensuit que, en conséquence, la raison pour ceci est que, il en résulte que…

Ex: *Moins de gens achètent de la viande de bœuf. C'est **parce qu'**ils ont peur d'attraper la maladie de la vache folle. **Il en résulte que** le cours de la viande de bœuf a baissé.*

*__Comme__ il pleut, nous n'irons pas au bord de la mer; **ainsi** nous aurons plus de temps pour visiter la ville.*

c) **An additive link:**

Additive connectors signal the presentation of additional information. The connectors can be:
et, aussi, en d'autres termes, en particulier, par exemple…

Ex: *Jean peut jongler avec vingt balles à la fois.*
*__Et__ il peut **aussi** faire des bulles avec son nez?*

d) **An adversative/concessive link:**

Adversative connectors indicate that what follows is in some sense opposed to, or contrasted with, what has come before. The connectors can be:
cependant, d'un autre côté, mais, néanmoins, en dépit de, alors que, bien que, toutefois…

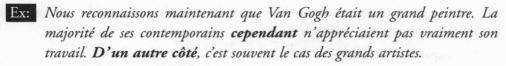 *Nous reconnaissons maintenant que Van Gogh était un grand peintre. La majorité de ses contemporains **cependant** n'appréciaient pas vraiment son travail. **D'un autre côté**, c'est souvent le cas des grands artistes.*

e) **A purpose/consequential link:**

Purpose or consequential connectors indicate an aim or a consequence. The connectors used are: *pour, afin de/que, avec l'intention de...*

Ex: *Il a agi ainsi **pour** vous plaire.*

Worked example:

Read the following extract:

1. ***Quand**, à Paris, une femme a résolu de faire métier et marchandise de sa beauté, ce n'est pas une raison **pour** qu'elle fasse fortune. On y rencontre d'admirables créatures, très spirituelles, dans une affreuse médiocrité, finissant très mal une vie commencée par les plaisirs. **Voici pourquoi:** se destiner à la carrière*
5. *honteuse des courtisanes, **avec l'intention d**'en palper les avantages, tout en gardant la robe d'une honnête bourgeoise mariée, ne suffit pas. Le Vice n'obtient pas facilement ses triomphes; il a cette similitude avec le Génie, qu'ils exigent tous deux un concours de circonstances heureuses **pour** opérer le cumul de la fortune et du talent. Supprimez les phases étranges de la Révolution, l'Empereur n'existe*
10. *plus, il n'aurait plus été qu'une seconde édition de Fabert. La beauté vénale sans amateurs, sans célébrité, sans la croix de déshonneur qui lui valent des fortunes dissipées, c'est un Corrège dans un grenier, c'est le Génie expirant dans sa mansarde. Une Laïs à Paris doit **donc**, avant tout, trouver un homme riche qui se passionne assez **pour** lui donner son prix. Elle doit surtout conserver une*
15. *grande élégance qui, pour elle, est une enseigne, avoir d'assez bonnes manières **pour** flatter l'amour-propre des hommes, posséder cet esprit à la Sophie Arnoud, qui réveille l'apathie des riches; **enfin** elle doit se faire désirer par les libertins en paraissant être fidèle à un seul, dont le bonheur est alors envié.*

Balzac, *La Cousine Bette*

The above passage is characterised by an abundant use of connectors, establishing explicit links between parts of the text. As we shall see, these connectors serve to construct a discourse of an explanatory and pedagogical nature. In this text, the connectors are used for:

– expressing hypothesis: ***quand***

The passage opens with the subordinate conjunction *quand: Quand, à Paris, une femme a résolu de faire métier et marchandise de sa beauté...* A hypothesis/consequence link is thus established with the main clause that follows (*ce n'est pas une raison pour qu'elle fasse fortune*), the neutral demonstrative pronoun *ce* functioning here as an anaphora, referring back to the whole of the previous clause. The positioning of the subordinate clause of hypothesis/consequence at the beginning of the passage adds to the general 'truth value' of the text: what is being said is valid for all times.

We also have an implicit subordination with

supprimez les phases étranges de la Révolution, l'Empereur n'existe plus (meaning: ***Si*** *vous supprimez...*)

The relationship between subordinate and main clause in lines 9-10 is again one of hypothesis/consequence. The choice of the second person plural here (*supprimez*) directly addressing a general audience (the reader) reinforces the pedagogical and explanatory impact of the discourse.

– introducing the last one in a list: ***enfin***

The final sentence opens with the connector *enfin* (line 17): *enfin elle doit se faire désirer par les libertins en paraissant être fidèle...* This connector not only constructs a link with the preceding sentence, it also imposes on the last section of the passage (from *Une Laïs à Paris...*, line 13 onwards) a sense of progression, establishing the necessary stages to be followed if a courtesan wishes to enjoy a financially rewarding career. The effect produced by these last lines is that of a recipe: we are being given a list of instructions to be followed.

– expressing an aim, a result to be obtained: ***pour***

There are four occurrences of *pour* in this passage.

The first sentence contains a subordinate clause of result (line 2): *pour qu'elle fasse fortune...* A link is thereby established both with the main clause and with the subordinate clause of hypothesis. The presence of this connector in the opening sentence sets the tone of the passage as a whole, that is one of rational explanation and argumentation. The extract clearly assumes the ability of the speaker to explain human behaviour in clear and simple patterns of 'if' and 'then'. On a semantic level, the principal theme is introduced here: pursuing the life of a courtesan does not automatically bring financial reward.

Line 8 contains the preposition *pour* followed by an infinitive, *pour opérer le cumul* (equivalent to a conjunction followed by a conjugated verb). A link is established with the preceding subordinate clause and in particular with the noun phrase *un concours de circonstances heureuses.* The discourse pretends to be of a highly rational and analytical nature: as in a scientific experiment, only the right circumstances can produce the correct results.

Line 14 contains a *pour* + infinitive clause, expressing result (what needs to be achieved in order to obtain a certain result): *pour lui donner son prix.*

Finally, line 16 contains a similar construction: *pour flatter l'amour-propre des hommes.*

　　– expressing an explanation: ***voici pourquoi***
The third sentence opens with an explanation: *Voici pourquoi* (line 4). A logical and cataphoric link is established with what is to come, that is, with the next ten lines (up to *expirant dans sa mansarde,* lines 12-13). The reader interprets each utterance within this section therefore as a reason why adopting the life of a courtesan does not automatically produce wealth.

　　– expressing purpose: ***avec l'intention de***
The third sentence also contains the prepositional phrase of purpose *avec l'intention de* + infinitive (line 5). On the semantic level, we have a repetition of the information given in lines 1-4.

　　– expressing causality: ***donc***
The causal connector *donc* in line 13 establishes not only a logical link of consequence with the sentence immediately preceding but also with the whole of the preceding text. Up to line 13, the text has presented us with the problem, we are now being informed of the solution - the right course of action to be pursued: *Une Laïs à Paris doit donc, avant tout...*

The frequent use of causal connectors in the description of human behaviour in this passage conveys the notion of calculation and of psychological manipulation, which constitutes one of the principal themes of *La Cousine Bette.*

2. Punctuation

Punctuation is a standard cohesive tool used to reinforce other connective means. (This is why some authors have made a point of not using punctuation so as to exploit other means of cohesion). Though the use of punctuation is characterised by flexibility and a certain degree of indeterminacy, it is essential to the structure of sentences and to the cohesion of the written text. Wrongly used punctuation marks can indeed seriously endanger the understanding of the message. Consider for instance the ambiguous meaning created by the lack of a comma after *lapin* in the following example:

Paul a tué un lapin et Pierre aussi.

More often, wrongly used punctuation will lead to nonsense, as created by the place of the comma in the following examples:

Il est interdit de jouer au ballon, avec les pieds sur la plage.

(cited in *La grammaire du français contemporain*, Larousse, 1964)

Les chiens doivent être tenus, en laisse dans les allées du parc.

On the other hand, the systematic use of **commas** can have a linking function and can replace an additive connector. This is called an asyndeton.

Ex: *La mer est basse, calme, la saison est indéfinie, le temps, lent.*

(*L'Amour*, Marguerite Duras)

In this poetic use, which closely resembles the style of theatre directions, the first comma replaces the additive connector *et* while the last one is substituted for the ellipsis of the verb form *est*.

Commas are often used to separate the elements of a list:

Ex: *Pierre, Paul, Marie, ma sœur et ses amies sont tous allés au cinéma.*

Commas always precede the presence of a reporting clause after direct reported speech:

Ex: *«Je veux jouer», a dit l'enfant.*

Commas can also signal the presence of an apposition: (see also Chapter 2, Section 1):

Ex: *«Avez-vous eu le L?», demande Charles Kline,* **étudiant en premier cycle de l'Université de Californie à Los Angeles** *(UCLA), à un chercheur de l'équipe de Doug Engelbart [. . .]. «J'ai eu un 1-4», répond celui-ci. Dans le codage en base 8, il s'agit bien d'un L. Suivent le O et le G. «Log»,* **le nom sésame de l'informatique**, *a été transmis entre deux ordinateurs distants de 600 kilomètres.*

(*Le Monde*, 10-11 October 1999)

Colons establish a semantic relation between what precedes them and what follows. This relation can be:

– an explanation or a development:

Ex: *Et ce n'est pas tout: une fois utilisée, l'eau doit être collectée et retraitée avant d'être rendue à la nature.*

(advertisement, *Questions de femmes*)

Pour beaucoup le constat s'impose: le rock est au pied du mur.

(*Libération*, 15-16 November 1997)

– the introduction of a list of examples:

Ex: *Nous sommes tous allés au cinéma: Pierre, Paul, Marie, ma sœur et ses amies.*

J'ai trois animaux domestiques: deux chats et un chien.

– a relation of cause or consequence:

Ex: *Prends ce panier: nous avons beaucoup d'achats à faire.*

– the introduction of direct reported speech (compare with the use of commas above):

Ex: *Il m'a dit: « Je viendrai te voir dès mon retour ».*

Colons can also introduce a cataphora:

Ex: *Je l'avais deviné: il ne viendra pas ce soir.*

Speech marks, often associated with the use of italics, or dashes in a dialogue, signal the presence of a voice other than that of the narrator, which in itself can help to reinforce the coherence of the text by strengthening or illustrating the argument made by the narrator:

Ex: *Ce boom des effets secondaires est à mettre en rapport avec la surconsommation des médicaments. « En France » a poursuivi le ministre, « il y aurait [...] deux fois plus d'antibiotiques qu'en Angleterre... »*

(d'après *Libération*, 15-16 November 1997)

Alternatively, speech marks can stress the narrator's dissociation from a specific utterance or word(s):

Ex: *Certains experts ont estimé que cette réforme fait la part trop belle « aux laboratoires », les plaçant au dessus de la santé des patients.*

(idem)

Suspension marks have a purely conventional meaning, indicating that the sentence is not finished or that there is a pause:

Ex: *«Mais qu'est-ce qu'il me…,»* a-t-elle commencé à murmurer.

«J'ai pensé que ça vous serait agréable… et puis vous m'aviez offert de l'orangeade…»

(Colette, *Le Blé en herbe*)

They can also stress the emphatic prolongation of a sentence:

Ex: *Et je retrouve une dame qui se confesse, mon rêve qui s'écroule, une horreur sans nom…*

(Cocteau, *Les Parents terribles*)

Question marks often signal the presence of the narrator's or another voice's direct speech. They can also have a connective function when they are used to introduce a rhetorical question which contributes to the argumentative structure of the text.

For instance, compare:

– the cohesive function of the question mark after *un peu cher* in the following example, which expresses the reader's implicit thought and as such allows the text to be further developed:

Ex: *Une firme américano-suisse envisage la construction d'une réplique du Titanic pour l'an 2002; il en coûtera entre 10000 et 100 000 dollars. Un peu cher? La White Star Line rentabiliserait ensuite le paquebot en lui faisant effectuer des croisières classiques.*

(d'après *Le Figaro*, 9 April 1998)

– with the use of the rhetorical question in the example below:

Ex: *Qu'est-ce que la plainte? La version dégradée de la révolte, la parole démocratisée par excellence dans une société qui nous laisse entrevoir la révolte.*

(Pascal Bruckner, *La Tentation de l'innocence*)

The question has a cohesive value since it allows writers to structure their discourse and to introduce their subject.

Exclamation marks are often used to insist on the narrator's (or sometimes someone else's) expression of emotion or surprise, hence signalling their presence, often compounded by the presence of interjections:

Ex: *On a le droit d'écrire ce qu'on veut, et tous les goûts des lecteurs sont dans la nature, non mais sans blague!*
(Daniel Pennac, *Comme un roman*)

Les bancs étaient tous en bois brun écaillé semblables les uns aux autres, égalitaires en somme!
(Rachid Boudjedra, *Topographie idéale pour une agression caractérisée*)

Finally, exclamation marks are often found after interjections used by themselves:

Ex: *Génial! Extraordinaire!*

Brackets and dashes can signal the inclusion of complementary information, non-essential to the general structure of the sentence:

Ex: *Depuis son quartier général futuriste – une ancienne base sous-marine à Bordeaux – ce groupe, composé de trois musiciens, un ingénieur du son et un infographiste, se place à l'avant-garde.*
(*Libération*, 15-16 November 1997)

Here, *une ancienne base* is in apposition to *son quartier général futuriste*.
Note on the contrary that *un ingénieur du son* and *un infographiste* are not in apposition to *trois musiciens* but are part of the list which starts with *trois musiciens*.

Brackets can also indicate the direct voice of the speaker:

Ex: *On est prié (je vous supplie) de ne pas utiliser ces pages comme instrument de torture pédagogique.*
(Exergue à *Comme un roman* by Daniel Pennac)

Note that in the following example, the dashes introduce a comment:
J'ai vu les deux hommes – mon frère les a vus bien après moi – et me suis immédiatement cachée derrière la voiture.

As already mentioned in Chapter 1, the **absence** or **non-normative use of punctuation** is sometimes used by writers as a creative device to reinforce or introduce the lexical fields of a text.

Look for instance at the opening sentences of Robert Pinget's novel *Cette Voix* and see how the absence or unusual use of punctuation illustrates the narrator's state of mind.

Cette voix.
Coupure de la nuit des temps.
Ou cette lettre adressée on ne sait plus à qui dont on trouve des brouillons disséminés partout.
Demander Théodore classer papiers.
Son nom chuchoté il hurle il se réveille en sueur dans cette chambre où tout recommence cette table la nuit il est sorti et refaisait le trajet de la cour jusqu'aux champs il suivait un étroit sentier.

The full-stops in the first four utterances do not punctuate a full sentence as is normally the case, since there is no main verb. This truncated style is used to reproduce a current of consciousness. In the last sentence, the full stop, as a contrast, regains its conventional usage. The absence of commas in that sentence suggests speed and impulsive action, conveying a feeling of breathlessness.

ASSIGNMENTS

1. Connectors

1. Link together the following clauses and/or sentences choosing suitable connectors from the examples given in Section 1:

In b), also include the following temporal connectors: *cette année, souvent, à cette époque, pour le moment.*

> **a)** *Bien des gens craignent la nourriture génétiquement modifiée. Trop peu de recherches ont été effectuées sur la sûreté de ces aliments. La culture et la consommation de ces produits ont été l'ojet de réactions négatives de la part du public.*
>
> **b)** *Nous allons au bord de la mer. Il fait un temps abominable. Nous avons décidé de rester en ville.*

2. How many temporal, causal and adversative connectors can you find in the following extract? Make three lists.

1. *Il alla ensuite à l'Hôtel de Ville pour l'achat du terrain. Une concession de deux mètres en longueur sur un de largeur coûtait cinq cents francs. Etait-ce une concession mi-séculaire ou perpétuelle?*

— Oh! perpétuelle! dit Frédéric.

5. *Il prenait la chose au sérieux, se donnait du mal. Dans la cour de l'hôtel, un marbrier l'attendait pour lui montrer des devis et plans de tombeaux grecs, égyptiens, mauresques; mais l'architecte de la maison en avait déjà conféré avec Madame; et, sur la table, dans le vestibule, il y avait toutes sortes de prospectus relatifs au nettoyage des matelas, à la*

10. *désinfection des chambres, à divers procédés d'embaumement.*

Après son dîner, il retourna chez le tailleur pour le deuil des domestiques; et il dut faire une dernière course, car il avait commandé des gants de castor, et c'étaient des gants de filoselle qui convenaient.

Quand il arriva le lendemain, à dix heures, le grand salon s'emplissait de

15. *monde, et presque tous, en s'abordant d'un air mélancolique, disaient:*

— Moi qui l'ai encore vu il y a un mois! Mon Dieu! C'est notre sort à tous!

— Oui; mais tâchons que ce soit le plus tard possible!

Alors on poussait un petit rire de satisfaction, et même on engageait des dialogues parfaitement étrangers à la circonstance. Enfin, le maître des

20. *cérémonies, en habit noir à la française et culotte courte, avec manteau, pleureuses, brette au côté et tricorne sous le bras, articula, en saluant, les mots d'usage: «Messieurs, quand il vous fera plaisir.»*

Flaubert, *L'Education sentimentale*

3. List the adversative/concessive connectors present in the following text. Can you find equivalent connective terms to replace some of them?

1. *Quand a paru mon essai,* La Vieillesse, *quelques critiques, quelques lecteurs, m'ont reproché de n'avoir pas parlé davantage de ma vieillesse. Cette curiosité m'a souvent semblé relever d'une sorte de cannibalisme plutôt que d'un véritable intérêt. Elle m'encourage néanmoins à continuer mon autobiographie. Plus je me rapproche*
5. *du terme de mon existence, plus il me devient possible d'embrasser dans son ensemble cet étrange objet qu'est une vie: je tenterai de le faire au début de ce livre. D'autre part dix années se sont écoulées depuis le moment où j'ai arrêté mon récit: j'ai certaines choses à raconter. […] En la contenant dans des phrases, mon récit fait de mon histoire une réalité finie, qu'elle n'est pas. Mais aussi il l'éparpille,*
10. *la dissociant en un chapelet d'instants figés, alors qu'en chacun passé, présent et avenir étaient indissolublement liés.*

Simone de Beauvoir, *Tout compte fait*

4. Read the following extract:

1. *Le pharmacien répondit:*
— J'ai une religion, ma religion, et même j'en ai plus qu'eux tous, avec leurs momeries et leurs jongleries! J'adore Dieu, au contraire! Je crois en l'Etre suprême, un Créateur, quel qu'il soit, peu m'importe, qui nous a placés ici-bas
5. *pour y remplir nos devoirs de citoyen et de père de famille; mais je n'ai pas besoin d'aller, dans une église, baiser des plats d'argent, et engraisser de ma poche un tas de farceurs qui se nourrissent mieux que nous! Car on peut l'honorer aussi bien dans un bois, dans un champ, ou même en contemplant la voûte éthérée, comme les anciens. Mon Dieu, à moi, c'est le Dieu de Socrate,*
10. *de Franklin, de Voltaire et de Béranger! Je suis pour la Profession de foi du vicaire savoyard et les immortels principes de 89! Aussi, je n'admets pas un bonhomme de bon Dieu qui se promène dans son parterre la canne à la main, loge ses amis dans le ventre des baleines, meurt en poussant un cri et ressuscite au bout de trois jours: choses absurdes en elles-mêmes et complètement opposées,*
15. *d'ailleurs, à toutes les lois de la physique; ce qui nous démontre, en passant, que les prêtres ont toujours croupi dans une ignorance turpide, où ils s'efforcent d'engloutir avec eux les populations.*
Il se tut, cherchant des yeux un public autour de lui car, dans son effervescence, le pharmacien un moment s'était cru en plein conseil municipal. Mais la
20. *maîtresse d'auberge ne l'écoutait plus; elle tendait son oreille à un roulement éloigné. On distingua le bruit d'une voiture mêlé à un claquement de fers lâches qui battaient la terre, et l'Hirondelle enfin s'arrêta devant la porte.*

Flaubert, *Madame Bovary*

a) Find one example of the following:
   (i)   additive connector
   (ii) adversative connector
   (iii) purpose connector
   (iv) temporal connector
   (v)   causal connector
b) How would you describe a discourse such as the one above?

c) Look carefully at the following use of *mais* occuring towards the beginning of the text:

mais je n'ai pas besoin d'aller, dans une église, ... (lines 5-6)

Here, the *mais* serves to implicitly link together two opposing arguments or viewpoints relating to the subject of religion. What are they?

d) What is the function of *mais* in the last paragraph (*Mais la maîtresse d'auberge...*, lines 19-20)?

e) What stylistic effect is achieved through the abundant use of logical connectors (adversative and causal) in this passage?

5. In what kinds of situations (or types of discourse) do you think causal connectors might predominate?

6. In what kind of discourse situation do you think temporal connectors might play a key role?

2. Punctuation

1. a) Analyse the function of brackets and dashes in the second and third paragraphs of the following extract (line 5 onwards).

    b) What is the function of the first question-mark in the text (line 3)? Which other devices are used to structure the argumentation?

    c) Comment on the use of commas in this article.

    d) Comment on the use of the full stop which separates sentences 4 and 5 (line 14).

Le soja génétiquement modifié affole les étiquettes.

1. *Faut-il parler « d'aliment modifié par les biotechnologies modernes», d'«aliment amélioré grâce au génie génétique» ou d'«aliment modifié par le génie génétique»..? Tandis que les membres du Comité permanent des denrées alimentaires*
5. *(CPDA) de l'Union européenne tergiversent, les industriels de l'agro-alimentaire s'énervent. [...] A quelques semaines de la mise sur le marché de ces produits – que Nestlé fixe à la fin novembre début décembre pour certains plats surgelés Findus – ils ne savent toujours pas précisément ce qui devra être porté sur*
10. *l'étiquette. Faute d'une consigne claire de la part de Bruxelles, les Nestlé et autre Danone, qui n'ont aucune envie d'avoir des ennuis avec des consommateurs que tous les sondages montrent plutôt réticents à l'idée de boulotter des aliments transgéniques, vont donc devoir se livrer chacun à un petit exercice d'écriture. A*
15. *moins qu'ils n'adoptent une position commune, ce qui n'est pas exclu. S'ils veulent noyer le poisson, ils choisiront la première formulation («modifié par les biotechnologies modernes...»).*
Les mêmes enquêtes ont montré, en effet, que les gens ne savaient pas exactement ce qu'étaient les biotechnologies, voire les
20. *confondaient avec l'agriculture biologique. S'ils veulent positiver, ils choisiront la seconde («amélioré grâce au génie génétique...»). S'ils veulent rester neutres, ils choisiront la troisième («modifié par...»).*

Libération 15-16 November 1997

2. Comment on the use of punctuation in this article extract.

> **1.** Jérémy Irons le Chinois…
> – *Vous jouez la plupart du temps des rôles dramatiques. Vous n'aimeriez pas tourner des comédies, pour changer?*
> – J'adorerais! J'en ai fait une, il y a longtemps . . . Mais quand un
> **5.** réalisateur veut faire une comédie, il pense spontanément à Steve Martin ou à Robin Williams. Jamais à Jérémy Irons! Même toi, Wayne, je suis sûr que tu n'aurais jamais pensé à moi pour un tel rôle! Avoue! (*Wayne Wang acquiesce en riant*). Tous les comédiens sont prisonniers de leur image! [...]
> *Journal du dimanche,* 16 November 1997

3. Restore the punctuation to the title and text of this passage (inserting capital letters as necessary) and compare your punctuated version with the original text at the end of this chapter. Examine to what extent your version provides a different cohesive meaning to the text.

> **1.** *Médicaments trop d'effets indésirables c'est une étude passionnante sur le danger des médicaments qu'a rendue publique Bernard Kouchner la semaine dernière lors d'un colloque sur la médecine générale elle révèle que sur l'ensemble des*
> **5.** *patients hospitalisés un jour donné dans un service de médecine de chirurgie ou de long séjour plus de 10% d'entre eux souffrent d'effets indésirables liés à la prise d'un médicament et parmi ces effets indésirables le tiers sont des effets indésirables graves et 1,4% auront été la cause probable d'un décès a même*
> **10.** *précisé le ministre selon cette étude une des plus importantes jamais effectuées par 31 centres régionaux de pharmacovigilance et sous l'égide de l'agence du médicament on estime à plus de 1,3 million le nombre de malades hospitalisés présentant chaque année au moins un effet indésirable.*
>
> *Libération,* 16 November 1997

4. Rewrite this short passage by replacing some of the punctuation marks, wherever you can, with connectors: conjunctions, pronouns or adverbs.

Que Hoffmann n'a-t-il vécu à notre époque! Il y aurait vu ce qui lui semblait inconcevable en son temps: la réconciliation du quantifiable avec le merveilleux; des Lumières avec le romantisme. On est loin ici de l'esprit de calcul rationnel qui formait selon Max Weber l'ethos du capitalisme à ses débuts: la production marchande est mise au service d'une féérie universelle, le consumérisme culmine dans « l'animisme des objets ».

Pascal Bruckner, *La Tentation de l'innocence*

SUGGESTED ANSWERS TO ASSIGNMENTS

1. Connectors

1. Link together the clauses/sentences:

a) *Bien des gens craignent la nourriture génétiquement modifiée* **car en effet**, *trop peu de recherches ont été effectuées sur la sûreté de ces aliments* **et donc** (or: **en conséquence**) *la culture et la consommation de ces produits ont été l'objet de réactions négatives de la part du public.*

b) *Nous allons* **souvent** *au bord de la mer* **à cette époque. Cette année** *il fait* **cependant** *un temps abominable, nous avons* **donc pour le moment** *décidé de rester en ville.*

2. *L'Education sentimentale*

Temporal, causal and adversative connectors:

a. Temporal   b. Causal   c. Adversative

   ensuite (1)   *pour* (1, 6, 11)   *mais* (7, 17)

   déjà (8)   *car* (12)

   après (11)

   quand (14)

   alors (18)

   enfin (19)

3. *Tout compte fait*

The adversative/concessive connectors are:

   néanmoins (= *quoiqu'il en soit, quand même*), line 4

   d'autre part (= *par ailleurs*), line 7

   mais aussi, line 9

   alors que, line 10

4. *Madame Bovary*

a) Find one example of:

   (i) additive connector: e.g. the conjunction *et* in the first sentence (*et même j'en ai plus qu'eux tous*, line 2); the conjunction *ou* (*ou même en contemplant...*, line 8)

    (ii) adversative connector: e.g. *au contraire* (line 3), *mais* (*mais je n'ai pas besoin d'aller*, line 5; *Mais la maîtresse d'auberge ne l'écoutait plus*, line 19), *d'ailleurs*, (line 15)

    (iii) purpose connector: e.g. *pour* (*pour y remplir nos devoirs*, line 5)

    (iv) temporal connector: e.g. *enfin* (*et l'Hirondelle enfin s'arrêta*, line 22)

    (v) causal connector: e.g. *car* (*Car on peut l'honorer aussi bien*, line 7)

b) It can be described as a discourse of argumentation. The speaker - here a character in a story - is defending one point of view in opposition to another. He is trying to convince his audience - the woman in charge of the inn - of the validity of his position.

c) Use of *mais* (to link two opposing arguments):

    (i) it is not necessary to go to church to be religious. One can believe in and worship God anywhere.

    (ii) to be religious, it is necessary to attend church and to belong to a religious institution.

d) By referring backward, the *mais* (here equivalent to *cependant* and not e.g. *par contre*) establishes a semantic link with the preceding sentence. For instance, 'attentiveness' (*en plein conseil municipal*) is contrasted with 'inattentiveness' (*ne l'écoutait plus*). At the same time, the *mais* provides a smooth transition from one character to another – the pharmacist to the person running the inn.

e) The use of connectors here contributes to the element of parody. It serves, for example, to construct a distance between the speaker – the pharmacist – and the authorial stance of the narrator, Flaubert. The arguments are thereby being undermined or discredited.

5. In the courtroom (legal discourse) and in all those situations where someone is trying to prove something to someone else. In all forms of argumentative discourse, therefore, patterns of logic (cause and effect, consequence, result, etc.) are necessarily brought into play.

6. Examples would include the following:

    a) when composing a recipe (*D'abord vous prenez...*, etc.)

    b) when a teacher gives instructions to a pupil on how to construct a model aeroplane, etc.

    c) when telling someone a story.

2. Punctuation

1. *Le soja génétiquement modifié* . . .

a) Brackets or dashes are used:
   - to give complementary information: here to point to the existence of an acronym (*CPDA*, line 5) and to specify the sale date of the products (*que Nestlé fixe à la fin novembre*. . ., lines 7-8)
   - to recall the information already stated in the first paragraph of the article cf. *modifié par les biotechnologies modernes*. . . line 17, *amélioré grâce au génie génétique*. . . lines 21-22, and *modifié par*. . . line 23. As such, brackets contribute to the clarity of the argumentation and reinforce the structure of the text.

b) The first question mark in the text (*Faut-il parler*. . . *par le génie génétique*. . .? lines 1-3) signals a rhetorical question which is used to introduce the subject of the article, already announced by its main title: the reference to the three labelling alternatives directly recalls the expression *affole les étiquettes* of the title.

The other devices used to structure the argumentation in the article are the many connectors: temporal ones (*Tandis que*. . . line 3, *A quelques semaines de*. . . line 6), consequential connectors (*donc*. . . line 14, *en effet*. . . line 18), conditional links (*S'ils veulent*. . . lines 16, 20 & 22), privative preposition (*Faute de*. . . line 10) and concessive conjunction (*A moins que*. . . lines 14-15).

The dominant connectors, temporal and conditional, reflect the principal theme of the article: when and how will the new product be presented to the public? The last three conditional clauses create an effect of parallellism recalling the alternatives presented in the rhetorical question:
- *S'il veulent noyer le poisson* . . .
- *S'ils veulent positiver* . . .
- *S'ils veulent rester neutres* . . .

c) The first comma in sentence 1 (line 2) is used to separate the elements of a list, that of the three ways of labelling the product.

The comma in sentence 2 (line 5) separates the two parts of the sentence (subordinate clause followed by main clause) and reinforces the meaning of parallel actions, introduced by the temporal connector *tandis que*.

The commas in sentence 4, before *qui n'ont aucune envie*. . . (line 11) and after *transgéniques* (line 13), signal additional information and have the function of brackets.

In sentences 6, 8 and 9, the commas serve to emphasize the position of the conditional clauses (lines 16, 21 & 23). The commas which accompany the same syntactic structure and the repeated use of brackets has, as already shown in b), a structural function in the argumentation.

In sentence 7, the commas around *en effet* (line 18) emphasize the affirmative meaning of the connector while reinforcing the argumentative nature of the text.

d) The full stop which separates sentences 4 and 5 (line 14) should normally have been a comma since sentence 5, which starts with a subordinate clause introduced by the concessive conjunction *à moins que,* does not have a main clause: this is a very common feature in journalism, as a means of foregrounding the counter argument introduced by the subordinate clause.

2. Jérémy Irons le Chinois . . .

The first full stop, after *rôles dramatiques* (line 2), and the second one, after *Robin Williams* (line 6) are used to complete the statements made.

The question mark in line 3 stresses the presence of a question in the context of a dialogue.

The comma in line 3 isolates the sentence sequence *pour changer* and as such emphasizes it.

While the comma in line 5 is used to detach the temporal clause: *mais quand un réalisateur...* from the main clause, the third and fourth commas in *Même toi, Wayne,...* (line 6) stress the proper noun in apposition.

The suspension marks in *J'en ai fait une, il y a longtemps...* (line 4) are used to emphasize the allusion to the passage of time.

The brackets with the sentence in italics (*Wayne Wang acquiesce en riant,* line 8) signal the interviewer's direct intervention.

The many exclamation marks add emphasis and a strong personal involvement in the dialogue. They either stress:
   – a wish in *J'adorerais!* (line 4)
   – an expression of regret and disapproval in *Jamais à Jérémy Irons!* (line 6),
      ... je suis sûr que tu n'aurais jamais pensé à moi pour un tel rôle! (line 7),
      Tous les comédiens sont prisonniers de leur image! (line 8)
   – the speaker's direct address with the imperative form *Avoue!* (line 7).

93

3. *Médicaments trop d'effets indésirables...*

1. *Médicaments: trop d'effets indésirables.*
C'est une étude passionnante sur le danger des médicaments qu'a rendue publique Bernard Kouchner, la semaine dernière, lors d'un colloque sur la médecine générale.
5. *Elle révèle que, sur l'ensemble des patients hospitalisés un jour donné dans un service de médecine, de chirurgie ou de long séjour, plus de 10% d'entre eux souffrent «d'effets indésirables» liés à la prise d'un médicament.*
«Et parmi ces effets indésirables, le tiers sont des effets indésirables graves, et 1,4% auront été la cause probable d'un décès», a même précisé le
10. *ministre.*
Selon cette étude - une des plus importantes jamais effectuées par 31 centres régionaux de pharmacovigilance et sous l'égide de l'Agence du médicament - on estime à plus de 1,3 million le nombre de malades hospitalisés «présentant chaque année au moins un effet indésirable».

4. Extract from *La Tentation de l'innocence*

***Si seulement** Hoffmann avait vécu à notre époque, il y aurait vu ce qui lui semblait inconcevable en son temps **c'est-à-dire** la réconciliation du quantifiable avec le merveilleux **et celle** des Lumières avec le romantisme. On est loin ici de l'esprit de calcul rationnel qui formait selon Max Weber l'ethos du capitalisme à ses débuts **car** la production marchande est **maintenant** mise au service d'une féérie universelle **tandis que** le consumérisme culmine dans «l'animisme des objets».*

CHAPTER 4

TENSE COHESION; ASPECT AND MODALITY

INTRODUCTION

This chapter seeks to examine the role of **tenses** in the production of textual cohesion. It will focus on the notion of **aspect** – the way the process described by the verb takes place in time – and on that of **modality** – the attitude of the speaker to what is being said.

Any **verb form** is characterised by a certain amount of grammatical information, shared in variable proportions with the forms to which it is opposed. For instance, *je savais* (imperfect tense, indicative mood) is opposed to *tu savais, il savait*, etc. through the person, to *j'avais su* (its compound form) through the aspect, and to *je saurai* or *je sais* through the tense.

What is expressed by the verb when conjugated, whether it be an action, a state, a transformation, etc. is called a **process**.

1. Tenses of the conjugation

Tenses of the conjugations ('imperfect', 'future anterior', etc.) are further classified into **moods**, corresponding to the **attitudes of the speaker** towards what she/he is saying (see also Section 4, Modality). These are the personal moods, i.e. the indicative, the subjunctive, the conditional and the imperative, to which should be added two impersonal moods, the infinitive and the participles (present and past). It is also important to be aware of the notion of **aspect**, which describes the **way the process** described by the verb **takes place in time** (see Section 3, Aspect):

a) The indicative expresses notions of person (first, second or third), tense (i.e. past, present or future) and aspect. It is referred to as the mood of maximum actualisation. The tenses of its conjugation are:

- simple tenses:

present *(je marche)*   future *(je marcherai)*
imperfect *(je marchais)*   past historic *(je marchai)*

- compound tenses:

perfect *(j'ai marché)*   past anterior *(j'eus marché)*
pluperfect *(j'avais marché)*   future anterior/future perfect
double compound past   *(j'aurai marché)*
   (j'ai eu marché)

b) The subjunctive: only the present and the perfect are still widely used in modern French, i.e. the simple and the corresponding compound form. The subjunctive can express notions of person and aspect but has no temporal value. This can be seen when looking at the main clause in the following examples: *J'ai regretté*
                        Je regrette   *que Paul soit là.*
                        Je regretterai

The subjunctive is generally used to express what 'might be' rather than what 'is' (for which the indicative is used, although there are a number of exceptions). For instance, in *Bien qu'il **pleuve**, je sors*, there is nothing 'virtual' about the rain: it is actually raining!

The imperfect and pluperfect forms of the subjunctive are still used by some authors in narratives. The tenses of the conjugation are:

- simple tenses:

present *(que je prenne)*   imperfect *(que je prisse)*

- compound tenses:

perfect *(que j'aie pris)*   pluperfect *(que j'eusse pris)*

c) The conditional exists mainly in the present form (non-accomplished aspect, see also Section 3, Aspect) and in the perfect form (accomplished aspect).

Compare for instance:

*Si je **gagnais** le gros lot au loto, j'**achèterais** une Ferrari.*

    and:

*Si j'**avais gagné** le gros lot au loto, j'**aurais acheté** une Ferrari.*

In the first example, it is still possible to win: I am talking about what **will happen if**... The possibility of winning has not taken place yet, it is non-accomplished.

In the second example, I am talking about what **would have happened if**... but it did not happen. The possibility of winning has already happened and did not materialise: the event (here a non-event!) is accomplished.

The pluperfect (also called 'second form of the perfect') conditional is still used in narratives and has the same morphology as the pluperfect subjunctive.

Compare:

*Il aurait fallu qu'il lui **eût dit** la vérité.*

    and:

*S'il avait su ce qui allait se passer, il lui **eût dit** la vérité.*

The conditional is considered as either a mood in its own right or part of the indicative, depending on the context.

As a mood, it is used to express hypotheses.

Ex: *A votre place, je **travaillerais** davantage.*

As a tense of the indicative, it is used to express the future seen from the past (i.e. the process could have taken place before the moment of speaking).

Ex: *Je pensais que vous **viendriez** hier/demain.*

The tenses are:
- simple tense:

present *(je prendrais)*
- compound tenses:

perfect *(j'aurais pris)*   pluperfect *(j'eusse pris)*

d) The imperative also expresses notions of aspect with its simple and corresponding compound form: *terminez; ayez terminé*. The person is either the second person *(tu/vous)* or the first person plural *(nous)* which itself necessarily includes a second person in the imperative *(nous = je + tu/vous)*.

It is used to express orders but also advice, suggestion, wish, apology, etc. and presupposes the simultaneous presence of speaker and addressee.

e) The infinitive and the participles (present and past) express notions of accomplished or non-accomplished aspect:

avoir mangé vs *manger* or *ayant mangé* vs *mangeant*.

2. Linguistic tenses

The **present** is defined as the coincidence between the moment of speaking and the moment when the action (or state or transformation) described by the verb is happening. It is from that present that the **past** and the **future** are defined. Hence the present is the 'unmarked' tense. However, there is no exact symmetry between the past and the future in their relation to the present. As far as past events are concerned, the most important thing is to determine HOW these events took place, which is an **aspectual** problem, whereas for future events, the most important thing is to know WHETHER or not they will take place and HOW they are presented by the speaker, which is a **modality** problem. These 'referential tenses' (i.e. which take the present as their point of reference) are not to be confused with the 'grammatical tenses' as described by the conjugations of the verb (imperfect, pluperfect, etc.: see above). Indeed, consider the following utterances:

*Il n'est pas encore arrivé: il **aura manqué** son train.*

where the future anterior expresses a probability in the past (= he has probably missed his train).

*Un pas de plus et je **tombais**.*

where the imperfect does not refer to an event in the past but to a mere hypothesis (Another step and I would have fallen).

*Demain il y **aura** du soleil.*

where the future expresses a prediction (Tomorrow will be sunny).

*Demain, tu **feras** les courses.*

where the future expresses an order (Tomorrow, you will do the shopping).

See also Section 4, Modality.

Note also the existence of a 'historical' present where events (with dates) can be made more vivid when told in the present tense (instead of e.g. a past historic).

Ex: *Mais la vie de la duchesse à la cour n'**est** bientôt plus qu'un calvaire. Le roi **se détache** d'elle et Mme de Montespan **devient** maîtresse en titre. Les courtisans **accablent** Louise de vexations. En 1671, elle **s'enfuit** à nouveau au couvent Sainte-Marie de Chaillot, mais Louis XIV l'en **fait** sortir encore, cette fois par Colbert.*

(Christian Melchior-Bonnet, *Le grand livre de l'histoire de France*)

The present is also used to express 'general truths', hence it is found in proverbs (e.g. *Pauvreté n'est pas vice; Pierre qui roule n'amasse pas mousse*) but also in scientific statements (e.g. *La terre tourne autour du soleil*) and other statements considered as 'accepted truths'. Thus this present can be used by speakers who want to express their own feelings and opinions (including criticisms of others) whilst making these statements pass for general truths (e.g. *Les gens qui se disent honnêtes le sont rarement*).

Compound forms, apart from expressing the aspectual value of accomplished (see below), are also used with a temporal value of anteriority. The pluperfect, for instance, can be used to show that a process is anterior to (i.e. happened before) another one also in the past.

Ex: *Le matin il **avait nagé** et après le déjeuner, il **fit/ a fait** une promenade.*

Finally, the notion of time can also be expressed by adjectives:

Ex: *un **ancien** ministre* (past)
*l'**actuel** président* (present)
*le **futur** champion du monde* (future)

Worked example:

Name, and justify, the use of the various verb forms (in bold) in the following passage:

*Ancien videur d'une discothèque, il **se crut** menacé. Mais cela ne **fit** que décupler son agressivité, alimentée par l'usage massif d'amphétamines et d'alcool. Quelques années auparavant, lors d'une bagarre de rue à Cannes, il **avait foncé** sur un adversaire qui **déchargeait** sur lui un révolver. Ce soir-là, il **saisit** un pied de table qui **traînait** derrière le bar du club et l'**abattit** sur le crâne de Roch Isnard.*
Le Monde, 23 January 1991

101

Suggested answers:

- *se crut, fit:* chronology of events (past historic)
- *avait foncé:* event anterior to the previous two events (pluperfect)
- *déchargeait:* background (imperfect) on which another event took place: *avait foncé*
- *saisit, abattit:* chronology of events (past historic)
- *traînait:* state (imperfect)

Note that since this is a narrative, the adverbs (here of time) are NOT deictic (*ce soir-là*; *quelques années auparavant*). See also Chapter 7, Presence of the speaker.

3. Aspect

Aspect concerns the way the process described by the verb **takes place in time**.

Lexical aspect

Some aspectual phenomena are particular to each verb. For instance, *habiter* or *dormir* imply a lasting process, whereas *saisir* or *éclater* imply a punctual, instantaneous, process: this is also referred to as the **'lexical'** aspect (based on the lexis), or **'mode of action'** of the verb. Note that these 'modes of action' are related to the meaning of each **use** of the verb concerned with a particular subject or object. Compare for instance *je prends un livre* (punctual process), *je prends le frais* (lasting process) and *le ciment prend* (transformation): we can say that the mode of action is imposed by the **meaning** of the verb.

Grammatical aspect

A distinction should be made between the notions of accomplished and non-accomplished process, corresponding in French to the compound and the simple forms. For instance, in *il chante* the process is non-accomplished (he is still singing as we are saying *il chante*) whereas in *il a chanté* the process is accomplished (he is no longer singing when we say *il a chanté*). This is also called the **'grammatical'** aspect and is considered by some linguists as the only genuine form of expression of aspect. Indeed, the choice of aspect here depends on nothing else but the speaker.

In addition, to express the past, the speaker can use e.g. *il marchait* (**imperfective aspect**), to describe for instance an ongoing process seen in the past, without any consideration of its beginning or its end, or *il marcha/a marché* (**perfective aspect**), to describe an event seen as completed in the past, whatever its duration.

As we said earlier, there are affinities between aspect and mode of action. However, aspect is based on a particular point of view on the process. Hence a so-called 'conclusive' verb such as *mourir* can only be conclusive when associated to a perfective aspect *(Paul **mourut** du choléra)*. Compare for instance with *Je **meurs** de froid avec tous ces courants d'air!* which is a metaphoric use of *mourir* and means: *J'ai très froid / Je souffre du froid*. Finally, the **context** in which the verb is used will determine the mode of action. For instance *ramasser un champignon* is punctual whereas *ramasser des champignons* could be punctual, durative or iterative.

Compare: *Je ramasse un champignon*   (punctual)

             Je ramasse des champignons   (durative)

             Tous les dimanches, je ramasse des champignons (iterative)

Worked example:

a) What aspectual distinction do you make between *La pluie tombe* and *L'enfant tombe*, *La pluie est tombée pendant des heures* and *L'enfant est tombé pendant des heures?*

b) What is 'wrong' about the following sentences?

  – **Il pleut en un instant.*   – **La pluie tombe en un instant.*

  – **Il ferme longtemps la porte.*   – **L'enfant tombe pendant des heures.*

Suggested answers:

a) In *La pluie tombe*, we have an extended present, where the rain may have started falling before the moment of speaking and is likely to continue after. The present here refers to the continuous fall of different drops of water; in *L'enfant tombe*, we have a punctual, single event, happening at the moment of speaking.

Hence *La pluie est tombée pendant des heures* refers quite naturally to a period of time during which rain fell, whereas *?L'enfant est tombé pendant des heures*, is difficult to understand: how can a punctual event 'last' for hours? Unless of course this utterance refers to a **repetition** of events: the child fell again and again for hours …

b) *pleuvoir* is a durative verb, hence is incompatible with the adverb phrase *en un instant*; *fermer* is punctual, hence is incompatible with an adverb such as *longtemps*; *tomber* is punctual hence is incompatible with *pendant des heures* (but see above).

Aspect is often neglected in French because (unlike in e.g. Slavonic languages) aspect markers cannot be distinguished morphologically from tense markers. For instance, the markers of the imperfect show both tense (past) and aspect (imperfective).

Grammatical tenses are associated to a particular aspect. For instance, both the past historic (*passé simple*) and the perfect (*passé composé*) are opposed to the imperfect as the perfective and imperfective forms respectively. The *passé composé* is the perfective form of the discourse (*discours*) while the *passé simple* is the perfective form of the narrative (*récit*). In a *récit*, there is no presence of the speaker, hence no modalisation and no deictics, i.e. nothing that can only be interpreted in relation to the speaker (e.g. *ici* = next to the speaker; *maintenant* = at the time when the speaker says *maintenant*, etc.). In a *discours* on the contrary, all these elements can be present.

Such an opposition (perfective/imperfective) cannot be established as far as the present and the future are concerned. Although as a rule the present is imperfective, it still depends on the mode of action and the context. For instance, with so-called 'performative' verbs, when the action is actually accomplished at the very moment when the utterance takes place, the present is perfective.

Ex: *Je **déclare** la séance ouverte. (l'action de déclarer est accomplie)*

*Je **promets** d'être fidèle (l'action de promettre est accomplie).*

Conversely, the future as a rule is perfective, except in subordinate clauses of time. Compare for instance:

*Demain, tu **feras** les courses* (where *feras les courses* is perfective)

*Pendant que tu **feras** les courses, j'irai chercher grand-mère à la gare* (where *feras les courses* is imperfective).

Worked example:

Comment on the following uses of the present tense:
(i)   *J'allume le gaz.*
(ii) *Il neige.*
(iii) *Paul et Marie se détestent.*
(iv) *Les cerises se récoltent en juin.*
(v)   *Paul fait du vélo.*
(vi) *Un et un font deux.*
(vii) *Nul n'est censé ignorer la loi.*
(viii) *Je vais aux Etats-Unis l'année prochaine.*
(ix) *Emile Zola meurt en 1902.*

Suggested answers:

(i)   event likely to be happening at the precise moment of speaking

(ii)   action taking place at or around the time of speaking

(iii) state of affairs: the present is 'extended' in the past as well as in the future

(iv)   action which takes place regularly (iterative present) at the time indicated by the adverb phrase of time, here *en juin*

(v)   this one is ambiguous: it could mean that right now, Paul is on his bicycle, OR that he is a cyclist (i.e. goes cycling on a regular basis)

(vi)   generic present, stating a general, 'accepted' truth

(vii) another form of generic present, usually found in proverbs, but also in philosophical or legal documents

(viii) the present here is interpreted as a future, thanks to the adverb phrase of time, here *l'année prochaine*

(ix)   this is an instance of literary or historic present, where the present is used to describe something which happened in the past; note that relevant adverb phrases of time are essential (here *en 1902*).

Worked example:

Compare the different aspectual values of the verbs *parler* and *arriver* in the following examples:

(i)   *Il parlait à ses amis quand sa mère arriva.*

(ii)   *Il parla à ses amis quand sa mère arriva.*

(iii) *Il parlait à ses amis quand sa mère arrivait.*

(iv)   *Il parla à ses amis quand sa mère arrivait.*

Suggested answers:

(i)   *parlait* is an on-going process and forms the background for *arriva*, a punctual event

(He was talking to his friends when his mother arrived.)

(ii)   *parla* is a punctual event which occurred at the precise moment when another punctual event took place: *arriva*

(He started talking to his friends when his mother arrived.)

(iii) *parlait* is an on-going event, taking place each time *arrivait* was taking place

(He would talk to his friends whenever his mother arrived.)

(iv)   This last combination is a little difficult to interpret, unless *quand* is understood as *alors que*, so that *parla* is a punctual event, taking place sometimes during the process of *arrivait*.

(He started talking to his friends (just) as his mother was arriving.)

4. Modality

This is where the speaker expresses her/his attitude towards what she/he is saying and also establishes a particular relation with the addressee. Hence the utterance is anchored in relation to what is (e.g. true or false, possible or impossible, necessary or optional, allowed or forbidden, etc.). It can be used to communicate value judgements or appreciations. It can be expressed in various ways, for instance with:

- the so-called 'modal verbs' *devoir, pouvoir* and *vouloir*:

Ex: *Vous **devez** être de retour à six heures.*
(expressing an obligation: You **must** be back by six o'clock.)

*Je **devais** le voir hier.*
(expressing intention/expectation: I **was supposed to** see him yesterday.)

*Nous **aurions dû** y aller.*
(expressing regret: We **should have** gone there.)

*Tu **aurais pu** me le dire!*
(expressing reproach: You **could have** told me!)

*Il **ne veut pas** y aller.*
(expressing determination: He **won't** go.)

- verbal moods:

Ex: subjunctive: *Qu'ils attendent!*
(expressing an order: Let them wait!)

conditional: *A votre place, j'attendrais!*
(expressing a suggestion: If I were you, I would wait!)

imperative: *Attendez-moi!*
(expressing a plea: Wait for me!)

- the use of grammatical tenses :

Ex: imperfect: *Et si on allait prendre un verre?*
(expressing a suggestion: How about going for a drink?)

future: *Ça ne marchera jamais!*
(expressing a prediction: It will never work!)

- impersonal constructions:

Ex: *Il est vrai/possible/probable/certain,* etc. *que…*

(expressing a judgement, through the adjective used: the selection of the subjunctive or indicative after *que* depends on the meaning of the adjective: does it express something probable or even certain (indicative) or merely possible or even impossible (subjunctive)?)

- adverbs:

Ex: *peut-être,* expressing a possibility
heureusement, expressing a judgement, etc.

In addition, any sentence is presented as either declarative, interrogative, imperative or exclamative. However, the particular **structure** of an utterance should not be confused with its **interpretation** in a particular context, in which, when speaking, the intonation of the speaker also plays a role. For instance, the **interrogative** sentence *Voulez-vous vous taire?* is likely to be interpreted as an **order** rather than a question, whereas the **declarative** sentence *Je voudrais deux croissants* will be understood as a **request**. This scope for interpretation is often used as a source of humour.

ASSIGNMENTS

1. What is the main tense in the following passage? What is expressed by the other tenses used?

*Je n'**avais** pas douze ans lorsque je **perdis** mon père. Ma mère, que plus rien ne **retenait** au Havre, où mon père **avait été** médecin, **décida** de venir habiter Paris, estimant que j'y **finirais** mieux mes études. Elle **loua**, près du Luxembourg, un petit appartement que Miss Ashburton **vint** occuper avec nous. Miss Flora Ashburton, qui n'**avait** plus de famille, **avait été** d'abord l'institutrice de ma mère, puis sa compagne et bientôt son amie. Je **vivais** auprès de ces deux femmes à l'air également doux et triste, et que je ne **puis** revoir qu'en deuil. Un jour, et, je **pense**, assez longtemps après la mort de mon père, ma mère **avait remplacé** par un ruban mauve le ruban noir de son bonnet du matin.*

*— O maman! m'**étais**-je **écrié**; comme cette couleur te **va** mal! Le lendemain, elle **avait remis** un ruban noir.*

André Gide, *La Porte étroite*

2. Comment on the meanings of the verbs *pouvoir* and *devoir* in the following extract:

*Quand Philippe sortit de chez la dame en blanc, il **pouvait** être une heure et demie du matin.*

*Il **avait dû** attendre, pour quitter la villa familiale, que tous les bruits et les lumières y fussent éteints [...]. Il avait marché vers Ker-Anna [...]. En haut de la côte, il s'était retourné, pour apercevoir à mi-falaise la maison où dormaient ses parents, les parents de Vinca - et Vinca... La troisième fenêtre, le petit balcon de bois... Elle **devait dormir** derrière cette paire de volets clos. Elle **devait dormir**, tournée un peu de côté, la figure sur son bras, comme une enfant qui se cache pour pleurer, ses cheveux égaux ouverts en éventail de la nuque à la joue.*

Colette, *Le Blé en herbe*

3. Comment on the meaning of the conditional in the following passage:

> *Le lendemain je me relevai, poursuivi des mêmes idées qui m'avaient agité la veille. Mon agitation redoubla les jours suivants; Elléonore voulut inutilement en pénétrer la cause: je répondais par des monosyllabes contraints à ses questions impétueuses; je me raidissais contre son insistance, sachant trop qu'à ma franchise **succéderait** sa douleur, et que sa douleur m'**imposerait** une dissimulation nouvelle.*
>
> Benjamin Constant, *Adolphe*, Ch. VIII

4. Comment on modality, as expressed by moods and tenses, in the following passage (present imperative, present indicative and future indicative).

> *Dany, Mademoiselle, ne **partez** pas sans donner la réponse… Et **prenez** ces violettes, au moins!* (Dany sort. Bérenger les bras ballants, est près de la sortie.) *Oh…* (A l'architecte.) *Vous qui **connaissez** le cœur humain, quand une femme ne **répond** ni oui ni non, cela **veut** dire «oui» n'est-ce pas?* (En direction de la coulisse de droite.) *Vous **serez** mon inspiratrice, vous **serez** ma muse. Je **travaillerai**.* (Tandis qu'on entend un vague écho répétant ces dernières syllabes, Bérenger fait deux pas vers l'Architecte et montre dans le vide.) *Je ne **renonce** pas. Je **m'installe** ici, avec Dany. J'**achèterai** cette maison blanche, au milieu de la verdure et qui **a l'air** d'être abandonnée par ses constructeurs… Je n'**ai** pas beaucoup d'argent, vous m'**accorderez** des facilités de paiement.*
>
> Ionesco, *Tueur sans gages*

5. What is the main tense of the following passage? What is expressed aspectually by the other tenses?

> Télérama: *Y **aura**-t-il d'autres albums de Gaston?*
> André Franquin: *Je ne **crois** pas. Celui-ci **sera** le dernier. Je **suis tombé** en panne de Gaston. J'**ai perdu** le rythme quotidien en 1989, pendant que je **me consacrais** à la réalisation des Tifous, un dessin animé qui me **tenait** énormément à cœur. C'**était** un travail fou! Soixante-quatorze épisodes de six minutes. Il **fallait** être en grande forme. Cela m'**a pris** tout mon temps et **a cassé** le rythme quotidien que j'**avais adopté** pour dessiner Gaston. Un ressort **s'est brisé**. J'**ai tenté** de recommencer plusieurs fois. J'**ai** plusieurs ébauches de gags que je n'**arrive** pas à terminer. Ils **risquent** de rester dans mes tiroirs.*
>
> *Télérama*, No 2453, 18-25 January 1997

6. Comment on the meaning of the future in the following passage:

> *Un coquillage est une petite chose mais je peux la démesurer en la replaçant où je la trouve, posée sur l'étendue du sable. Car alors je **prendrai** une poignée de sable et j'**observerai** le peu qui me reste dans la main après que par les interstices de mes doigts presque toute la poignée **aura filé**, j'**observerai** quelques grains, et aucun de ces grains de sable à ce moment ne m'**apparaîtra** plus une petite chose, et bientôt le coquillage formel, cette coquille d'huître ou cette tiare bâtarde, ou ce «couteau», m'**impressionnera** comme un énorme monument, en même temps colossal et précieux, quelque chose comme le temple d'Angkor, Saint-Maclou, ou les Pyramides, avec une signification beaucoup plus étrange que ces trop incontestables produits d'hommes.*
>
> Francis Ponge, *Notes pour un coquillage,* in *Le parti pris des choses*

7. Comment on the use of tenses (past historic, imperfect, present), in particular the shifts between discourse and narrative, in the following passage:

> *Ce **fut** ma nièce qui **alla** ouvrir quand on **frappa**. Elle **venait de** me servir mon café, comme chaque soir (le café me **fait** dormir). J'**étais** assis au fond de la pièce, relativement dans l'ombre. La porte **donne** sur le jardin, de plain pied. Tout le long de la maison **court** un trottoir de carreaux rouges très commode quand il **pleut**. Nous **entendîmes** marcher, le bruit des talons sur le carreau. Ma nièce me **regarda** et **posa** sa tasse. Je **gardai** la mienne dans mes mains.*
>
> Vercors, *Le Silence de la mer*

8. Comment on the use of the conditional (present and perfect) and the imperfect subjunctive in the following passage:

> *Quant à Marie-Ange, elle **aurait** également **souhaité** rentrer à pied, parce qu'alors elle **aurait pu** savoir quelle impression on retirait d'être suivie dans la rue ainsi que la fille aux cheveux jaunes affirmait l'avoir été souvent. Marie-Ange se demandait si elle **oserait** jamais embrasser un garçon sur la bouche, et si elle ne devait pas faire l'expérience une fois avec sa camarade.*
> *Ainsi, pour les deux enfants [...] apparaissaient de manière permanente, angoissante, les soucis de leur orgueil et de leur sexe. Il suffisait que, certaines nuits, ils **craignissent** en s'endormant de ne point se réveiller, que chaque jour, sur le plateau d'argent du courrier, ils **vissent** le cadre noir de quelque faire-part de décès, et que certains matins ils **se demandassent** soudain pourquoi ils étaient au monde, sous le grand ciel nuageux, et pourquoi leur père n'y était plus quand tant de vieillards s'y trouvaient encore, pour que **vînt** s'ajouter la troisième angoisse, celle de la mort.*
>
> Maurice Druon, *La Chute des corps*

SUGGESTED ANSWERS TO ASSIGNMENTS

1. *La Porte étroite*

The main tense is the past historic, as we are told a story:
- *je **perdis** mon père*
- *ma mère **décida***
- *Elle **loua***
- *Miss Ashburton **vint**.*

Around the past historic, signalling events, are instances of the imperfect expressing properties or states of affairs:
- *je n'**avais** pas douze ans*
- *plus rien ne **retenait***
- *qui n'**avait** plus de famille*
- *je **vivais**.*

The pluperfect refers to events and states prior to those expressed by the past historic and imperfect respectively:
- *mon père **avait été** médecin* (i.e. was no longer a doctor when *ma mère décida de venir habiter Paris*)
- *Miss Flora Ashburton **avait été** d'abord l'institutrice . . .* (i.e. was no longer *l'institutrice* at the time of the story).

There is one conditional:
- *que j'y **finirais***

expressing a future in the past (see Section 1(c)). Compare with:
- *Ma mère **décide**. . . estimant que j'y **finirai** mieux . . .*

There are two present tenses:
- *que je ne **puis** revoir*, corresponding to the present of the speaker, hence we have a deictic tense in the middle of a story in the past historic, suggesting that the speaker intervenes in his own story.
- The same applies to *je **pense***, which expresses what the speaker thinks NOW of events which happened THEN.

2. *Le Blé en herbe*

  pouvoir: il pouvait être une heure et demie

here, *pouvoir* expresses a possibility

  devoir: il avait dû attendre

here, *devoir* expresses an obligation

  elle devait dormir (twice)

here, *devoir* expresses a probability.

3. *Adolphe*

The two conditionals (*succéderait* and *m'imposerait*) are used to express the future in the past. Compare with:

> *Je me raidis... succédera... m'imposera...*

4. *Tueur sans gages*

Moods and tenses:

> • imperative present:

> *ne partez pas*   *prenez ces violettes*

to express here a plea and an offer respectively

> • indicative present:

vous qui connaissez: state of affairs

quand une femme ne répond: present of iteration (= whenever . . .)

cela veut dire: state of affairs

je ne renonce pas: state of mind

je m'installe ici: with a value of immediate future (= *je vais m'installer ici*)

je n'ai pas beaucoup d'argent: state

cette maison blanche qui a l'air: descriptive

> • indicative future:

> *vous serez* (twice)   *j'achèterai*
> *je travaillerai*   *vous m'accorderez*

Whilst with the first person, we have a prediction, with the second person, we are very much nearer the expression of an order.

5. *Télérama*

The main tense here is the perfect *(je suis tombé, j'ai perdu, cela m'a pris, a cassé, s'est brisé, ai tenté)* around which are organised:

> • imperfect:

pendant que je me consacrais: background on which the event *j'ai perdu le rythme* took place

un dessin qui me tenait à cœur: description of a state of affairs in the past

c'était un travail fou: ditto

il fallait être en forme: ditto

• pluperfect:

le rythme que j'avais adopté: event anterior to *cela a cassé (= j'avais adopté un rythme → cela a cassé ce rythme)*

• indicative present:

we have four, one at the beginning of André Franquin's reply:

je ne crois pas

and the other three at the end:

j'ai plusieurs ébauches   je n'arrive pas   ils risquent de rester

all referring to the present of the speaker, André Franquin

• future:

finally, we have two futures, both referring to events which may happen yet:

the question of Télérama: *Y aura-t-il d'autres albums?*

André Franquin's reply: *celui-ci sera le dernier* (prediction).

6. *Notes pour un coquillage*

The future here has a value of conditional: [...] *je peux la démesurer. Comment? En prenant une poignée de sable,* etc. Hence the speaker imagines what will happen **if** he adopts a particular course of action: *je prendrai, j'observerai, m'apparaîtra, m'impressionnera.*

The future anterior refers to a future in the past:

toute la poignée aura filé: refers to an event imagined as happening in the future, **before** *j'observerai.*

7. *Le Silence de la mer*

The main tense in this text is the past historic *(fut, alla, frappa, entendîmes, regarda, posa, gardai)*, all expressing events in the story, with the exception of *ce fut* where the past historic is there to 'match' the others. Note that *ce fut... qui* is just a presentative form whose aim is to focus on a particular element of the sentence. Compare with the plain:

Ma nièce alla...

The recent past *(Elle venait de me servir...)* refers to an event which happened just prior to the events *alla* and *frappa.*

The imperfect expresses a state *(j'étais assis).*

Then we have a few presents:

(le café me fait dormir): between brackets, indicates an intervention of the

speaker in the narration, to express something which is true regardless of time: a property of coffee for him. Then after the background *(étais assis)*, the speaker suddenly intervenes again in the narration with a description of the scene, as if it were there before his eyes:

la porte donne sur le jardin

un trottoir court

quand il pleut: iterative present (= whenever).

Then he returns to the narration with the past historic *(entendîmes, regarda,* etc.).

8. *La Chute des corps*

There are two perfect conditionals in the first paragraph, both expressing regret, i.e. a wish which cannot ever be fulfilled now: *elle **aurait** également **souhaité** rentrer à pied parce qu'alors elle **aurait pu** savoir*[...] On the contrary, the present conditional of *elle se demandait si elle **oserait***[...] expresses a possibility in the future.

There are four imperfect subjunctives in the second paragraph: the first three **(craignissent, vissent, demandassent)** are governed by the impersonal expression *il suffisait que* and the last one **(vînt)** by the conjunction *pour que*. The author applies the rule whereby in a literary text, an imperfect or conditional in the main clause entails the use of the **imperfect subjunctive** in the subordinate clause (in standard French, the present subjunctive would be used: *il suffisait qu'ils craignent..., qu'ils voient..., et qu'ils se demandent..., pour que vienne...*).

CHAPTER 5
REITERATION

INTRODUCTION

Lexical cohesion occurs when two or more words in a text are linked primarily in terms of their **meaning**. A grammatical relationship between these items may not always be apparent.

There are two major categories of lexical cohesion. These are **reiteration** (treated in this chapter) and the construction of **lexical fields** (treated in Chapter 6).

Reiteration is a basic device for establishing the cohesion of a text: if lexical items did not refer back to previously mentioned entities with same or similar meanings, there would be no textual continuity. Reiteration, therefore, fulfils a similar function to anaphoric reference (see Chapter 2, Coreference and contrast).

Reiteration includes the following devices:
1. Repetition
2. Synonymy and lexical anaphora
3. Superordinates, hyponyms and generals

1. Repetition

By repetition is meant the repeating of the **same** key word or phrase. Example:

> *En cette époque antérieure à la philosophie des Lumières, la **tolérance** n'est pas celle que l'on croit. Il s'agit de **tolérer** ce qu'on ne peut empêcher, en espérant que le temps le corrigera. La **tolérance** n'interdit pas de souhaiter très fort une correction des mentalités, une évolution des situations. La **tolérance** n'est ni équanimité ni acception fataliste, elle est simple résignation jusqu'à meilleure fortune. La **tolérance** au sens plein, celle d'une acception assumée, marque le message de l'ère des Lumières, elle n'est pas antérieure.*
>
> *Le Monde,* 22 August 1998

In the above example, the repetition of the word *tolérance* has the effect of highlighting and of drawing constant attention to the theme of the passage. The function of repetition here, therefore, is primarily didactic.

At the same time, however, the use of repetition in the passage carries, for some readers, echoes of Biblical discourse, in particular of the Sermon on the Mount. Thus, from this intertextual perspective, repetition also becomes a strategy for strengthening the emotive and evaluative dimensions of the discourse.

2. Synonymy and lexical anaphora

Instead of repeating exactly the same word, which can sometimes produce monotony, some texts employ a different cohesive device. They use:

– a word that has the same meaning as another word. Example:

> *Sur le marché des changes, la livre sterling s'est effondrée à son plus bas niveau historique face au **deutschmark** à 2,2950 pour 1 **mark**. La **devise allemande** a battu de nouveaux records...*
>
> *Le Monde,* 28 February 1995

– or a word which, in the context in which it appears, has a similar or related meaning to another one and refers to the same 'object of the world'. This lends the text greater variety. Example:

*Engin réputé tout-terrain — et donc destiné à l'origine à de lointaines expéditions dans des conditions difficiles —, **le 4x4** est devenu, de plus en plus, un véhicule de loisirs. Les constructeurs ont donc, d'année en année, civilisé **leurs modèles** en trahissant parfois les vertus d'origine qui avaient doté **ces engins rustiques et inusables** d'une vocation plus militaire ou agricole que familiale.*

Le Monde, 28 February 1995

Worked example:

Read the following passage:

1. *Une mouche maigre tournait, depuis un moment, dans l'autocar aux glaces pourtant relevées. Insolite, elle allait et venait sans bruit, d'un vol exténué. Janine la perdit de vue, puis la vit atterrir sur la main immobile de son mari. Il faisait froid. La mouche frissonnait à chaque rafale du vent* **5.** *sableux qui crissait contre les vitres. Dans la lumière rare du matin d'hiver, à grand bruit de tôles et d'essieux, le véhicule roulait, tanguait, avançait à peine. Janine regarda son mari. Des épis de cheveux grisonnants plantés bas sur un front serré, le nez large, la bouche irrégulière, Marcel avait l'air d'un faune boudeur. A chaque défoncement de la chaussée, elle* **10.** *le sentait sursauter contre elle. Puis il laissait retomber son torse pesant sur ses jambes écartées, le regard fixe, inerte de nouveau, et absent. Seules, ses grosses mains imberbes, rendues plus courtes encore par la flanelle grise qui dépassait les manches de chemise et couvrait les poignets, semblaient en action. Elles serraient si fortement une petite valise de toile, placée entre ses* **15.** *genoux, qu'elles ne paraissaient pas sentir la course hésitante de la mouche.*

Albert Camus, *La Femme adultère*, in *L'Exil et le royaume*

a) List as many synonyms or lexical anaphoras as you can from this passage.
b) What effects are achieved through their use in this text? What is their function?

Suggested answers:

a) *allait et venait* (line 2) describing the movement of the fly, is close in meaning to *tournait* (line 1)

d'un vol (line 2) can also refer back to *allait et venait*

les vitres (line 5) is a synonym of *aux glaces* (lines 1-2)

le véhicule (line 6) is actually a superordinate (see Section 3, Superordinates, hyponyms and generals) referring back to the hyponym *l'autocar* (line 1)

both *tanguait* (line 6) and *roulait* (line 6) refer to the movement of the bus but note that they are lexical anaphoras rather than synonyms

both *inerte* (line 11) and *fixe* (line 11) express an absence of movement

la course hésitante in the last sentence (line 15) refers back to *allait et venait* and *tournait* of the opening lines.

b) The use of synonyms and lexical anaphoras in this passage have the following functions:

– Firstly, the device serves to introduce and reinforce a select number of key themes and of oppositions. These are, for instance:

movement: *tournait, allait et venait, la course, tanguait, roulait*
vs immobility: *fixe, inerte*

inside: *aux glaces relevées*
vs outside: *contre les vitres*

– Secondly, as two words can never possess exactly the same meaning (synonyms), lexical anaphoras can be particularly effective in evoking the myriad of nuances and shades that, for a writer like Camus, constitute the very nature of sensorial reality.

Worked example:

Read the following extract:

Agression sous la tente
Un motard danois qui passait sa nuit sous une tente au bord de la nationale 89, à Milhac-d'Auberoche, a été dépouillé par deux hommes et une femme armés de pistolets. Les agresseurs se sont emparés de la moto de grosse cylindrée, des papiers et des vêtements du touriste, qui a été légèrement blessé.
Libération, 9 August 1998

a. Identify two lexical anaphoras. To what do they refer in this particular context?

b. How do you think the choice of lexical anaphora contributes to rendering the account more vivid and more immediate for the reader?

Suggested answers:

a. The term *les agresseurs* at the beginning of the second sentence is a lexical anaphora referring back to *deux hommes et une femme armés de pistolets*. Similarly, in the last line, the word *touriste* refers back to *un motard danois* in the opening sentence.

b. The choice of lexical anaphora strengthens the dramatic impact of the passage. The oppositional grouping of characters (aggressors vs victim, innocent vs guilty, etc.) is also rendered apparent. This particular use of lexical anaphora to oppose different groups of people is a characteristic feature of much media discourse.

3. Superordinates, hyponyms and generals

Another way of establishing links in a text is the use of superordinates and hyponyms. A superordinate expresses a whole, it denotes a class. The part is expressed by a hyponym, a more specific term. For instance, 'Brazil', 'Spain', 'England', etc. are hyponyms of the superordinate 'country'. Similarly the superordinate 'animal' can have as its hyponyms 'dog', 'elephant', 'lion', 'cat', etc.

Generals are a little vaguer (i.e. more general) than superordinates, and are expressed in words such as 'things' or 'place'.

Ex: *Il a étalé ses vêtements et ses livres sur le lit, puis il a soigneusement mis toutes ses affaires dans sa valise.*
affaires here is a general term referring back to *vêtements* and *livres*.

Superordinates and generals can have an anaphoric or cataphoric function. Note however that it is a common mistake to use a hyponym instead of a superordinate in a list after *et autres*. The following example was heard on the radio:

> [...]*où il chassait lions, tigres et autres leopards.*

instead of, for instance: [...]*où il chassait lions, tigres et autres grands fauves.*

You will find another example of erroneous use of hyponyms in the text from *Libération* entitled *Le soja génétiquement modifié...*, (Chapter 3, Assignments

127

for Section 2, Punctuation), line 11: [...] *les Nestlé et autres Danone* [...] (i.e. two brands), and a 'proper' example of use in the text from *Le Monde* which begins with *Une agriculture monstrueuse* [...] (Chapter 6, Section 1, Lexical fields), line 9: [...] *gavées d'antibiotiques et autres bonnes choses* (with a certain ironical note!).

ASSIGNMENTS

1. Look at the following extract taken from a newspaper article:

> **1.** *Le plan Marshall était un projet profondément marqué par les thèses interventionnistes de l'économiste britannique John Meynard Keynes et par sa* General Theory of Employment, Interest and Money, *selon laquelle les gouvernements ne doivent pas seulement* **5.** *miser sur le marché, mais tout mettre en œuvre pour assurer le plein emploi grâce à une meilleure redistribution des revenus. Le plan fut aussi une manière de populariser chez les Européens le modèle du New Deal expérimenté avant la guerre par les Etats-Unis pour mettre fin, avec succès, à la récession provoquée par la crise de 1929.*
>
> **10.** *En célébrant, le 28 mai dernier à La Haye, le 50ème anniversaire du plan, le président William Clinton n'a pas manqué de replacer l'aide Marshall au cœur des débats actuels sur le rôle de l'Etat dans l'économie. Comme l'avait déjà fait M. Jacques Delors en affirmant:* «Le plan Marshall exprimait l'idée qu'un rattrapage **15.** économique fondé sur les seules forces du marché devait s'accompagner d'un dispositif volontariste d'aide et d'assistance, de nature à surmonter les principaux obstacles structurels».
>
> *Le Monde diplomatique,* June 1997

a) Which key word or lexical item is repeated most?
b) Do you think it would be possible to replace this lexical item by a pronoun? Give your reasons.

2. Look at the text of the advert below:

> *Entre 1 et 3 ans, votre enfant se construit, il change et grandit à vue d'œil.*
> *Pendant ces années, qui sont déterminantes pour son développement physique*
> *et intellectuel, le lait est encore à la base de son alimentation et doit répondre*
> *à ses besoins nutritionnels très spécifiques.*
> *C'est pourquoi le lait Croissance de Candia contient 20 fois plus de fer qu'un*
> *lait ordinaire, car le fer, il en faut beaucoup à votre enfant pour devenir fort.*
> *Et dans Croissance, il trouvera aussi des vitamines, du calcium et des lipides*
> *essentiels, tout ce qu'il lui faut pour bien grandir.*
> **Croissance met toutes les chances dans son biberon.**
> $\qquad\qquad\qquad\qquad$ **CANDIA fait du bien au lait.**
>
> *Marie-Claire, October 1995*

a) Identify examples of repetition.

b) What effect is produced by the use of this device? Why do you think repetition is so common in adverts?

3. Look at the following passages:

> **1.** *Turquie: combats*
> *Quatorze rebelles kurdes ont été tués hier par l'armée turque lors d'un*
> *affrontement à Erzincan, dans l'est de la Turquie, selon l'agence Anatolie.*
> *Cet affrontement a eu lieu dans le cadre d'une vaste opération militaire*
> *lancée voilà trois semaines contre les bases rebelles kurdes du PKK (Parti des*
> *travailleurs du Kurdistan, séparatistes) au nord de l'Irak.*
>
> *Libération, 6 June 1997*

> **2.** *Il n'y avait rien d'autre sur la terre, rien, ni personne. Ils étaient nés du*
> *désert, aucun autre chemin ne pouvait les conduire. Ils ne disaient rien. Ils*
> *ne voulaient rien. Le vent passait sur eux, à travers eux, comme s'il n'y avait*
> *personne sur les dunes.*
> Le Clézio, *Désert*

a) Identify examples of repetition in each of the above texts.

b) Compare and contrast the effects produced by repetition in these two texts.

4. Look at the following extract:

> *Les Irlandais élisent aujourd'hui leurs 166 députés.*
> *L'Irlande nouvelle relève la tête.*
>
> *Chez les McInerney, l'exil est un peu comme une tradition familiale. Dans les années 50, les oncles de John allèrent tenter leur chance à l'étranger. Puis, ce fut au tour de ses quatre frères et sœurs de prendre le large. John, lui, est parti en 1980, son diplôme de physique sous le bras. «A l'époque, il n'y avait aucun avenir en Irlande, aucun travail qui correspondait à mes qualifications. Alors, j'ai atterri à Londres. Après, j'ai eu une proposition pour participer à la création d'un centre de recherches au Nouveau-Mexique. J'y ai consacré huit ans de mon existence, et j'avais l'intention de rester là-bas pour longtemps...». Aujourd'hui, John est de retour sur sa terre natale. Depuis 1993, il est le président du département de physique de l'université de Cork. A 37 ans, il parle de fonder une famille « là où sont ses racines ». « Parce que ce pays a changé et qu'enfin on s'y sent bien ».*
> *Pour John McInerney comme pour beaucoup d'autres, l'Irlande, qui vote aujourd'hui afin de renouveler son Parlement et de désigner son Premier ministre, est une «Irlande nouvelle». Après des décennies durant lesquelles elle n'avait pas les moyens de retenir ses forces vives, l'île d'émeraude a su inverser la tendance. Là où le pays n'arrivait plus à se défaire de son sobriquet «d'homme malade» de l'Europe dans les années 80, il est devenu le «tigre celtique» de l'Union dans les années 90. La croissance y est désormais établie autour de 6%, l'inflation est sous contrôle, les investissements affluent et les Irlandais n'ont plus peur de se dire «optimistes». Résultat: depuis cinq ans, l'Irlande a vu plus de nationaux revenir sur son sol qu'émigrer hors de ses frontières.*
>
> *Libération*, 6 June 1997

a) Identify the use of lexical anaphoras and synonymous expressions in this extract.

b) What effect is produced on the reader through the use of such synonymy?

c) What other reiterative device can you detect in this passage?

5. Read the following extract:

> *Quelques-uns portaient des costumes de ville, tout à fait neufs, mais presque tous étaient vêtus de blouses noires à l'étoffe amollie par l'usure, étoilées d'accrocs, et mal boutonnées faute de boutons. La mienne, trop bien repassée, descendait en plis raides, et luisait de toute sa lustrine, tandis que mes chaussures neuves, qui me serraient un peu les chevilles, disaient à chaque pas: «huit, huit, huit, huit!»*
>
> *Je craignais que cet équipement ne signalât ma nouveauté: mais ces garçons – dont plusieurs avaient un ou deux ans de plus que moi – avaient déjà organisé des jeux qui retenaient toute leur attention.*
>
> *Il y avait des parties de bille, de saute-mouton, de cheval fondu. Au beau milieu de la cour, un tournoi de chevalerie réunissait une vingtaine de participants.*
>
> Marcel Pagnol, *Le Temps des secrets*

a) Identify the use of superordinates and generals in this passage.
b) What effect is produced by the use of superordinates and generals? Do they tell us something about the narrator?

SUGGESTED ANSWERS TO ASSIGNMENTS

1. *Le plan Marshall*

a) The word *plan* occurs in each of the four sentences.

b) It would in most cases not be possible to replace this item by a pronoun. The reference would thereby become ambiguous: within its immediate context, a pronoun such as *il* could refer grammatically to a person (*John Maynard Keynes* or *William Clinton*) rather to the *plan*. Owing to the length of the sentences, there is a textual distance between each mention of *le plan*. The repetition of this word is therefore essential in order to remind the reader of the subject or theme of the article.

Note however that *le plan Marshall* only appears once, at the beginning of the text (and then when quoting Jacques Delors). Thereafter, it is sufficient to say *le plan* and still have an identified item. Note also the presence of a lexical anaphora, *l'aide Marshall* (line 12).

2. *Le lait Candia*

a) Examples of repetition are: *Croissance* (three times)
Candia (two times)
lait (four times)

b) The effects produced by repetition are that:
   – It draws attention to the product and fixes its name in the reader's mind.

   – It turns a basically ordinary product like milk into a superior product, mainly thanks to *Croissance*.

   – The incantatory effect of the repetition draws the reader into the text: a spell is being cast to compel the reader to buy the product.

   – Attention is thereby being focused on language itself - on sound and rhythm (note the use of alliteration with the words *fer, fer, faut, enfant* and *fort*). The text may be similar to a jingle: its use of repetition makes it easier to remember and hence easier for the reader to recognise next time she/he sees it.

Note: these effects are all persuasive devices inducing the reader (or viewer) to buy a particular product. As has often been pointed out, they contribute to the strengthening of the economic status quo, i.e. consumer capitalism.

3. Text 1. *Turquie: combats.* Text 2. Le Clézio, *Désert*

a) Examples of repetition in Text 1 are:
   rebelles kurdes (twice)
   affrontement (twice)

Examples in Text 2 are:
  rien (four times)
  ils (three times)
  personne (twice)
  eux (twice)
  autre (twice)

b) The effects produced by repetition in Text 1 are:
  – Clarity in the communication of the message – there is no ambiguity. The tone is one of a factual report where information is being communicated to the reader.

  – The repetition of the item *rebelles kurdes* has the effect of focusing the reader's attention on this group and on the dominant theme of the passage: that a number of rebels were killed by a stronger military power – the official Turkish army.

  – The repetition of *affrontement* has the additional effect of highlighting the actual physical conflict between the two sides and hence rendering the news story more dramatic and more vivid for the reader.

The above uses of repetition belong to the conventions of newsreporting and in particular to those adopted by the news agencies. Repetition helps to construct the ideological position of these agencies, i.e. to contribute to focusing the reader's attention on minority and socially subversive groups. These groups are almost always presented, as in this article:
  • in physical conflict with the forces of law and order
  • as essentially weak and a victim of these forces.

The effects produced by repetition in Text 2 are quite different. The primary effect of repetition is not to produce clarity or to communicate facts or information but rather to create a particular state of mind or emotion in the reader: the feeling of absolute nothingness (physical and mental). The repetition of words evoking this nothingness suggests the permanency of the state - there can be no change or difference.

4. *L'Irlande nouvelle relève la tête*
a) The expressions *tenter leur chance à l'étranger* and *prendre le large* are loosely synonymous in that both suggest a departure.
  L'Irlande, l'île d'émeraude and *le pays* here also refer to the same object of the world.

Les McInerney is also a lexical anaphora referring to *les oncles de John, ses quatre frères et sœurs* and *John*.

b) In the first example, the effect is poetic. The speaker is not simply concerned with imparting factual information to the reader. The aim is to evoke the sense of anticipation when leaving a country in the hope of a better future. Similarly, in the second example, the choice of the lexical anaphora *l'île d'émeraude* referring to Ireland evokes a poetic mood – that of physical beauty. In the third example, the effect is to emphasize the theme of emigration.

c) Another reiterative device is the use of repetition, for instance *Irlande nouvelle* in italics refers back to the title.

5. *Le Temps des secrets*

a) *cet équipement* is a general referring back to *la mienne* (i.e. *la blouse*) and *mes chaussures neuves; des jeux* is a superordinate referring forward to the hyponyms *des parties de bille, de saute-mouton, de cheval fondu* and *un tournoi de chevalerie*.

b) The passage is predominantly descriptive, giving the reader detailed information relating to the general areas of clothing and of games. It is told from the point of view of a narrator who is also a character in the story. The focus on detail and the choice of the general *cet équipement* may reflect his inner mood of physical embarrassment and self-consciousness.

CHAPTER 6
LEXICAL FIELDS, FIGURES OF SPEECH AND VISUAL REPRESENTATION

INTRODUCTION

An important contribution to lexical cohesion is the process whereby a text sets up its own internal network of semantic associations. These associations can be verbal in the case of written language, or visual in the case of pictorial representation.

Figures of speech such as the metaphor or simile may strengthen lexical cohesion in verbal discourse.

1. Lexical fields

A lexical field is formed by grouping together words or phrases in a text that possess a meaning in common. In other words, it is the name we give to such a set of words. For instance, in a meteorological report, we might say that the words 'ice', 'snow', 'blizzard', etc. all relate to the **lexical field** of weather.

Worked examples:

1. Look at the passage below:

> **1.** *Une agriculture monstrueuse est née. Une agriculture contre nature. On a retourné* **des prairies** *pour* **planter du blé et du maïs,** *au risque d'abîmer* **les sols** *et de polluer* **l'eau souterraine.** *On a construit de véritables cathédrales de métal et de ciment pour*
> **5.** *l'engraissement des* **veaux, vaches, cochons, couvées. Les étables** *sont devenues des forceries; les élevages porcins, des ateliers à mille truies;* **les poules** *de basse-cour, les passagers involontaires d'immenses vaisseaux éclairés jour et nuit à l'ampoule électrique (pour favoriser la ponte), gavées d'antibiotiques et autres bonnes choses. Sous couvert de*
> **10.** *rentabilité, d'économies d'échelle, de «seuils minimum d'activité» qui conduisent à concentrer les élevages en même temps que leur alimentation, le système est à son tour devenu fou, ou plutôt absurde à force de logique marchande poussée toujours plus loin.*
>
> Eric Fottorino, *Le Monde*, April 1995

a) How are the words in bold related? What meaning do they have in common?

b) Can you find another group of words which contrasts with this first group? What are they associated with?

c) Which lexical items suggest a negative evaluation or judgement on the part of the narrator?

d) What ideological stance (beliefs, ideas) do you think is suggested by these patterns? Of what is the text trying to convince the reader?

Suggested answers:

a) The underlined words all have some idea of 'nature' in common. They all belong to the lexical field of 'nature'.

b) A second group is *métal, ciment, ateliers, vaisseaux éclairés* . . . *à l'ampoule électrique, antibiotiques.* These terms can all be associated with modern farming methods.

c) Lexical items suggesting a negative evaluation include: *monstrueuse, contre nature, abîmer les sols, polluer l'eau, gavées d'antibiotiques, des forceries, fou, absurde.*

Note: the above listed group of evaluative terms provides a cohesive tie between our first two groups; this cohesive tie is one of **opposition**: nature or the natural (the positive) is clearly being opposed to the human-made or artificial (the negative).

d) The lexical patterns suggest a condemnation of modern agricultural methods. The text is trying to persuade the reader of their destructive power.

2. How many groups of related words can you identify in the passage below?

> *Ce que Michaux trouve dans la peinture, c'est une liberté. Il l'a répété mille fois, c'est échapper aux mots et laisser vivre en soi une voix simple et primitive qui ne doit rien à cette obligation du sens qui naît dès le moment qu'on parle. Merleau-Ponty le disait, le peintre a l'innocence, il est l'homme du plus grand privilège car à la fois il peut tout dire et rester silencieux. Michaux a exercé ce privilège jusqu'au bout, avec l'ivresse de qui échappe à une emprise et s'abandonne à soi.*
>
> *Magazine littéraire,* No 220, June 1985

Suggested answer:

Painting	**Freedom**	**Innocence**
la peinture	*une liberté*	*une voix simple et primitive*
le peintre	*échapper aux mots*	*l'innocence*
	ne doit rien à cette obligation du sens	
	qui échappe à une emprise	
	s'abandonne à soi	

Communication/Speech

l'a répété mille fois	*dès le moment qu'on parle*
mots	*Merleau-Ponty le disait*
une voix	*tout dire et rester silencieux*

2. Figures of speech

The use of figures of speech may contribute to the semantic density of a text. They can play an important role in the construction of the lexical fields.

2.1. Metaphor

The term metaphor designates the procedure whereby a given sentential unit (item) is substituted for another, thereby transforming its original semantic charge. A substitute name or descriptive expression is transferred to some object or person to which it is not literally applicable. For instance, in the extract from *Le Monde* given in Section 1, there are two examples of metaphor: *cathédrales de métal et de ciment* and *les passagers involontaires d'immenses vaisseaux éclairés jour et nuit à l'ampoule électrique*, both contributing to the negative evaluation of modern agricultural methods.

The use of metaphor may heighten the emotional impact of a text. It is associated in particular with the poetic register of language. However, metaphor is not only widely used in fiction but also in discourse types such as argumentative discourse (see Chapter 9, Textual schemata) and sometimes in advertisements.

Worked example:

Read the following extract from a novel:

Personne n'a vu Monopol, *parce qu'il se cache derrière ses murailles de béton, et qu'il n'est jamais deux fois au même endroit. Simplement, il bâtit, il bâtit tout le temps ses édifices somptueux, et il donne ses ordres à l'armée des flics et des esclaves. Il possède des usines où des millions de gens travaillent, et lui, il n'a jamais assez de richesses. Il aime l'or et l'argent, il les enferme dans de grandes bâtisses silencieuses qui sont gardées par ses flics. Il aime la guerre aussi, parce que ses esclaves se tuent entre eux, avec les fusils qu'il fabrique. Et il aime le pouvoir, parce qu'il est le seul à savoir ce qu'il veut, et comment l'obtenir. Il y a des gens qui veulent tuer* Monopol, *alors ils jettent des grenades sur les magasins et sous les roues de ses voitures. Mais* Monopol *est invincible. Il a des quantités de corps, des quantités de vies. Il est partout à la fois, il est derrière les miroirs sans tain, à l'écoute des téléphones, de l'autre côté des écrans des télévisions. Il sait tout ce qui se passe. Peut-être qu'un jour* Monopol *n'existera plus. Mais il faudra d'abord qu'il ne reste pas une pierre, pas une vitre de ses gigantesques bâtisses. Il faudra que la terre brûle pendant un an jour et nuit, pour que tout soit détruit jusqu'à la racine.*

J.M.G. Le Clézio, *La Guerre*

a) What is the principal metaphor in this passage?

b) Suggest at least two other lexical fields in the text that reinforce (or extend) this initial choice of metaphor.

c) Why do you think this metaphor is so apt?

d) What socio-political position is conveyed through this poetic presentation of monopoly forces?

Suggested answers:

a) The principal metaphor is the evocation of the monopoly system as a totalitarian despot with absolute power over his subjects.

b) Other lexical fields might be:
   – quantity: *l'armée des flics et des esclaves, des millions de gens, jamais assez de richesses, des quantités de corps, des quantités de vies*
   – construction: *il bâtit, il bâtit, de grandes bâtisses, il est partout à la fois, gigantesques bâtisses*
   – absolute knowledge: *il est le seul à savoir ce qu'il veut et comment l'obtenir, il sait tout ce qui se passe*
   – absolute power: *il aime le pouvoir, il donne ses ordres, mais* Monopol *est invincible.*

c) The metaphor of a totalitarian leader is particularly apt as the monopoly system is one in which a few individual enterprises take over all the others, thereby acquiring an absolute power - political and economic - over the lives of the citizens.

d) The choice of metaphor suggests a very powerful indictment of monopoly capitalism, a characteristic feature of contemporary Western societies.

2.2. Simile

A simile is an explicit comparison between two different items that share a common quality. It is most frequently introduced by 'like' (*comme*). Terms such as 'as if', 'resembling', 'suggesting', that introduce descriptions, are termed quasi-similes (Leech & Short 1981). Note that a simile can sometimes be introduced by a comparative structure (*plus/moins/aussi... que*) but not necessarily so.

   Compare: *Il est aussi grand qu'un arbre,*
      and: *Il est grand comme un arbre.*

Like metaphor, simile belongs mainly to the poetic register of language but can be present in all discourse types.

Worked example:

Look at the following passage:

> *Quelquefois les vents alisés du nord-est, qui y soufflent constamment, cardent les nuages comme si c'étaient des flocons de soie; puis ils les chassent à l'occident, en les croisant les uns sur les autres, comme les mailles d'un panier à jour. Ils jettent, sur les côtés de ce réseau, les nuages qu'ils n'ont pas employés, et qui ne sont pas en petit nombre; ils les roulent en énormes masses blanches comme la neige, les contournent sur leurs bords en forme de croupes, et les entassent les uns sur les autres comme les Cordillières du Pérou, en leur donnant des formes de montagnes, de cavernes et de rochers; ensuite, vers le soir, ils calmissent un peu, comme s'ils craignaient de déranger leur ouvrage.*
>
> Bernardin de Saint-Pierre, *Etudes de la nature*

a) How many similes can you find in this passage?

b) What other stylistic device is employed in association with the first simile?

c) Suggest two lexical fields evoked by these similes.

d) What do you think is the overall effect of the repeated use of simile in this passage?

Suggested answers:

a) There are six similes:
   - *comme si c'étaient des flocons de soie*
   - *comme les mailles d'un panier à jour*
   - *masses blanches comme la neige*
   - *leurs bords en forme de croupes*
   - *comme les Cordillières du Pérou*
   - *des formes de montagnes, de cavernes et de rochers.*

b) Personnification is used in the contèxt of the first simile (*les vents* [...] *cardent les nuages comme si c'étaient des flocons de soie;* [...]). Here the clouds become people dressed in silk.

c) Possible lexical fields are:
   - size: *comme les Cordillières du Pérou, des formes de montagnes, de cavernes et de rochers*
   - shape: *comme les mailles d'un panier à jour, flocons de soie, des formes de cavernes et de rochers, leurs bords en forme de croupes*
   - colour: *blanches comme la neige*
   - texture: *flocons de soie.*

d) The effect is to evoke a description of the clouds which emphasizes their sensory qualities: colour, size, shape and texture. The impact is strongly visual. The dramatic nature of the description with its stress on size and contrast may suggest the preromantic aesthetic of the sublime.

2.3. Metonymy

Metonymy designates the procedure whereby a given lexical unit is substituted for another with which it entertains a relationship of contiguity, e.g. cause for effect, container for contained, part for the whole, concrete for abstract.

Examples:
- part for the whole: *la voile* for *le voilier* (pour prendre un exemple 'bateau'…)
- container for contained: *boire un verre* instead of e.g. *boire du vin*
- cause for effect: *lire un Balzac* for a *un roman de Balzac*
- concrete for abstract: *avoir du nez* meaning 'to be intuitive'. This device is frequently used with parts of the body. Other examples: *avoir du coffre* for *avoir de la voix* (i.e. to have a strong/powerful voice); *avoir de l'oreille* for having a musical sense.

Worked example:

Identify and explain the use of metonymy in the following sentences:
a. *Ils ont bu une bonne bouteille.*
b. *Elle a vraiment du cœur.*
c. *Le pays avait été dévasté par cinq ans de guerre par le feu.*
d. *Elle a éteint l'électricité.*
e. *Il écrit d'une belle main.*

Suggested answers:

a. container *(bouteille)* for contained
b. concrete for abstract = she is kind-hearted
c. part for the whole: *le feu* refers to *armes à feu*
d. whole for the part: *l'électricité* refers to *la lumière électrique*
e. cause for effect: *d'une belle main* means *d'une belle écriture*

2.4. Hyperbole

Hyperbole is a figure of speech expressing an exaggeration. Its meaning should not be taken literally. It is frequently used to convey intensity of emotion as well as humour and irony.

Ex: *Je suis **mort(e)** de honte.*
 *Elle a **des milliers** d'amis.*

Hyperbole appears in all discourse types but most of all, it is a characteristic feature of sensational news reporting (e.g. headlines) and of advertising.

Worked examples:

1. Identify the use of hyperbole in the following extract from Balzac. What is the effect produced?

> *1. Veuillez excuser la rigueur de notre ministère, monsieur le baron! dit le commissaire, nous sommes requis par un plaignant. Monsieur le juge de paix assiste à l'ouverture du domicile. Je sais qui vous êtes, et qui est la délinquante.*
>
> *5. Valérie ouvrit des yeux étonnés, jeta le cri perçant que les actrices ont inventé pour annoncer la folie au théâtre, elle se tordit en convulsions sur le lit, comme une démoniaque du Moyen-Age dans sa chemise de soufre, sur un lit de fagots.*
>
> *— La mort!... mon cher Hector, mais la police correctionnelle? oh!*
>
> *10. jamais! Elle bondit, elle passa comme un nuage blanc entre les trois spectateurs, et alla se blottir sous le bonheur-du-jour, en se cachant la tête dans ses mains.*
>
> *— Perdue! morte!... cria-t-elle.*
>
> *— Monsieur, dit Marneffe à Hulot, si madame Marneffe devenait folle, vous seriez plus qu'un libertin, vous seriez un assassin...*
>
> Balzac, *La Cousine Bette*

Suggested answer:

Line 6-7: ... *elle se tordit en convulsions sur le lit, comme une démoniaque du Moyen-Age...*
Line 13: *Perdue! morte!... cria-t-elle*
The effect achieved through the choice of hyperbole in these examples is twofold:
- the intensity of Valérie's own surprise and embarrassment is very aptly evoked
- a farcical impression is also conveyed to the reader.

Line 15: ... *vous seriez un assassin*
The effect here is to convey the sense of anger and conflict experienced by the characters. A humorous impression is also communicated to the reader.

2. Identify the use of hyperbole in the following comment on a new perfume. What effect is produced on the reader?

Marie Claire, September 1998

▼ **PARFUM DE MATHEUX**

Pour la majorité des femmes, le symbole et le nom rappellent de douloureuses prises de tête, flash-back de CM1. La plupart des hommes le reconnaissent infailliblement et frétillent de l'intelligence dès que son nom magique est prononcé. C'est Pi. Le 3,14! L'infini, le nombre d'or, le monde magique des mathématiques poétiques. Givenchy en a fait son affaire en mettant tout cela en parfum. On nage dans la galaxie aux côtés de Neil Armstrong et de Jules Verne. Pas facile, l'approche, et cela nous change un peu. Compte à rebours commencé. Mise en orbite tout de suite!

GIVENCHY
PARIS

Suggested answer:

Examples of hyperbole are:

Line 4: *et frétillent de l'intelligence*

Line 12: the extended image of the space flight, from line 12 to the end of the paragraph, can also be seen as an example of hyperbole.

The effect of the use of hyperbole is to strengthen the association that is being made between the magic/irrational and the rational/intelligent or mechanical. It is the perfume that embodies these traditional opposite, contrasting qualities.

3. Visual representation

3.1. Visual representation and pictures

As is the case for a written message, semantic associations can also be established by visual representation. Visual representation is a means used by designers, publicists and sometimes writers to create various meanings. In an attempt to make sense of a visual representation, viewers will in turn attempt to establish semantic links based on their own cultural assumptions. These may or may not be the same as the ones intended by the author.

a) Example from advertisements
Look at this BNP advert: what links can you establish between the message and its illustration?

Unexpected connections can be established between the object of the advert – to sell a new investment deal – and its visual representation. Even if the contemporary French reader is unlikely to recognise any particular film (and even if the older reader may think of the Bernard Borderie 1952 film *La Môme Vert-de-Gris,* which tells the adventure of the FBI agent Lemmy Caution played by the American actor Eddie Constantine), the illustration clearly alludes to the world of cinema. The younger reader faced with this posed photograph may think of a James Bond scenario in which the male hero is surrounded by typically voluptuous women; but in an ironical and humorous twist it is the women who possess the guns.

If we examine the link between the picture and the text which follows, the use of the intertextual field of cinema to entice the potential customer into investing in the new BNP bank placement, *Natio-Vie,* develops further the oppositional link between the semantic field of fiction (=cinema) and reality (=financial investments). For detailed analysis of this aspect, see Chapter 7.

When examining the relation between the titular phrase *En 10 ans nous multiplions votre capital par 2. Ça tombe bien, non?* and the picture, one becomes aware of the effect of an unexpected reversal. In the attempt to make sense of the unusual link between the product and its visual representation, the reader is not only likely to attribute the dialogue of the titular phrase to the implicit voice of the company (see Chapter 7 Presence of the Speaker for more details), but to the male character of the picture. The two women of the picture could, besides, be seen as the representation of the customers: contrary to what happens in thriller films centred around an FBI agent, the two women empowered with masculine attributes (guns), and no longer sex objects, are in a position to make the man/the company answerable to his/its claim.

Visual representation is often used in relation to a text in advertisements, book covers, newspapers (sometimes with the use of cartoons) and can either illustrate or reinforce the message given, or create contradictory meanings. Elements such as colour, choice of typography, size and layout of the illustration and of its message can contribute to the creation of semantic fields.

As a contrast to the title, the illustration used for the Tahar Ben Jelloun book *Les Yeux baissés* tends to create oppositional meanings. The positioning of the titular message at the centre of the realistic setting of the photograph, next to the anonymous shape of a female character, links the two elements together. The reader, who associates *les yeux baissés* with the representation of this non-western female figure, is likely to link by association the meanings of the title to the situation of Muslim women, *les yeux baissés,* thus ***connoting*** respect and submission.

The female character of the cover who, although faceless, is nevertheless the focus of attention, is captured in a brisk walking movement with space stretching out in front of her. The connoted determination and implied activity of this female character create therefore oppositional meanings which counteract those of the title. Such contradictory meanings, created by the interaction between the message and the visual illustration, encapsulate the story and dilemma of the central female character. The visual representation of the cover thus functions as a mirror, a *mise en abyme*, of the whole narrative.

3.2. Visual representation and typography

Typography refers to the choice of characters and layout of the page. The resources of typography to create, illustrate or reinforce meaning(s) have been particularly used by surrealist French poets such as Apollinaire.

Worked example:

Study the link established between the title and the pictural representation of Apollinaire's *La Colombe poignardée*.

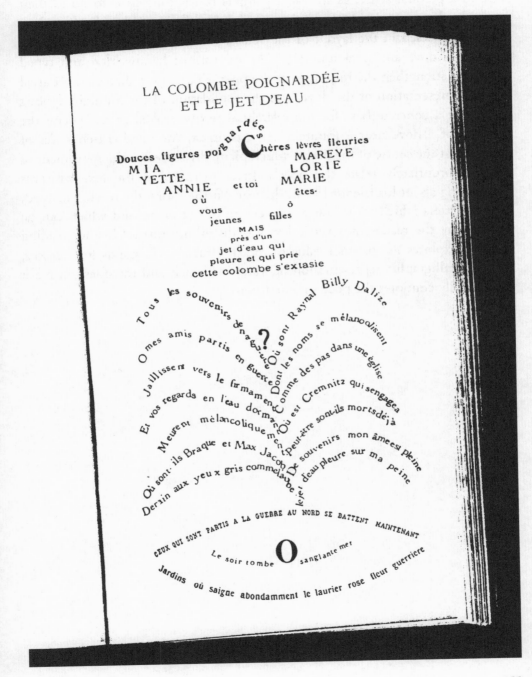

Suggested answer:

The link established between the words of the title and the layout of the poem is mostly pictural. Apollinaire wanted to use the figurative possibilities of the verse in a pictural sense, as surrealist painters of his time used to do in their works. In this example, the figurative possibilities of the words *colombe* and *jet d'eau* are realised in the layout of the verses, which indeed mirrors the visual shape of a dove and of a fountain. The mixture of handwritten and typed characters strengthen the meanings of the poem. The typed characters are used for the representation of the dove, and the foundation of the fountain appears to provide a concrete base for the referential reality evoked in the poem: the presence of a dove near a fountain. As a contrast, the handwritten series of questions at the centre of the poem, which picturally represent the movement of water, appropriately relate the poet's direct presence in the text with his questioning about his friends lost in the war. Furthermore, the use of enlarged, isolated letters which stand out at the centre of the poem and which can be decoded by the reader in a vertical way – disturbing further his/her reading habits – explores the pictural value of the title further: C stands for *colombe*, O is the calligraphic representation of water in French and the question mark semantically connotes the poet's mental state.

ASSIGNMENTS

1. Look at this advert for *Candia* milk and study the meanings created by the visual illustration chosen for this advert. Which links can you establish between the message and the picture?

UNE FEMME QUI B

Voyez-vous, Silhouette est un lait écrémé qui a su préserver ses vitamines, son calcium
de notre corps. Et quand tous les jours on apporte à son corps ce dont il a besoin, il vous

Une femme qui boit Silhouette, ça se voit
(*Elle*, 6 April 1998, no 2127)

2. How many groups of related words can you identify in the passage below?

> *Tenir un journal est chose courante mais le poursuivre pendant presque trente ans l'est moins. Surtout lorqu'au matin l'on se souvient de ses rêves et qu'on les note sur une période de dix-sept ans. Des rêves qui un beau jour («beau» retrouve alors son sens d'origine) prennent dans leur enchaînement entre eux et avec la vie diurne une signification enfin acceptable. Ils peuvent révéler le sens d'une vie, peut-être davantage.*
>
> *Magazine Littéraire,* 1985

3. Look at the illustration of the book cover of Driss Chraïbi's *Les Boucs*. What types of meaning are created?

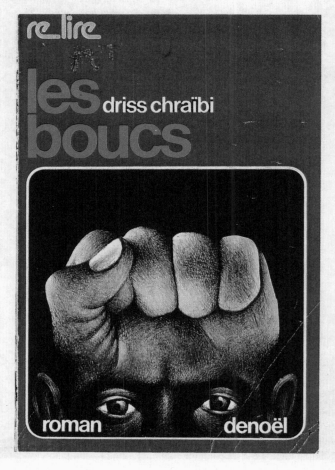

SUGGESTED ANSWERS TO ASSIGNMENTS

1. *Une femme qui boit Silhouette, ça se voit*

The visual representation of this advertisement reinforces the main message: the full-page illustration representing the realistic summary setting of a garden or park connotes calm, peace and harmony. The natural shades of colours used (light and dark greens, yellow and cream), the rounded shapes evident in the choice of handwritten typography and also constructed in the picture by the rounded shape of the hammock, geometrically reinforced by the horizontal line of the written message, all these elements contribute to making the illustration a symbolic metaphor of the benefits offered to customers by the *Candia* milk *Silhouette*, namely balance and harmony. Furthermore, the witty interplay between seeing and not seeing, between the *ça se voit* of the message and the central element of the picture, a hammock in which a woman is precisely not visible - her presence just hinted at by her bent arm - reduced to a *silhouette*, no doubt the result of drinking *Candia Silhouette*, reinforces in a punning effect the claim of the message: 'if you drink *Candia Silhouette*, it will be noticed'.

2. *Tenir un journal . . .*

Groups of related words:

Dreams
de ses rêves
des rêves

Time
pendant presque trente ans
au matin
une période de dix-sept ans
un beau jour

Meaning
son sens d'origine
une signification
le sens d'une vie

Writing
tenir un journal
le poursuivre
on les note

3. *Les Boucs*

The cover illustration which accompanies the title *Les Boucs* is unusual in so far as it both reinforces the enigmatic connotation of the book title and that it reactivates the seme of foreignness present in the author's name: Driss Chraïbi. Indeed, the representation of what appears to be half a non-white face, whose fixed eyes stare at the reader and whose look is rendered even more striking by the delineation of the square box in which it is framed, gives a meaning of foreignness to the whole picture. This effect is reinforced by its contextual juxtaposition to the French title *Les Boucs*, the use of French of the title indicating its French targetted readership.

The shape of a clenched fist which continues the forehead and replaces the skull gives the human representation a rather grotesque appearance. Such an illustration aims at triggering the imagination of the reader and can be broadly seen as evoking the representation of a billy-goat, echoing the denoted title. In such a context, the clenched fist functions as the metaphorical representation of the horns – the main defence of the male goat.

The reader suspects that the illustration is likely to refer to one of the *boucs* mentioned in the title. Beyond the title's literal meaning of animality lies a human presence: that of a foreigner whose clenched fist constitutes his main defence and the determination of whose fixed gaze embodies the sign of his inner resistance. As such, the illustration functions as a perfect *mise en abyme* of the novel.

Production Exercises

a) Design an advertisement or a slogan employing at least one **metaphor**.

b) Write a short text to be included in an instruction booklet. Use as many **metonymies** as possible.

c) Briefly describe your ideal man/woman, using as many **similes** as possible. You might even like to add a touch of **hyperbole**!

d) Choose one of your photographs, a painting, an advertisement or any other visual representation and analyse the **semantic associations** or connotations suggested by the **visual representations**.

CHAPTER 7

PRESENCE OF THE SPEAKER

INTRODUCTION

The presence of the speaker can contribute to the coherence of a text. It can be detected through various, explicit, linguistic items, or it can be implicit. The following illustrative examples are taken from literature, newspaper articles and product advertisements.

1. Literature

1.1. *L'Étranger*

Read the following passage, which is the opening paragraph to *L'Étranger*, by Albert Camus.

> *Aujourd'hui, maman est morte. Ou peut-être hier, je ne sais pas. J'ai reçu un télégramme de l'asile: «Mère décédée. Enterrement demain. Sentiments distingués.» Cela ne veut rien dire. C'était peut-être hier.*
>
> Albert Camus, *L'Étranger*

a) Identify the presence of the speaker in the opening sentence.
b) Comment on the tenses used in the passage.
c) What effect is produced by the use of the modalizing term *peut-être*?
d) How does the choice of narrative device, i.e. the explicit traces of a speaker, help to construct what could become the fundamental theme(s) of the novel? What message(s) is being communicated in the opening paragraph?

On reading this short passage, the reader is struck by the abundance of deictics (e.g. *aujourd'hui, hier*) revealing the explicit presence of the speaker. Indeed, this famous opening to Camus's *L'Étranger* is an excellent example of the 'inappropriate' use of deictics: the recipient, Meursault, is not sure what the words are referring to, he cannot understand their referents:

Aujourd'hui, *maman est morte. Ou peut-être* **hier**, *je ne sais pas.*

The reason for Meursault's doubt is that the information comes from a telegram: *«Mère décédée. Enterrement demain...»* Since Meursault does not know when the telegram was written (i.e. since he does not share the present of the speaker - the person who wrote the telegram), he cannot interpret *demain*. For instance, if the telegram were written the day before Meursault receives it, the *demain* of the speaker would be *aujourd'hui* for Meursault, a fact Meursault is aware of when he points out: *Cela ne veut rien dire. C'était peut-être hier.*

The use of deictics in this passage has the effect of abolishing the conventional distance between text and reader and between fiction and reality. A sense of immediacy is thereby conveyed.

The deictics and modalizers also possess a strong thematic function. The modalizing term *peut-être* for example, at the beginning of the second sentence, together with the utterance *je ne sais pas*, suggest a position of uncertainty on the part of the speaker. This position of uncertainty is reiterated in the last sentence, *c'était peut-être hier*, where our attention is again drawn to the speaker in the use of the deictic *hier*. The theme of narratorial uncertainty, of the inadequacy of our knowledge – a key component of Camus's philosophy of the absurd - is thus established at the outset.

In addition to the presence of deictics, of modalizing terms and of what Benveniste calls the tenses of discourse (i.e. the present and the perfect in this case), the opening paragraph of *L'Étranger* is characterised by an evaluative utterance, *cela ne veut rien dire*, referring back to the contents of the telegram from the residential home. Indeed, as the novel unfolds, references to meaning or absence of meaning, to the difficulties of interpretation, become characteristic utterances of the speaker.

The message contained in this telegram is itself presented in quotation marks: in other words, we have an additional speaker in the text – the anonymous voice of the residential home. The use of the deictic *demain* within this quoted statement serves to strengthen the blurring of temporal boundaries that we have already noted, contributing to the overall temporal confusion and uncertainty.

1.2. *Le Curé de Tours*

In the following extract, what traces of the speaker can be found?

> *Sans trop sonder le vide, la nullité de Mademoiselle Gamard, ni sans s'expliquer la petitesse de ses idées, le pauvre abbé Birotteau s'aperçut un peu tard, pour son malheur, des défauts qu'elle partageait avec toutes les vieilles filles et de ceux qui lui étaient particuliers. Le mal, chez autrui, tranche si vigoureusement sur le bien, qu'il nous frappe presque toujours la vue avant de nous blesser.*
>
> Balzac, *Le Curé de Tours*

The direct intervention of the narrator in the last sentence, generally referring to human experience with the presence of a *nous*, signals in a typical Balzacian manner the presence of the speaker. In addition, the choice of the terms *vide*, *nullité*, *petitesse* and *pauvre* betrays the narrator's judgement and opinion about his characters. This is known as implicit presence of the speaker.

169

2. Newspaper articles

2.1. *Le chant des coucous*

Read the following article from *Le Figaro*:

LE CHANT DES COUCOUS

Personne ne peut prétendre que la situation politique soit bonne. Sauf à se boucher les oreilles, fermer les yeux et taire ses observations. Examinez les sondages: ils indiquent, pour le moins, un désenchantement. Ecoutez les rumeurs de la ville: elle bruisse de mille suppositions toutes alarmistes.

Tel est le microcosme, comme dirait M. Barre: à l'image des coucous suisses, il vient régulièrement caqueter, pour amplifier ce qu'il croit sentir de l'opinion. M. Juppé et les siens auraient tort de s'en alarmer: pour peu que le balancier prenne la direction inverse, ces gens-là chanteront aussi vigoureusement l'air du triomphe qu'ils entonnent, ces temps-ci, celui de la déception. C'est ainsi: il faut l'accepter, à moins de renoncer à la politique et à ses intrigues.

Le calendrier lui-même ne favorise pas la tâche du gouvernement. Voilà les grands d'Espagne de retour sur la scène: MM. Balladur, Pasqua, Sarkozy, Léotard, Rocard, Badinter, et d'autres, viennent d'être élus, qui au Sénat, qui à l'Assemblée. Les uns et les autres ont trop de talent, trop d'idées et trop d'originalité pour rester muets. Ils ont besoin également de se manifester. Quoi de plus facile alors que de critiquer, plus ou moins vivement, la politique gouvernementale? Une situation monétaire grave – la France n'y est pour rien –, des experts réservés, un rapport alarmant, autant d'éléments qui permettent, sans grand mal, de faire entendre sa différence.

M. Juppé peut invoquer, avec raison, la nouveauté de son gouvernement: ce n'est pas en quelques mois qu'une politique porte ses fruits. Le premier ministre n'a d'ailleurs jamais caché que le redressement et le renouveau qu'il proposait exigeaient trois bonnes années. D'autant que la situation économique reste très difficile - voyez le poids de la dette - et que les résultats encourageants, comme la lente diminution du chômage, sont occultés par d'autres polémiques, telle celle sur l'ampleur de la réduction des déficits. Marier l'espérance née de la victoire de M. Chirac au credo de M. Mitterrand – « laissez du temps au temps» – n'est pas aisé. Il y a toujours de l'impatience dans les démocraties et de l'injustice dans tout jugement politique.

Au-delà des ronchonnements de l'opinion; au-delà des grognements de circonstance de dirigeants patronaux et syndicaux; au-delà de quelques maladresses ministérielles, il reste des réformes à mener et des débats à ouvrir. Celui sur les retraites et leurs différences entre les secteurs privé et public en est un. Il est essentiel. C'est un des exemples où la réflexion ne doit pas vaciller devant les conservatismes et où, comme lors de la campagne présidentielle, l'apport de tous à la discussion est nécessaire. M. Juppé, juge-t-on, a de la ténacité, du pragmatisme et le goût de l'innovation. C'est sa tâche, redoutable, de le prouver au quotidien.

Michel Schifres, *Le Figaro*, 25 September 1995

In what way(s) is the presence (implicit and explicit) of the speaker felt in this text?

The presence of the speaker is immediately apparent (though implicit) with the very first word, the indefinite pronoun *personne*, which introduces a judgement:

Personne ne peut prétendre que . . .

Then follows a string of infinitives, with the restrictive preposition *sauf à*, giving a conditional meaning:

se boucher les oreilles   fermer les yeux   taire ses observations.

(i.e. except **if** you close your eyes and ears and **if** you do not say what you think.)

The intervention of the speaker then becomes more direct, with two imperatives:

examinez les sondages   écoutez les rumeurs de la ville

both rhetorical questions to which the speaker immediately gives an answer:

ils indiquent . . . un désenchantement   elle bruisse de mille suppositions . . .

The way people are quoted reveals the presence of the speaker:

Tel est le microcosme, **comme dirait M. Barre.**

(i.e. it is something that the speaker **knows** about M. Barre, about what M. Barre might say.)

Conclusions are offered subjectively, in the shape of suggestions to others about what to think:

M. Juppé et les siens **auraient tort** *de s'en alarmer*

or of predictions about how some will behave:

. . . ces gens-là **chanteront** *. . .*

The conclusion of the second paragraph, although using an impersonal verb, is the voice of the speaker who incites his readers to share it.

C'est ainsi: il faut l'accepter

(i.e. **I** accept it and **you** should do the same)

Facts, events, **are tinted with the speaker's judgement:**

le calendrier **ne favorise pas** *la tâche du gouvernement.*

Les uns et les autres (Balladur, Rocard . . .) **ont trop de** *talent,* **trop d'** *idées et* **trop d'** *originalité pour rester muets.*

Ils **ont besoin** *également de se manifester.*

The speaker comments further on some of the facts:

M. Juppé peut invoquer, **avec raison** *. . .*

Then the speaker goes back to a straight presentation of his own opinions, with the occasional imperative of suggestion, to establish further a link with his reader. The speaker is thus asking for the reader's views on his own (the speaker's) preoccupations:

> ...**voyez** le poids de la dette...

Finally, he uses the 'universal truth' structure, characterized by the use of the present tense (cf proverbs), adverbs such as *toujours* and/or determiners such as *tout* (any):

> Il y **a toujours** de l'impatience dans les démocraties et de l'injustice dans **tout** jugement politique.

This is a well-used method of expressing one's thoughts or feelings, by making them look as if they were universally recognized truths, with the same power as an old proverb or popular *dicton*.

The author's subjectivity appears throughout, up to and including the last paragraph, with nouns *(ronchonnements, grognements)* and an impersonal expression *(il est essentiel)* denoting a personal judgement.

2.2. *A la rencontre des pauvretés*

Read the following article by Bruno Chenu from *La Croix*:

A LA RENCONTRE DES PAUVRETÉS

Il ne fait pas bon être pauvre au temps de Noël. Tout vous agresse: les lumières, les vitrines, les paquets, la publicité. Les projecteurs de la fête exaltent la bonne chère, le clinquant et les paillettes. Malheur à ceux qui ne peuvent faire front! Vous vous demanderez alors ce que vous avez bien pu faire au Bon Dieu pour vous retrouver faisant la queue au resto du cœur, cherchant un coin abrité pour la nuit et éprouvant la terrible morsure de la solitude. Vos sabots n'ont pas dû être bien placés dans la cheminée de la fortune.

Noël des riches, Noël des pauvres. Deux planètes différentes. Deux fêtes qui se vivent à des années-lumière. L'une célèbre le Dieu qui a comblé la terre de la pluie de ses bénédictions, l'autre a toutes les raisons de maudire l'auteur d'un monde aussi mal fichu. La profusion et le dénuement: deux situations qui rendent aussi difficile l'écoute du message de Noël. Car notre société de tradition chrétienne a tellement acclimaté cette fête que nous croyons le message de Noël facile d'accès, et nous-mêmes à niveau. Il n'en est rien.

La Croix, 29-30 December 1991

a. Examine the following uses of *vous* in the first paragraph:
   — *Tout vous agresse*
   — *Vous vous demandez . . . ce que vous avez bien pu faire . . . pour vous retrouver . . .*
   — *Vos sabots . . .*

Who exactly does the speaker address?

b. How is the speaker's subjectivity more implicitly expressed?

c. Examine the following uses of *nous* in the second paragraph:
   — *notre société . . .*
   — *nous croyons le message . . . et nous-mêmes.*

Who do these *nous* refer to?

The *vous* in the text are ambiguous: the speaker seems to address the reader. However, the reader of *La Croix* is unlikely to be a *sans-logis*. These *vous* are in fact generic. They refer to a third party.

Note that the function of generic *vous* is to 'personalize' utterances which have a general value by replacing the universal subject (often *on*) by a *tu* or a *vous*. Thus the speaker creates the impression that the reader is participating in the process (be it as a beneficiary or a victim).
Here, we may wonder if this use of *vous* is not **also** some sort of warning: the reader could one day be in a similar position to that described in the article.

The speaker's subjectivity is more implicitly expressed by the use of expressions connoting his attitude towards the situation described:
   — *Il ne fait pas bon être pauvre . . .*
   — *Malheur à ceux . . .*
   — *L'auteur d'un monde aussi mal fichu . . .*

In the second paragraph, several *nous* show the speaker and the reader joined together, as they are deemed to share the same culture (*notre société de tradition chrétienne*), particularly as the article comes from *La Croix*, a Catholic daily. The speaker thus establishes a kind of solidarity with his reader, in order to promote a greater awareness of what Christmas is all about.

3. Product advertisements

3.1. *L'alarme Daitem*

SYSTÈME DE SÉCURITÉ SANS FIL ULTRA-FIABLE POUR LA MAISON

"Ma tranquillité, je ne l'ai pas volée : je l'ai enfin trouvée avec l'alarme Daitem."

Personne n'est à l'abri d'une tentative de cambriolage. Pour bien protéger ma maison, j'ai choisi Daitem, le spécialiste de la sécurité totalement sans fil. Quoi qu'il arrive, je suis tranquille.

"... tranquille parce que mon alarme est très efficace"

Il me suffit d'appuyer sur une touche pour que ma maison soit efficacement protégée contre le cambriolage. Des détecteurs surveillent les portes et les fenêtres ainsi que tout mouvement anormal. A la moindre tentative d'intrusion, les sirènes et flashs clignotants feront fuir les voleurs et nous serons prévenus automatiquement par téléphone, moi, mes proches ou la société d'intervention de Daitem.

"... tranquille parce que Daitem va plus loin pour ma sécurité"

Fondé il y a 20 ans, Daitem est l'inventeur de la sécurité totalement sans fil qu'il ne cesse de perfectionner. Mon alarme bénéficie des innovations qui la rendent ultra-fiable : c'est le seul système qui utilise la double transmission radio TwinPass® et dispose d'une autonomie supérieure à 5 ans. Non raccordé au secteur EDF, il ne craint ni la foudre ni les coupures de courant.

"... tranquille parce que l'Installateur Partenaire Daitem s'occupe de tout"

Garantie supplémentaire, mon alarme a été installée par un professionnel de confiance, membre du réseau des Installateurs Partenaires Daitem. Il m'a conseillé, proposé la protection la mieux adaptée et a réalisé une installation très performante. En cas de besoin, je sais que je peux compter sur lui. La preuve de son engagement : la Charte Consommateurs Daitem qui me garantit la plus totale satisfaction.

VU A LA TV

"... tranquille parce que ma famille aussi est protégée"

Même lorsque nous sommes chez nous, la nuit par exemple, nous sommes protégés : les issues et les pièces inoccupées sont sous surveillance. En cas de malaise ou d'agression, nous pouvons prévenir très rapidement nos proches ou la société d'intervention avec la télécommande ou le clavier.

"... tranquille parce qu'il n'y a aucune dégradation"

Grand Prix du Design Janus 1995

Pas de fil, donc pas de travaux, pas de trous inutiles. Mon installation reste simple et esthétique tout en m'apportant une très large protection qui englobe aussi les risques d'incendie et d'inondation. C'est ce qui a achevé de me convaincre : oui, le système Daitem est le meilleur pour ma maison.

DEMANDE D'INFORMATION GRATUITE

Oui, je souhaite recevoir une information détaillée et confidentielle sur le système d'alarme Daitem D14000, sans engagement de ma part.

Retournez ce coupon sous enveloppe non-affranchie à :
Daitem - Service Consommateurs - Libre réponse n°38 - 38926 Crolles Cedex

Nom........................ Prénom........................

Adresse........................

Code postal └┴┴┴┴┘ Ville........................

Tél. dom........................ Tél. pro........................

❏ Résidence Principale
❏ Résidence secondaire, préciser le département : └┴┘
❏ Local professionnel

Télérama, no 2421, 8-14 June 1996

a) Identify the presence of the speaker in the title. By which type of coreference devices is that presence emphasised?

b) List all the marks of the speaker's presence. Which shifts can you identify and what effects do they have?

c) Does the *je* in the advertisement always refer to the same person?

d) What effect could the accumulation of first person markers have on the reader?

This advertisement for a home radio security system which appeared in the French TV magazine *Télérama* is structured and centred around the presence of the speaker.

The presence of the speaker is felt from the very first word of the title with the possessive adjective *ma* used in connection with the word *tranquillité* which constitutes a keyword in the context of the product advertised. The presence of the speaker is immediately emphasised with the repetition of the first person singular pronoun *je* and foregrounded by the anaphoric context in which it appears:

> *Ma tranquillité: je ne l'ai pas volée, je l'ai enfin trouvée . . .*

(the direct object *l'* anaphorically refers to *ma tranquillité*)

The identity of the speaker is clarified if the reader glances at the nearby picture showing a relaxed middle-aged man looking confidently at the reader. The product advertised – an alarm system which implies valuable property to be protected – and the emphasis placed on the word *tranquillité* connote the fact that this middle-aged man is likely to be retired, and present an attractive image of comfortable retirement. The visual representation thus reinforces the presence of the speaker in the advertisement by giving reality to its linguistic expression.

Throughout the text of the advertisement, the repeated use of *je* in direct speech reinforces the sense of immediacy conveyed by the present tense. The text starts with a general statement introduced by the indefinite pronoun *personne*:

> *Personne n'est à l'abri d'une tentative de cambriolage.*

One can detect the opinion of the speaker behind the impression of universal truth given by the statement. The speaker's presence is immediately reasserted in the sentence which follows with the possessive adjective *ma* followed again by the *je*:

> *Pour bien protéger ma maison, j'ai choisi Daitem*

The presence of *je* is reinforced in sharp contrast with the indefinite value of *personne* in the preceding sentence. An opposition personal/impersonal is asserted in the next sentence:

Quoiqu'il arrive (= general/impersonal), **je** suis tranquille (= personal).

In the next subtitles:

*tranquille parce que **mon** alarme est très efficace*
*tranquille parce que Daitem va plus loin pour **ma** sécurité*
*tranquille parce que **ma** famille aussi est protégée*
tranquille parce qu'il n'y a aucune dégradation.

The *je* disappears in favour of the foregrounding of the adjective *tranquille* ('peace of mind' being a major feature in the evoked saleable value of the product). The speaker's disappearance is only partial since in three subtitles the possessive adjective *(**mon** alarme, **ma** sécurité, **ma** famille)* reasserts it.

The speaker's presence remains central in the paragraphs which follow the subtitles:

*Il **me** suffit d'appuyer… pour que **ma** maison soit suffisamment protégée*
***mon** installation reste simple… tout en m'apportant une très large protection.*

As in the subtitles, we also notice the repetition of possessive adjectives: **ma** *maison*, **ma** *famille*, **mon** *installation* which signal a possessive link identifying the speaker's voice as that of the authoritative head of the family. The speaker's strong presence, decoded as male, mostly because of the juxtaposed picture, is supposed to be attractive to the potential buyer, who is also likely to be male. A controversial strategy, however, which no doubt reflects the market situation but which can also be counterproductive for readers, and potential customers, aware of gender equality.

From the fourth paragraph onwards, the first person singular (*je, mon, ma*) changes into the first person plural (*nous, nos…*):

*A la moindre tentative d'intrusion… **nous** serons prévenus automatiquement…;*
*lorsque **nous** sommes chez **nous**… **nous** sommes protégés…*
*… **nous** pouvons prévenir très vite **nos** proches ou la société d'intervention…*

The *je* has now become a *nous* which includes the speaker himself, his family and, in a clever device, the company itself. The company is therefore put on the same level as that of a close family, reinforcing the reassurance factor.

The advert ends with the authoritative opinion of the family head:

*oui, le système Daitem est le meilleur pour **ma** maison.*

A last phenomenon, that of a linguistic contamination centred around the speaker's presence, is evident in the last part of the advertisement entitled *Demande d'information gratuite*:

Oui, **je** *souhaite recevoir une information détaillée... sans engagement de* **ma** *part.* The speaker has changed; the *je* is no longer the voice of the retired man of the picture as in the preceding main text of the advertisement, but is supposed to be that of the potential targetted buyer/the reader of the advertisement. It is as if the repetition of the *je* of the speaker throughout the main text of the advert had suddenly entered or invaded the box entitled *demande d'information gratuite*. The assertion of the *oui, je* with the foregrounded first person marker, which suggests a definite enthusiastic answer to an implied question, stresses a type of personality shift from that of the speaker to that of the potential customer, a clever strategy used to reinforce the reader's identification with the authoritative speaking voice.

3.2. *BNP*

a) Who is the speaker in this advertisement?

b) What can you say about the presence of the speaker in the title?

c) List all the marks of the speaker's presence in the rest of the advertisement.

d) Show how the presence of the speaker has a structuring value in the text.

The speaker in this advertisement is the *BNP*.

The presence of the speaker in the title is shown by the use of *nous*, representing the company. The company is speaking directly to the reader/potential customer, with a rhetorical question: *ça tombe bien, non?*, implying the speaker's knowledge of the reader's situation. This device introduces an element of complicity.

In the rest of the advertisement, the speaker's presence is marked by the use of direct speech and the present tense, and especially the use of present imperatives: *Imaginez un investissement, passez vite du rêve à la réalité*. At the beginning of the text, the speaker prompts the reader to picture what is offered with the imperative *imaginez*. The connotation of the verb *imaginer* gives a dream value to the investment offered. The speaker's authoritative voice in *cela existe* brings the reader back to reality, followed by the speaker/company's advice given to the reader/potential customer on how to make the dream come true. The last sentence, *Alors passez du rêve à la réalité*, echoes the first imperative but this time prompts the reader to act and definitely make the dream come true.

ASSIGNMENTS

1. Job advertisements

Encyclopaedia Universalis

Comment on the choice of
   a) 1st person plural markers
   b) 2nd person plural markers
   c) verb tenses
used in this job advertisement.

ENCYCLOPAEDIA UNIVERSALIS lance sa *Nouvelle Édition et son* **CD-ROM** et recherche sur toute la France DÉLÉGUÉS CULTURELS H/F

Pour poste à caractère commercial. Une solide formation à nos produits et méthodes, votre culture générale et vos qualités humaines vous permettront de présenter notre nouveau programme culturel auprès d'un large public (pas de porte à porte). Votre rémunération sera à la hauteur de vos compétences et comportera un minimum garanti progressif. Perspectives d'évolution rapide pour candidat de valeur.
Appelez le 05 31 74 00

Télérama, no 2384, 20 September 1995

Production exercise:

Take into account the main components in this advertisement and create a new one in which the presence of the speaker will be more obvious:

La ville de PRADES (6500 habitants), sous-préfecture des Pyrénées Orientales, recherche par voie de mutation ou de détachement

BIBLIOTHÉCAIRE TERRITORIAL EXPÉRIMENTÉ (H/F)

pour prendre en charge la conception puis l'ouverture d'un équipement de lecture publique. La connaissance du Catalan (écrit, parlé) sera un atout pour le (la) candidat(e). Une expérience réussie de création d'équipement (participation à la définition des objectifs et à la programmation, relations avec les architectes, etc) est indispensable. Adresser un dossier de candidature (lettre manuscrite, curriculum vitae) à Monsieur le Sénateur-Maire, Hôtel de ville, 66500 Prades.

Télérama, no 2384, 20 September 1995

2. Product advertisements

2.1. *SFR*

a) How is the author's presence explicitly felt?

b) What product is being advertised? How do we find out?

c) What does the *charade* 'trick' enable the publicist to do?

2.2. Simply Palm

a) Who is the question «*Pourquoi as-tu…*» addressed to?

b) Who is *Jérémie*?

c) What are the connotations attached to *collection de timbres*?

d) Is there an answer to the question? How is it given? Can you tell now who *Jérémie* is and who is asking the question?

3. Literature

3.1. *Mme Bovary*

1. *De temps à autre, on entendait des coups de fouet derrière la haie; bientôt la barrière s'ouvrait: c'était une carriole qui entrait. Galopant jusqu'à la première marche du perron, elle s'y arrêtait court, et vidait son monde, qui sortait par tous les côtés en se frottant les genoux et en s'étirant les bras. Les* **5.** *dames, en bonnet, avaient des robes à la façon de la ville, des chaînes de montre en or, des pèlerines à bouts croisés dans la ceinture, ou de petits fichus de couleur attachés dans le dos avec une épingle, et qui leur découvraient le cou par derrière. Les gamins, vêtus pareillement à leurs papas, semblaient incommodés par leurs habits neufs (beaucoup même étrennèrent ce jour-là la* **10.** *première paire de bottes de leur existence), et l'on voyait à côté d'eux, ne soufflant mot dans la robe blanche de sa première communion rallongée pour la circonstance, quelque grande fillette de quatorze ou seize ans, leur cousine ou leur sœur aînée sans doute, rougeaude, ahurie, les cheveux gras de pommade à la rose, et ayant bien peur de salir ses gants. Comme il n'y avait* **15.** *point assez de valets d'écurie pour dételer toutes les voitures, les messieurs retroussaient leurs manches et s'y mettaient eux-mêmes. Suivant leur position sociale différente, ils avaient des habits, des redingotes, des vestes, des habits-vestes: — bons habits, entourés de toute la considération d'une famille, et qui ne sortaient de l'armoire que pour les solennités; redingotes à grandes basques* **20.** *flottant au vent, à collet cylindrique, à poches larges comme des sacs; vestes de gros drap, qui accompagnaient ordinairement quelque casquette cerclée de cuivre à la visière; habits-vestes très courts, ayant dans le dos deux boutons rapprochés comme une paire d'yeux, et dont les pans semblaient avoir été coupés à même un seul bloc, par la hache du charpentier. Quelques-uns encore* **25.** *(mais ceux-là, bien sûr, devaient dîner au bas bout de la table) portaient des blouses de cérémonie, c'est-à-dire dont le col était rabattu sur les épaules, le dos froncé à petits plis et la taille attachée très bas par une ceinture cousue.*

Flaubert, *Madame Bovary*

a) Identify one or two examples in Flaubert's description which reveal the satiric presence of the narrator.

b) In which part of the text does the narrator intervene more obviously? How is punctuation used to stress such an intervention?

c) To what extent do the images of the passage reveal the presence of the narrator?

3.2. *La Cousine Bette*

1. *La sculpture est comme l'art dramatique, à la fois le plus difficile et le plus facile de tous les arts. Copiez un modèle, et l'œuvre est accomplie; mais y imprimer une âme, faire un type en représentant un homme ou une femme, c'est le péché de Prométhée. On compte ce succès dans les annales de la* **5.** *sculpture, comme on compte les poètes dans l'humanité. Michel-Ange, Michel Columb, Jean Goujon, Phidias, Praxitèle, Polyclète, Puget, Canova, Albert Durer sont les frères de Milton, de Virgile, de Dante, de Shakespeare, du Tasse, d'Homère, et de Molière. Cette œuvre est si grandiose qu'une statue suffit à l'immortalité d'un homme, comme celles de Figaro, de Lovelace, de* **10.** *Manon Lescaut suffirent à immortaliser Beaumarchais, Richardson et l'abbé Prévost. Les gens superficiels (les artistes en comptent beaucoup trop dans leur sein) ont dit que la sculpture existait par le nu seulement, qu'elle était morte avec la Grèce et que le vêtement moderne la rendait impossible. D'abord, les anciens ont fait de sublimes statues entièrement voilées, comme* **15.** *la Polymnie, la Julie, etc., et nous n'avons pas trouvé la dixième partie de leurs œuvres. Puis, que les vrais amants de l'art aillent voir à Florence le* Penseur *de Michel-Ange, et dans la cathédrale de Mayence la Vierge d'Albert Durer, qui a fait, en ébène, une femme vivante sous ses triples robes, et la chevelure la plus ondoyante, la plus maniable que jamais femme de* **20.** *chambre ait peignée; que les ignorants y courent, et tous reconnaîtront que le génie peut imprégner l'habit, l'armure, la robe, d'une pensée et y mettre un corps, tout aussi bien que l'homme imprime son caractère et les habitudes de sa vie à son enveloppe.*

Balzac, *La Cousine Bette*

a) Discuss the use of the second person plural at the beginning of the second sentence *(Copiez un modèle…)*. To whom is the suggestion addressed? What is its modal value?

b) Comment on the use of *on* in the third sentence (*On compte ce succès...*)

c) Can you find another pronoun in the passage with a similar function?

d) Find examples of evaluative terms or expressions that express a judgement of the narrator.

e) Can you find words or phrases that suggest a tendency on the part of the narrator to categorize people in terms, for example, of good and bad?

f) What stylistic or rhetorical devices does the narrator employ to reinforce his own views?

3.3. *Germinal*

1. *Et, sous ses pieds, les coups profonds, les coups obstinés des rivelaines continuaient. Les camarades étaient tous là, il les entendait le suivre à chaque enjambée. N'était-ce pas la Maheude, sous cette pièce de betteraves, l'échine cassée, dont le souffle montait si rauque, accompagné par le ronflement du* **5.** *ventilateur? A gauche, à droite, plus loin, il croyait en reconnaître d'autres, sous les blés, les haies vives, les jeunes arbres. Maintenant, en plein ciel, le soleil d'avril rayonnait dans sa gloire, échauffant la terre qui enfantait. Du flanc nourricier jaillissait la vie, les bourgeons crevaient en feuilles vertes, les champs tressaillaient de la poussée des herbes. De toutes parts, des graines se gonflaient,* **10.** *s'allongeaient, gerçaient la plaine, travaillées d'un besoin de chaleur et de lumière. Un débordement de sève coulait avec des voix chuchotantes, le bruit des germes s'épandait en un grand baiser. Encore, encore, de plus en plus distinctement, comme s'ils se fussent rapprochés du sol, les camarades tapaient. Aux rayons enflammés de l'astre, par cette matinée de jeunesse, c'était de cette* **15.** *rumeur que la campagne était grosse. Des hommes poussaient, une armée noire, vengeresse, qui germait lentement dans les sillons, grandissant pour les récoltes du siècle futur, et dont la germination allait faire bientôt éclater la terre.*

Emile Zola, *Germinal*

a) Find two examples of the presence of the speaker in this passage.

b) Comment on the third sentence beginning *N'était-ce pas la Maheude* ...

c) Comment on the manner metaphor is being used in this passage to convey the narrator's point of view.

4. Newspaper article

Notre langue

1. *Parler une langue, c'est partager, adhérer à un système, c'est rejoindre une histoire, une mémoire, une communauté d'idées, de mythes, de rêves, de sensations, c'est prétendre à une identité de regard. Parler une langue, c'est faire acte d'amour [...]*

5. *Que dire d'une langue qui vous « broie du noir », ravale, qui vous nie, vous flétrit, vous accuse, condamne, qui ne cesse de vous déconsidérer, de vous maudire, de vous abêtir, de vous enchaîner, de vous détruire, de vous saper [...] ?*

Une langue qui, de vous, ne sait donner qu'une image négative, souterraine, animale, qui s'entend à célébrer un monde schizophrénique, où les uns sont là-
10. *haut et les autres là-bas, univers manichéen, où le « blanc » est un espace libre qui fonde sa présence au monde par sa pureté, sa propreté, sa virginité, sa chasteté, son homogénéité, sa cohérence, par tout ce qui n'est pas singé, souillé, « noirci » et, ainsi donc maître du commencement et de la puissance signifiante, par son fabuleux pouvoir de création, seul capable de concevoir le fils de Dieu,*
15. *Verbe fait homme; et de l'autre, à l'inverse, fantôme des ténèbres, l'« âme noire », désunie, privée de lumière, ne peut atteindre à une existence légale et innocentée qu'à condition d'être « blanchie » [...], condition qui fait « rougir » tout Noir, surtout s'il ne regarde pas son interlocuteur en face afin de se donner l'air « franc », c'est-à-dire Blanc, libre et conquérant.*
20. *Que penser d'une telle langue quand vous êtes un Noir et que cette langue occidentale est la vôtre? La quitter? Mais on ne quitte pas sa langue ainsi — autant se quitter. C'est le tragique de l'âme noire.*

Marcel Zang

a) How can we identify the presence of the speaker in this passage?

b) Who is *vous* in the text?

c) What is the effect produced by the use of infinitives in the first paragraph?

d) How does the development of the passage cause us to reassess our initial impression as to the identity of the reader, an identity that is, of course, constructed by the text?

e) What devices are employed by the author to create an effect of immediacy?

f) What can you say about the proliferation of *vous* in the second paragraph?

SUGGESTED ANSWERS TO ASSIGNMENTS

1. Job advertisements

Encyclopaedia Universalis

a) In the choice of the 1st person plural in the determiners – *une solide formation à **nos** produits et méthodes, **notre** nouveau programme culturel* – the *nous* represents the company hidden behind the personnification of the title: *Encyclopaedia Universalis lance... et recherche...* Many advertisements are characterised by a process of mystification, that is of hiding from the reader the true enunciative source. The choice of a *nous* can produce a familiar, chatty tone (register) involving the reader in an immediate, personal experience. The true source of the advertisement, the company, remains hidden behind this stance.

b) The use of the 2nd person plural pronouns and possessive adjectives ***votre** culture générale, **vos** qualités humaines, **vous** permettent, **votre** rémunération, **vos** compétences* is one of the many means by which the reader is being seduced into carrying out a specific action, i.e. applying for the job or making a particular purchase.

c) The tenses used are two sets of futures which respect the chronology of events: *vous permettront* and *sera à la hauteur, et comportera* (the first one referring to the results of the qualities that the potential candidate must have, while the second and third stress the ensuing salary). The futures respect the chronology of imagined events and give the reader a sense that the sequence of events between applying and getting the job is easy and automatic. These futures furthermore exist as a backdrop to the present of the title *(lance et recherche)* – a common tense used in advertisements to give a sense of immediacy – again stressing the link between reading the advertisement and getting the job.

2. Product advertisements

2.1. *SFR*

a) The author addresses the reader by telling him/her a riddle (*une charade*): *Mon 1er...* The attention of the reader is caught by what looks like an easy game.

b) The name of the product, *SFR*, is given as the answer to the riddle. It is given upside down, to mimic the way answers to riddles, crosswords, etc. are often given in television magazines or Sunday supplements.

c) The *charade* makes it possible to give a summary of the qualities of the product in very laudative terms (*meilleur réseau, s'engage à satisfaire, élu... la plus innovante*), whilst giving those qualities a flavour of generally accepted truth that a simple list would not yield: *charade* definitions are part of popular folklore!

2.2. Simply Palm

a) It is unlikely that the question directly addresses the reader, for two reasons:
   – use of familiar *tu*
   – the person addressed has a name: *Jérémie*.

b) We do not know who *Jérémie* is, except that he is likely to be a young boy of stamp-collecting age.

c) The connotations attached to *collection de timbres* are of a not very exciting, and certainly very low-tech, hobby.

d) The answer to the question is inferred from the list given on the right hand-side of the advert, a list of all the things one can do with the product advertised, the pocket computer 'Simply Palm'. The reader is thus made to feel that it is not surprising to find out that your young son is no longer interested in stamp-collecting, when there are so many exciting (and high-tech!) things to do with the product being advertised.

3. Literature

3.1. *Mme Bovary*

a) The satiric presence of the narrator is revealed by an emphasis on the ridiculous aspect of what is described. For instance the description of the tall girl *dans la robe blanche de sa première communion rallongée pour la circonstance* (lines 11-12), with *les cheveux gras de pommade à la rose*. The emphasis on *gras* and the reference to rose perfume reinforce the impression of the character's 'bad taste' given by the description, an indirect way for the narrator to reveal his implicit judgement. Similarly, *les gamins, vêtus pareillement à leurs papas* (line 8) signals the identification of children with adult roles; the narrator implicitly stresses their ridiculous appearance.

b) The use of brackets in *beaucoup même étrennèrent ce jour-là la première paire de bottes de leur existence* (lines 9-10) reveals the narrator's barely concealed social comment; similarly for *mais ceux-là, bien sûr, devaient dîner au bas bout de la table* (line 25) where the adverbial phrase *bien sûr* signals the narrator's implicit intervention in the text, hinted at here by a sense of slight irony.

c) In images such as *redingotes à grandes basques... à poches larges comme des sacs...* (lines 19-20) *dont les pans semblaient avoir été coupés à même un seul bloc, par la hache du charpentier* (lines 23-24) or *habits-vestes... ayant dans le dos deux boutons rapprochés... comme une paire d'yeux* (lines 22-23), the use of comparisons stresses the ridiculous or comical appearance of the characters described, revealing the hidden presence of a narrator who does not keep to what could be conceived as an objective description of the scene (though it could be pointed out that the concept of narrative objectivity is itself to be questioned).

3.2. *La Cousine Bette*

a) The second person plural at the beginning of the second sentence is generic, implying people in general. The coordination of imperative + declarative structures expresses an implicit condition. This rhetorical device is a characteristic of didactic and pedagogic discourse. It involves the reader as a possible actant: if you do 'this', then 'that' will happen.

b) In the third sentence, *On* also refers to people in general. But this time the narrator resorts to notions of public opinion to reinforce his own views: the voice of others – of authority and of truth – is very strong in the works of Balzac.

c) Another pronoun in the passage with a similar function is *nous* in *nous n'avons pas trouvé...* (line 15), involving both reader and speaker together as learned people.

d) Examples of evaluative terms or expressions that express a judgement of the narrator include *succès, grandiose, superficiels, sublimes, vrais,* etc. and a superlative *la plus ondoyante...*

e) Words and phrases that suggest a tendency on the part of the narrator to categorize people include *les gens superficiels, les vrais amants de l'art, les ignorants, le génie.*

f) The stylistic or rhetorical devices employed by the narrator to reinforce his own views are lists of historical examples and cultural allusions, the use of simile (e.g. *la sculpture est comme l'art dramatique,* line 1), the use of the structure of argumentation - presenting an alternative viewpoint only to be invalidated (e.g. the opinions of *les gens superficiels* concerning sculpture, given in lines 11-13, are contradicted by the sentences that follow).

3. *Germinal*

a) The presence of the speaker can be detected in the use of evaluative terms such as *obstinés* at the beginning, and in the metaphoric comparison of the miners with an avenging army towards the end.

b) The use of the interrogative form (lines 3-5) draws our attention to the narrator (free indirect speech). The reader is actually being addressed in the device of the rhetorical question. An effect of immediacy is achieved - we are being drawn into the fictive universe. The choice of the deictic *cette* reinforces this impression of reader involvement.

c) The metaphoric comparison of the earth to a body giving birth (Mother Earth) itself compared to an army of vengeance strikes a note of political optimism. The narrator envisages a future revolution produced by the workers - a Marxist and Messianic vision.

4. Newspaper article

Notre langue

a) The presence of the speaker in this passage is revealed by the use of the second person personal pronoun *vous* together with a large number of evaluative terms such as *condamne, sa pureté, le tragique*.

b) In the text, all the *vous* are generic, i.e. are used instead of *on, quelqu'un, les gens,* etc. in order to involve the reader more directly with the argument propounded by the speaker.

c) With the use of infinitives in the first paragraph, the reader is led to regard the statements as universally valid rather than simply as the subjective outpourings of an individual. This device will lend credibility to the speaker's overall position and render acceptable to the reader what is to follow.

d) Our initial impression (based on cultural assumptions) is that the reader – and narrator - is white and French. As the passage develops, however, it becomes clear that in this context, the *vous* refers to black French people.

e) The use of rhetorical questions (e.g. *Que dire d'une langue...*, para.2), the use of repetition (e.g. *parler une langue... langue...*), together with the use of lists (e.g. *qui vous broie du noir, ravale, qui vous nie...*), create a strong emotional impact on the reader. The violence and destructive power of language is rendered all the more vivid and concrete.

f) The *vous* in the second paragraph are all direct objects except for the first one, hence they could all be made passive. Indeed, all these *vous* undergo the actions expressed by the verbs, which all have an aggressive connotation, e.g. *ravale, nie, flétrit.* The statements feel much more personal. Even though these *vous* are generic (they could be replaced by *les gens* and then *les,* hence *broie du noir aux gens, les ravale . . .*), the reader now feels more involved. The overall impression is that the speaker is now talking about a different language from that in the first paragraph.

CHAPTER 8
SITUATIONAL REFERENCE,
CULTURAL KNOWLEDGE AND ASSUMPTIONS

INTRODUCTION

Reference is about being able to **identify** the objects of the discourse. Objects presented as immediately **identifiable** by both speaker and interlocutor are preceded by:

- a definite article: *le, la, les*
- a demonstrative adjective: *ce(t), cette, ces*
- a possessive adjective: *mon, ma, mes...*

Identification can be achieved either in the **linguistic context** (see Chapter 2, Coreference and contrast), or in the **situational context**, i.e. the 'surrounding world' and/or our knowledge of it. In any given text, there will normally be a mixture of both identification in situation and in context.

Identification in situation may also relate to knowledge that is culturally specific. Indeed, many texts rely for their coherence on the existence of a number of presuppositions or cultural assumptions. In the headline 'Lager Louts Cause Havoc' for example, the terms 'lager louts' assume a familiarity on the part of the reader with contemporary English drinking habits.

Similarly, *Une quarantaine de voitures brûlées à Strasbourg pour la Saint-Sylvestre* refers to predictable acts of violence perpetrated by some people every year in *Strasbourg* to 'celebrate' New Year's Eve. More generally, *week-end de la Toussaint: soixante morts sur les routes*, would assume a familiarity on the part of the reader with French driving habits.

1. Situational reference

The object mentioned may not have been introduced before in the discourse (i.e. in the linguistic context) but can be identified 'in the situation'. Objects which can be identified in the situation include:

a) objects which are physically present in the environment shared by speaker and interlocutor, or present in their minds.

Ex: *Ouvrez **la** fenêtre!*

One would assume there is a window present and visible to both speaker and interlocutor. In this example, the referent is identifiable in the discourse **situation** shared by them, hence the definite article can be used. This is often called the **deictic** use of the definite article and is equivalent to a demonstrative.

Ex: *Où sont **les** enfants?*

This could easily be said in the absence of any children in the field of vision of both speaker and interlocutor, provided the interlocutor knows which children the speaker has in mind.

b) objects which exist in the cultural knowledge (called 'extra-linguistic knowledge' or 'knowledge of the world'), shared by speaker and interlocutor. This knowledge includes:

  • abstract nouns:

Ex: *C'est **l'amour** qui nous fait rêver!*

  • abstractions of concrete nouns (i.e. taken in their generic sense)
       countable:

Ex: ***Le chat** est un petit mammifère à poils doux.*

       uncountable:

Ex: ***L'or** est un métal précieux.*

  • 'unique' objects:

Ex: *On a annoncé une éclipse de **la lune** pour demain.*

  • complete dates:

Ex: *La révolution française a eu lieu **le 14 juillet 1789**.*

  • proper nouns, with or without articles:

Ex: *Jacques Chirac, la France, le Sénat, Paris.*

In all those cases, there is a presumption of identification: the speaker presumes that the interlocutor can identify the entity referred to (but see also Chapter 2, Section 1, NB(2), where an apposition is needed).

2. Cultural assumptions

All texts are anchored in a specific historic and cultural context and they assume a knowledge of this context on the part of the addressee. A teenage magazine published in the year 2000 in England may take for granted (and thereby strengthen) a number of contemporary cultural phenomena such as the preoccupation of increasingly younger girls (10 years onwards) with make-up, going on dates, etc., trends (or presuppositions) which may not be applicable to a Muslim community in India or to a Mormon community in the USA.

Cultural assumptions and presuppositions are also an important ingredient of the ironic effect. It is the addressee's knowledge of given extra-linguistic reality, of a cultural situation or pre-existing cultural discourse that enables her/him to interpret what is being said as meaning exactly the opposite. An example would be the utterance 'That's Einstein speaking' when someone has just said something very stupid.

Indeed, cultural assumptions play a key role in the production of humour in general. In an episode ('The Germans') of the TV series 'Fawlty Towers', John Cleese's repeated injunction to his staff, upon the arrival at his hotel of a German couple, 'Don't mention the war' is only funny if the addressee is familiar with Germany's recent history and with a number of stereotypical representations of the Germans.

Worked example:

Look at the following newspaper headlines:

(i)   *Les dossiers sensibles; synchroton, CNRS, espace*
Le Monde, 5 May 2000

(ii)   *L'ennemi des totalitarismes*
Le Monde, 16 December 1997

(iii)   *Les avocats se mettent en grève pour dénoncer la misère de la justice*
Le Monde, 7 November 1997

(iv)   *Red Ken, roi de Londres*
Le Monde, 5 May 2000

(v)   www.dprk.com
Le Monde, 26 May 2000

a) In which of the above headlines does understanding depend on a specific and detailed background knowledge?

b) Which headlines can be understood without such detailed background knowledge?

Suggested answers:

a) In headlines (i) and (v), understanding depends on a very specific cultural knowledge. The utterances make very little sense on their own and there is a complete absence of any cohesive ties. To fully appreciate headline (iv) would also require a familiarity on the part of the reader with a particular historical event, i.e. the candidature of Ken Livingstone for Mayor of London, as well as knowledge of the political symbolism of the colour red. However the use of the general term *roi* may provide a clue for the reader. The seeds of a possible story-line – involving some heroic event of great importance – are already sown.

b) Headlines (ii) and (iii) can be understood without detailed background knowledge. Headline (iii) presents a summary of an event (we know who the principal actors were, what they did and why). The vocabulary is of a more general nature and the sentence makes sense on its own. It could be understood in most countries of Europe as well as in many of the developing countries. Headline (ii) is more elliptic. Nevertheless, the use of political vocabulary of a general nature, in association with words suggesting a battle *(l'ennemi)*, enables the reader to construct the outline of a story to come and to anticipate a particular course of events.

ASSIGNMENTS

1. The following text was given in Chapter 2, Coreference and contrast, to illustrate examples of identification in context. Using this same text, find examples of identification in situation.

Elle a levé la tête. Elle a suivi son idée sur mon pauvre visage. Elle ne le voyait pas. Alors, du fond des siècles, l'événement est arrivé. Elle lisait. Je suis revenue dans le café. Elle suivait d'autres idées sur d'autres visages. J'ai commandé une fine. Elle ne m'a pas remarquée. Elle s'occupait de ses lectures. Quand elle arrive on nettoie le café ou bien on finit de le nettoyer. Le carrelage sèche. On le voit sécher: un carreau trop pâle, un carreau trop rouge. Plus il est fade, plus il sèche. Les chaises sont sur les tables, deux par deux, renversées l'une sur l'autre. Les tables dégraissées supportent ces enlacements obscènes. On passe la main sur le marbre humide. On a un frisson. Cette propreté qui s'envole me calme. Le patron a déposé sa gueule de patron à la caisse. Il astique. Il a travesti la moitié de son corps avec un tablier. Son sexe, auquel on ne pensait pas, est derrière un paravent de toile bleue. Les garçons l'aident. Ils ont ressuscité des mouvements non automatiques. La porte du café est ouverte. L'odeur du tabac vadrouille. La rue a l'exclusivité des bruits.

Violette Leduc, *L'Affamée*

2. Read the following text:

Les Noirs ont obtenu l'indépendance. Les prolétaires se sont unis. Les femmes seulement demeurent soumises et désunies, handicapées par le lien très spécial et souvent délicieux qui les unit à leurs «oppresseurs». Pour elles seules le racisme reste un système honorable, appliqué dans la plupart des régions du globe et les «différentes formes d'aliénation dont elles sont victimes représentent actuellement la plus massive survivance de l'asservissement humain». D'elles seules les philosophes peuvent continuer à prétendre «qu'elles sont une propriété, un bien qu'il faut mettre sous clé, des êtres faits pour la domesticité et qui n'atteignent leur perfection que dans la situation subalterne». (Nietzsche).

Benoîte Groult, *Ainsi soit-elle*

a) Find examples of abstract words, or concrete words taken in their generic sense.

b) What effect is produced by this accumulation of abstract words?

c) Is there a reference to a 'unique' object?

3. Look at the following short extracts. To what extent does the humour depend on assumed knowledge? What is this assumed knowledge?

a) *Les nez ont été faits pour porter des lunettes, ainsi avons-nous des lunettes. Les jambes sont visiblement instituées pour être chaussées, et nous avons des chausses.*

Voltaire, *Candide*

b) *Le sucre serait trop cher, si l'on ne faisait travailler la plante qui le produit par des esclaves. Ceux dont il s'agit sont noirs depuis les pieds jusqu'à la tête; et ils ont le nez si écrasé qu'il est presque impossible de les plaindre [...]. On peut juger de la couleur de la peau par celle des cheveux qui, chez les Egyptiens, les meilleurs philosophes du monde, étaient d'une si grande conséquence, qu'ils faisaient mourir tous les hommes roux qui leur tombaient entre les mains.*

Montesquieu, *De l'Esprit des lois*, XV

4. Read the following text:

Mme Aubry et M. Strauss-Kahn s'opposent sur les modalités du passage aux 35 heures. Hostile à cette perspective, le patronat menace de boycotter la conférence du dix octobre. Une divergence sérieuse oppose la ministre de l'emploi au ministre de l'économie sur les modalités de réduction de la durée du travail. Attachée au respect des engagements de la campagne législative, Martine Aubry souhaite que la conférence sur l'emploi, les salaires et le temps de travail qui réunira les partenaires sociaux, le 10 octobre, à Paris, donne l'occasion au premier ministre de réaffirmer la volonté du gouvernement de présenter une loi-cadre permettant de parvenir aux trente-cinq heures de travail hebdomadaires à la fin de la législature. Au nom du pragmatisme, Dominique Strauss-Kahn estime, au contraire, que toutes les solutions, y compris l'absence de texte législatif dans l'immédiat, sont envisageables.

Le premier secrétaire délégué du Parti socialiste, François Hollande, avait lui-même évoqué, le 21 septembre, au «Grand Jury RTL-Le Monde», la possibilité de ne présenter une loi qu'après l'engagement de négociations entre le patronat et les syndicats. Pourtant, que ce soit dans le programme du PS ou dans le texte de son accord avec le PC, aussi bien que dans la déclaration de politique générale au lendemain des législatives, la gauche puis Lionel Jospin ont toujours affirmé leur intention de passer aux trente-cinq heures avant 2002. Le premier ministre devra trancher ce différend entre ses ministres avant le 10 octobre. Le chef du gouvernement pourrait aussi être conduit à répondre au CNPF, qui menace de boycotter cette conférence si le gouvernement lui impose un texte législatif. Mme Aubry a dénoncé «le chantage» exercé par le patronat, dont les porte-parole affirment qu'aucune divergence n'existe en son sein.

Les pouvoirs publics ont adressé aux partenaires sociaux, vendredi 26 septembre, un «diagnostic» économique pour préparer la conférence. [...]
Le Monde, 28-29 September 1997

a) A number of 'objects' appear preceded by the definite article, without previous introduction, thus assuming that the reader can identify them. What are they? Can **you** identify them?

b) Can you find instances of abstract words/abstractions of concrete words?

c) What essential piece of information is necessary to understand fully the article?

5. Read the following texts:

Le GIA revendique les derniers massacres commis en Algérie et menace la France.

La rédaction londonienne du quotidien de langue arabe Al Hayat a reçu, vendredi 26 septembre, un communiqué signé par le Groupe islamique armé (GIA) [...] Dans ce texte de trois pages écrites en arabe qui figure dans le dernier numéro du bulletin clandestin El Ansar, le GIA lance également une série de menaces et d'avertissements. Il s'en prend tout d'abord aux partisans de l'Armée islamique du salut (AIS), la branche armée de l'ex-Front islamique du salut (FIS).

Le Monde, 28-29 September 1997

Emma Bonino interpellée à Kaboul.

Le commissaire européen chargé de l'aide humanitaire, Mme Emma Bonino, et les dix-neuf membres de sa délégation, ont été interpellés, lundi 29 septembre, à Kaboul, par des talibans (milices islamistes) pour avoir photographié des femmes, ce qui est illégal dans la capitale afghane. [...]

Le Monde, 30 September 1997

What difference do you make between this and Text 4 (*Mme Aubry et M. Strauss-Kahn...*) as far as assumed knowledge is concerned? Why? What devices are used so that the reader does not feel that she/he is an ignoramus?

6. Examine the irony and other sources of humour in this extract from an article by Pierre Georges in *Le Monde*. What cultural assumptions are made?

Une grande manifestation de brebis – deux mille selon les bergers, mille pour la préfecture de police – était prévue ce lundi à Nice. Aux bêlements déchirants de « Non, non au loup du Mercantour », les braves bêtes entendaient ainsi signifier un désaccord fondamental avec les hommes qui militèrent pour le retour du loup dans les Alpes-de-Hautes-Provence.

D'un point de vue de brebis, cela se tient parfaitement. Des siècles pour se débarrasser de l'héréditaire ennemi. Des siècles pour en finir avec les fables qui tournaient inévitablement mal, selon le célèbre constat de M. de la Fontaine: « La raison du plus fort est toujours la meilleure. » Des siècles d'alliance avec l'homme pour, enfin, en finir avec l'ancestrale peur du loup.

Et voici que l'homme est devenu, par un renversement d'alliance, un loup pour la brebis. Comment voulez-vous, dans ces conditions, qu'une agnelle y retrouve ses petits? N'est-ce point trop demander aux agneaux que de faire silence sur leurs malheurs présents? Donc, tous dans la rue, sur la promenade des Anglais peut-être, ce qui serait d'un chic achevé [...]

Le Monde, 30 September 1997

Production exercise

Write four sentences in French that rely for much of their meaning on cultural assumptions and presuppositions.

SUGGESTED ANSWERS TO ASSIGNMENTS

1. *L'Affamée*

   Examples of identification in situation: *le café, le carrelage, les chaises, les tables, le marbre, le patron, la caisse, les garçons, la rue, les bruits*: this is what the speaker 'sees'.

2. *Ainsi soit-elle*

   a) – abstract words: *l'indépendance, le racisme, la domesticité*

   – concrete words taken in their generic sense: *les Noirs, les prolétaires, les femmes, les philosophes*

   b) The accumulation of abstract words (and abstractions of concrete words) establish a link of complicity with the reader, who is assumed to be able to identify them.

   c) Instance of a 'unique' object: *le globe*

3. a) *Candide*

   The irony of this extract depends largely on the reader's ability to associate what is being said with a pre-existing scientific and biblical discourse with the tendency, for example, to explain all the phenomena in terms of cause and effect or of intentionality, whether it be human or divine.

   b) *De l'Esprit des lois*

   The irony of this passage depends largely on the reader's familiarity with racist attitudes and patterns of discourse which are here being exaggerated *ad absurdum*.

4. *Mme Aubry...*

   a) *les trente-cinq heures* (two instances)
   refers to a government proposal whereby the 'normal' working week would amount by law to 35 hours.

   le patronat (three instances)
   refers to the representatives of the employers in France.

   la campagne législative
   refers to the legislative campaign that led to the victory of the left in the Spring of 1997. (Note that the text is dated September 1997).

les partenaires sociaux (two instances)
name given to the three representative bodies in France for social
negotiations: the government, the employers and the trade unions.

le premier ministre (two instances)
Lionel Jospin, also mentioned by name in the same article.

le gouvernement (two instances)
the government in power at the time of writing the article, i.e. Lionel
Jospin's left-wing government.

la législature
the lifespan of the present parliament, i.e. refers to the length of the
mandate of the parliament at the time of writing: 1997 to 2002.

les syndicats
the representatives of the trade unions, one of the *partenaires sociaux*.

le PS
the French Socialist Party, also the party of Lionel Jospin, Prime Minister.

le PC
the French Communist Party, political ally of the Socialist Party.

les législatives
refers to the last legislative elections date.

la gauche
the French left-wing.

le chef du gouvernement
a lexical anaphora for *le premier ministre*.

le CNPF
stands for *Conseil National du Patronat Français*, known also as *le patronat*.

les pouvoirs publics
a synonym for the government, as one of the *partenaires sociaux*.

b) *le pragmatisme, l'emploi, les salaires.*

c) The full date of publication of the article: 28-29 September 1997. This
enables us to understand the *vendredi 26 septembre*, towards the end of the
article: note the use of the past tense *(ont adressé)*, and why there are
speculations on the conference of 10th October (it has not happened yet).

5. *Le GIA...; Emma Bonino...*

Text 4 refers to a French context, known by French readers, as opposed to Texts 5, which refer to a less familiar context. Hence, unlike in Text 4, all proper nouns and acronyms are now explained. Although the proper nouns and acronyms mentioned are supposed to be known by a reasonably well educated *Le Monde* reader, they belong to foreign countries and/or cultures, and it is safer for the journalist to make them more explicit if she/he wants to be fully understood. However, in order not to make the reader feel too ignorant, and in order to spare the feelings of those readers who did not need the explanations, note that it is the acronyms that appear between brackets (*GIA, AIS, FIS*), as a mere supplement of information; similarly *Emma Bonino* is in apposition to *le commissaire européen chargé de l'aide humanitaire* (and not the other way round), *Al Hayat* and *El Hansar* appear as mere noun complements for *le quotidien de langue arabe* and *le bulletin clandestin* respectively. Finally *la capitale afghane* appears discreetly at the end of a paragraph describing events in *Kaboul*. The reader is supposed to know about events in these countries and is only 'reminded' of who is who and what the acronyms are.

6. *Une grande manifestation...*

Irony and cultural assumptions include:

– allusions to the fact that for demonstrations and other street protests, the number of demonstrators differ according to the source that gives it: the police or the demonstration organisers. Here, the police are supposed to have counted the number of sheep! (*deux mille selon les bergers, mille pour la préfecture de police*)

– various references to clichés regarding sheep and wolves in popular folklore, together with puns, e.g. *L'homme est devenu... un loup pour la brebis* (*l'homme est un loup pour l'homme*, meaning men are ruthless with one another), *Comment voulez-vous... qu'une agnelle y retrouve ses petits?* (*une vache n'y retrouverait pas son veau*, meaning it's such a mess that it's impossible to find/understand anything), and an allusion to the film *Le silence des agneaux* (*N'est-ce point trop demander aux agneaux que de faire silence...*)

– allusion to the famous fables by La Fontaine (17th century), as if they were telling 'true stories', as a newspaper would for instance

– political allusions with:
  - *la raison du plus fort est toujours la meilleure,* with a pun on *le plus fort*: the strongest vs the most powerful (from La Fontaine's *Le loup et l'agneau*)
  - *renversement d'alliance*
  - and a pun with the allusion to the dispute over lamb between France and England some time ago with *tous dans la rue, sur la promenade des Anglais peut-être, ce qui serait d'un chic achevé* since *la promenade des Anglais* is indeed a very elegant avenue in Nice.

Other sources of humour include:
  - personnification of the sheep, who demonstrate, shout slogans and explain the reasons for the demonstration (*Une grande manifestation de brebis...,* *Aux bêlements déchirants de «Non, non au loup du Mercantour»,* *les braves bêtes entendaient ainsi signifier..., D'un point de vue de brebis...*)
  - the poetic/comic anteposition of the adjective in *se débarrasser de l'héréditaire ennemi.*

CHAPTER 9

TEXTUAL SCHEMATA

INTRODUCTION

Textual schemata are models or *a-priori* structures of meaning that underly a text and that play a central role in the establishment of its coherence. This chapter will focus on two groups of models:

1. Narrative models
2. Models of argumentation

1. Narrative models

Narrative models play a central role in the production of meaning in all types of discourse (and indeed in all forms of human interaction). They express archetypal story-structures derived from myth and fairy tales.

Worked example:
Compare the following two short texts.
What do you think is the principal difference between them?

> **1.** *La femme gisait sur le plancher. Le sang s'écoulait de son flanc sur le tapis où le contenu de son sac se trouvait éparpillé. Derrière elle, le rideau battait au vent et un chien aboyait dehors.*

> **2.** *La femme lisait, confortablement assise dans son fauteuil, quand soudain, un homme est entré et a tiré dans sa direction. Elle s'est écroulée sur le plancher. Après avoir saisi l'argent de son sac, l'homme s'est échappé par la fenêtre.*

Suggested answer:

Text 1 is purely descriptive: nothing happens, no change takes place, it is entirely static.

Text 2 on the other hand, presents an event: the position of the woman at the end of the account is not the same as at the beginning. A transformation has taken place.

1.1. Narrative and transformation

The principal characteristic of a narrative text is that it expresses a **transformation** (a change of state). The state of affairs at the end of the account is different from that described at the beginning. Something has happened, an event has taken place.

The transformation is always a movement between opposites. In the previous example, the woman moves from intact to injured and from life to death. The man moves from absence to presence. The money likewise moves from presence to absence.

Worked example:

a) Can you find the principal transformations in the following passages?

> **1** *Dans la capitale serbe du Kosovo, Pristina, au moins trois cents policiers équipés de canons à eau et de véhicules blindés ont dispersé, mercredi 1er octobre, les trois mille étudiants qui voulaient défiler dans la capitale provinciale pour réclamer des cours en langue albanaise. Une trentaine d'entre eux auraient été blessés dans cette province où neuf habitants sur dix sont des Albanais de souche.*
>
> Le Monde, 3 October 1997

> **2** *Tout mon être s'est tendu et j'ai crispé ma main sur le révolver. La gâchette a cédé, j'ai touché le ventre poli de la crosse et c'est là, dans le bruit à la fois sec et assourdissant que tout a commencé. J'ai secoué la sueur et le soleil. J'ai compris que j'avais détruit l'équilibre du jour, le silence exceptionnel d'une plage où j'avais été heureux. Alors, j'ai tiré encore quatre fois sur un corps inerte où les balles s'enfonçaient sans qu'il y parût. Et c'était comme quatre coups brefs que je frappais sur la porte du malheur.*
>
> Albert Camus, *L'Étranger*

b) Now look back at the two passages at the beginning of this chapter. What other major differences can you spot in the presentation of the characters? Try to relate these differences to the notion of **desire** (i.e. goals, purpose).

Suggested answers:

a) In Text 1, the following transformations may be discerned:

demonstrators gathered ⟶ demonstrators dispersed

intact ⟶ injured

In Text 2, the transformations include:

silence ⟶ noise   balance ⟶ imbalance

happiness ⟶ unhappiness   absence of shots ⟶ presence of shots

life ⟶ death

b) In Text 1, the female character is passive: she is presented as possessing no purpose or goal. In Text 2 on the other hand, both characters are presented as possessing specific goals: the woman's aim is to read a book whereas the man's aim is to injure or incapacitate her in order to steal the money.

1.2. Narrative and the structure of the quest

The fundamental structure of meaning can be defined in terms of the **quest**. The quest can be articulated in two narrative models. These are a) the actantial narrative schema and b) the canonical narrative schema.

1.2.1.The actantial narrative schema

This schema presents the six key **narrative functions** or roles which together account for all possible relationships within a story and indeed within the sphere of human action in general. These are: the subject, the object, the helper, the opponent (known sometimes as the anti-subject) and the sender.

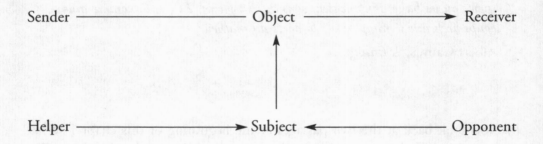

(i) The Subject and the Object

The main character (or characters) in a story is known as the subject. The subject is always in pursuit of an object or goal (without this fundamental orientation there can be no subject). Sometimes the goal is explicit, i.e. expressed in the actual words of the text, and sometimes it is implicit, i.e. the reader reconstructs an object calling on her/his knowledge of the world. An example of a text with an implicit goal would be the following:

> *Un homme marchait dans la montagne. Il commença à avoir soif. Il se dirigea vers le torrent.*

Here, the object of the man's quest is clearly to drink some water.

Worked example:
Can you find subjects and objects in these two sentences?

1. *Le gouvernement veut tourner le Massif Central vers un développement durable.*
Le Monde, 7 November 1997

2. *Au-delà de la fiabilité de leurs propres installations, les deux pays veulent contribuer à instaurer un niveau de sûreté homogène et renforcé sur l'ensemble du continent européen.*
Le Monde, 9 November 1997

Suggested answers:

Sentence 1: The subject of the quest is the French government. The object of the quest is to open the *Massif Central* to a more permanent development.

Sentence 2: The subject is the two countries (France and Germany). The object of the quest is to install common safety measures to be applied and strenghthened throughout the continent of Europe.

(ii) The Helper and the Opponent

The subject is frequently helped in its quest. The helper could be concrete such as money, or abstract such as courage. Courage, for example, can help you achieve your goal of sailing around the world single-handed. The subject may also have opponents: a lorry may block your way as you are driving to Heathrow, or your laziness may be an obstacle towards your goal of passing an examination.

(iii) The Anti-Subject

The anti-subject is an opponent with a quest of its own: this quest is always in opposition to that of the subject. If your subject in a general election campaign in England is the Labour Party, then the principal anti-subject will be the Conservative Party, as the goal of both - to be elected - is in opposition. Similarly, in accounts of strikes, management and unions are frequently presented in the relationship of subject and anti-subject.

(iv) The Sender and Receiver

The sender is the person, idea or emotion that motivates an action or causes something to happen. The receiver is the person to whom the motivation is given. Once the decision to act has been made, the **receiver** becomes a **subject**, ready to embark on a quest. Every quest must have a sender, whether it be explicit or implicit. For instance, in their quest to defeat the Argentinians, the soldiers who took part in the Falklands War had two senders:

a) an external sender in the figures of Margaret Thatcher and the British Government

and:

b) an internal sender in the belief in patriotism and in the traditional ideology of warfare.

Once the decision to act has been made, the **receiver** (the soldiers) becomes the subject of a quest.

Worked example:

How many narrative roles (subject, object, helper, opponent, anti-subject and sender) can you spot in the texts that follow?

1. *Le Président de la République Démocratique du Congo (RDC, ex-Zaïre), Laurent-Désiré Kabila, a annoncé, mercredi 1er octobre, l'envoi prochain de soldats à Brazzaville afin de localiser les pièces d'artillerie qui ont ouvert le feu sur Kinshasa.*
Le Monde, 3 October 1997

2. *La police vietnamienne dit aborder la question de la sécurité des nombreux chefs d'Etat et de gouvernement présents à Hanoï avec sérénité. Le chef de la police de la ville, Pham Chuyen, ne s'attend pas à des manifestations spontanées lors du sommet. Il refuse de communiquer les effectifs déployés pour la circonstance et indique simplement: «Nous avons simplement renforcé nos moyens techniques, avec 50 voitures et 50 motos supplémentaires, des équipements de détection des explosifs à l'aéroport et aussi de communication.»*
Le Monde, 14 November 1997

Suggested answers:

Text 1:

Subject: the soldiers
Object: to restrain the activities of the artillery
Sender: the President of the Republic

Text 2:

Subject: the Vietnamese police
Object: to ensure the security of Heads of State
Helpers: 50 additional cars
         50 additional motorbikes
         equipment for detecting explosives at the airport and for
         communication purposes

Anti-Subject (potential): the demonstrators

Sender(s) (implicit): the Vietnamese government
                  the obligation to carry out the professional role of keeper
                  of the peace and defender of the status quo.

1.2.2. The canonical narrative schema

This schema presents in detail the stages of the quest. It is composed of three tests: the qualifying test, the decisive test and the glorifying test, which always unfold in a logical progression. These tests are preceded by the stage of manipulation or the contract. The following schema is adapted from Groupe d'Entrevernes, *Analyse sémiotique des textes.*

contract	competence	performance	sanction
	qualifying test	**decisive test**	**glorifying test**
acquisition of a wanting-to-do or a having-to-do	acquisition of a being-able-to-do and/or of a knowing-how-to-do	the primary event where object of value is at stake	action of subject is evaluated: success/failure praise/blame

(i)   Contract

The sender transmits to the receiver the desire or obligation to act. What is known as a contract is established between the two and the subject embarks on a quest. The contract is followed by three tests. These tests mirror the fundamental logic of human action.

(ii)   The Qualifying Test (or stage of competence)

Here the subject acquires the competence needed to carry out the planned action or mission. The desire or obligation to act is not in itself sufficient: the subject must also possess the ability to act (*pouvoir-faire*) and/or the knowledge/skills to do so (*savoir-faire*). For example, if your intention is to shoot someone, you first of all need to acquire a gun; the gun functions as your helper, providing you with the necessary ability to act.

(iii)   The Decisive Test (or stage of performance)

This represents the principal event or action for which you have been preparing, where the object of the quest is at stake. In news articles, the decisive test frequently takes the form of a confrontation between a subject and an anti-subject.

(iv)   The Glorifying Test (or sanction)

The outcome of the event is now revealed; the decisive test has either succeeded or failed, the subject is acclaimed or punished. In other words, it is the point at which the performance of the subject is interpreted and evaluated by what is known as the sender-adjudicator.

1.3. Narrative models and text ideology

Narrative models are exploited by individual texts in a variety of ways. For instance, certain stages or tests in the canonical narrative schema may be foregrounded, others remain implicit: in adventure stories and in news stories, for example, the emphasis is on the decisive test, whereas in *avant-garde* fiction it is the qualifying test that is frequently foregrounded.

This exploitation of narrative models - together with the distribution of power relations that is implied - is one of the many means (see, for example, the use of connectors in Chapter 3) by which a text constructs its ideology and seeks to persuade the receiver (addressee) of a particular stance or world-view.

Worked example:

Read the following newspaper article:

> *LES ÉVÊQUES AVANCENT UN BILAN DE **400** MORTS APRÈS LA RÉVOLTE DES INDIENS DU CHIAPAS*
>
> *L'armée mexicaine, qui a engagé dans cette opération 12000 hommes — le cinquième de ses forces — appuyés par des chars, des hélicoptères et des avions, semblait sur le point, mercredi 5 janvier, de mettre fin au soulèvement paysan dans l'Etat du Chiapas, au sud du pays.*
>
> *Les rebelles se replient vers des zones montagneuses, où ils sont poursuivis par l'aviation. Le gouvernement a fixé ses conditions à un dialogue avec les rebelles «zapatistes»: cessez-le-feu et remise de leurs armes. Parmi les autres conditions, figurent également la libération de tous les prisonniers et l'identification des dirigeants de l'Armée zapatiste de libération nationale (AZLN), a indiqué un porte-parole officiel.*
>
> *L'armée fédérale était parvenue à entrer mardi dans la ville d'Ocosingo, où les rebelles de l'AZLN ont opposé une forte résistance. Selon plusieurs journalistes, les rues de la ville étaient jonchées de cadavres, certains pieds et mains liés. D'autres avaient reçu le coup de grâce. Les autorités militaires ont ouvert une enquête sur d'éventuels excès de la part des soldats.*
>
> *Depuis le début du soulèvement, le 1er janvier, le bilan officiel est de 93 tués, dont 59 rebelles, 7 soldats et 27 civils. Mais les évêques catholiques estiment que le bilan est bien plus lourd, de l'ordre de 400 morts. — (AFP, Reuter)*
>
> *Le Monde*, 7 January 1994

a) If we envisage **the Mexican army** as subject of a quest, who or what do you think is (or are):

   1) the object(s) of the quest?   3) the anti-subject?
   2) the helpers?   4) the sender?

Where possible, find the exact French words or phrases that suggest these narrative roles.

b) If we now envisage **the Indians** as subject of a quest, who or what do you think are:

   1) the object of the quest?   2) the sender?

c) Why do you think that the narrative roles in b) are not explicitly mentioned in the text? Do you think that this omission influences the way you think about the relationship between the Indians and the Mexican army?

d) In the quest of the Mexican army:
   1) Where in the article is the qualifying test suggested? In other words, where are we informed that this army is a fully competent subject capable of carrying out its quest?
   2) What do you think is the decisive test?
   3) Where do you think the glorifying test or the outcome of the quest is suggested?

Suggested answers:

a) 1) The object of the quest is the defeat of the Indians and the restoration of the status quo. This is suggested in *semblait sur le point... de mettre fin... au soulèvement paysan...* at the end of the first paragraph.
   2) The helpers are the tanks, helicopters and planes.
      This is suggested in *appuyés par des chars, des hélicoptères et des avions...,* again in paragraph one.
   3) The role of anti-subject is enacted by the Indian rebels or peasants. We deduce this fact from the word *paysan* and the reference to the state of Chiapas at the end of paragraph one. The term *les rebelles* at the beginning of paragraph two makes the relationship absolutely clear.
   4) The sender of the quest of the Mexican army is the Mexican government. This is suggested implicitly in *Le gouvernement a fixé ses conditions à un dialogue...* in paragraph two. This allocation of narrative roles is reinforced by reference to our own cultural knowledge and assumptions: national armies usually take their orders from the government in power. The sender (implicit) of the soldiers' quest may also be fear and/or a desire to maintain the status quo - an army can always disobey orders and refuse to carry out its mission.

b) 1) The object of the Indians' quest is social justice. This is not stated in the text: readers must draw on their own background knowledge to fill in the gaps and make sense of the article.
   2) The sender (implicit) is social justice. Again the reader may draw on background knowledge to reinforce the narrative coherence, such as an awareness of political corruption on the part of the Mexican government.

c) The narrative roles in b) are not explicitly mentioned in the text, as the principal focus is on the activities of the Mexican army. The omission of information about the Indians does influence the reader's assessment of the situation, suggesting a possible bias in favour of the Mexican army. If, for example, the object of the quest, i.e. social justice, and the reasons (the sender) for the Indian uprising, i.e. corruption and social injustice, were overtly stated, then the reader's sympathies for the Indians would undoubtedly be strengthened. The omission may suggest a reluctance on the part of the text producer (the authors) to show open sympathy for the Indians, thereby upsetting or challenging the status quo. Textual silence, the backgrounding of information, can therefore become a means of strengthening dominant ideologies (value-systems) and power structures.

d) 1) The qualifying test is evoked in the opening paragraph. We learn that the subject, the army, is in possession not only of the necessity *(devoir-faire)* or desire to act *(vouloir-faire)* but also of the capability to carry out the quest *(pouvoir-faire)* provided by the tanks, planes, etc. The army can therefore be viewed as a fully competent subject.

2) The decisive test is the confrontation with the Mexican army. This is suggested in particular in paragraphs two, three and four as well as in the headline.

3) The glorifying test or outcome of the quest (i.e. the defeat of the Indians) is suggested in particular in paragraph one *(de mettre fin au soulèvement paysan)*, in paragraph three where atrocities committed by the Mexican army are described, and finally in the last paragraph where several indications suggest the imminent defeat of the Indians.

Production exercises

1. Write a short account (100-200 words) of an unusual event for your local newspaper. Try to include as many of the following narrative roles as possible:
   a) subject   d) sender
   b) object   e) helper.
   c) anti-subject

   Then state what you think in your account represents:
   a) the decisive test   b) the glorifying test.

2. Attempt to re-write the article in Section 1.3 as if the source of information were the Indians rather than official news agencies.

2. Models of argumentation

An argumentative text is a text that puts forward and defends a particular point of view - that of the narrator. Its overall aim is to persuade the reader to adopt this point of view as opposed to any other.

2.1. Basic structure

Broadly speaking, the argumentative text can be divided into three parts. These are:

(i) Statement of position

The narrator presents the position she/he is taking in the argument.

(ii) Justification

This part includes the provision of evidence and the presentation of arguments for and against a position. It could also contain an elaboration or expansion of the initial position by referring to something more general or by resorting to a process of examplification (i.e. giving an example).

(iii) Conclusion

This part could formulate the narrator's acceptance or rejection of a particular argument. Or it might simply be an expansion of the second section or of the initial position in the light of what has been said.

Worked example:

Read the following article. Can you divide it broadly into three parts?
Homosexualité, famille, filiation
by Eric Dubreuil (président de l'APGL) and Maud Grad (ingénieur):

P.1 *Nous souhaitons, au nom de l'Association des parents et futurs parents gays et lesbiens (APGL), apporter notre point de vue sur les échanges parus dans* Le Monde *en réponse au texte d'Eric Fassin du 5 novembre, intitulé « Homosexualité, mariage et famille ». Serge Bakchine et Irène Théry sont intervenus (*Le Monde *des 19 et 25 novembre) dans ce débat en tant que professionnels, respectivement neuropsychologue et sociologue du droit, et non en tant que simples citoyens.*

P.2 *Les familles gays et lesbiennes, ou homoparentales, sont une réalité: 10% des gays et des lesbiennes déclarent avoir un enfant et 50% déclarent en vouloir un (sondage paru dans le magazine* Têtu *de janvier), ce qui représente plusieurs centaines de milliers de citoyens. Le temps est révolu où gays et lesbiennes faisaient leur deuil des enfants.*

P.3 *Certes, Irène Théry dénonce toute discrimination envers des homosexuels qui ont eu des enfants dans un cadre hétérosexuel. Nous nous en réjouissons. Mais si des gays ou des lesbiennes souhaitent devenir parents, elle parle alors de «personnes qui n'assument pas leur finitude » et de «régression biologique». Serge Bakchine écrit que tous les homosexuels ayant des enfants « les ont emmenés avec eux d'un précédent couple hétérosexuel». Si une partie des parents gays et lesbiens sont en effet divorcés, d'autres enfants sont nés dans un cadre homoparental. Avoir des enfants dans ce cadre ne se résume pas à l'utilisation de la procréation médicalement assistée (PMA), aujourd'hui pratiquée à l'étranger. Nombreux sont ceux qui élaborent des projets de coparentalité où hommes et femmes sont présents autour du berceau. Enfin, certains adoptent des enfants. Le droit français ne permettant pas aux couples de personnes de même sexe d'adopter, ils doivent se présenter en tant que célibataires «sexuellement corrects».*

P.4 *Dans tous les cas, la transparence vis-à-vis de l'enfant au sujet de sa conception est prônée. Tous ces projets sont ceux de personnes qui veulent, comme tant d'autres, apporter à un enfant sécurité et affection, et qui y engagent leur responsabilité.*

P.5 *En quoi donc une orientation sexuelle différente implique-t-elle que le désir d'enfant soit un «fantasme d'auto-engendrement»? Bien des couples inféconds n'assument pas leur finitude. Lorsqu'ils ont recours aux techniques de PMA, personne ne parle à leur sujet de «régression biologique». Pourquoi homosexualité et négation de l'autre sexe, voire négation de l'Autre, sont-ils si souvent confondus? Pour aimer autrement, on n'en aime pas moins un autre que soi.*

P.6 *Serge Bakchine avance ensuite qu'il n'existerait pas de travaux scientifiques démontrant qu'un couple homosexuel offrirait à un enfant les mêmes chances de développement harmonieux qu'une famille hétérosexuelle. Nous contestons cette affirmation. L'APGL a publié un Petit guide bibliographique à l'usage des familles homoparentales et des autres. Cet ouvrage recense plus de 200 références bibliographiques. On y trouvera des études comparatives rigoureuses concernant le développement des enfants et les attitudes parentales. Et nous ne demandons pas mieux que des recherches scientifiques soient publiées en France sur le sujet de l'homoparentalité.*

P.7 *Qui peut décider de la compétence parentale d'une partie de l'humanité? Peut-on refuser à certains d'être parents? Faudrait-il instituer des permis d'enfanter et de «parenter»? Combien de familles hétérosexuelles réussiraient-elles l'examen? On a déjà vu dans le passé les méfaits d'un tel tri…*

P.8 *Comme pour toute minorité, la société se doit d'assurer aux homosexuels les moyens de leur intégration. Brider leur désir de fonder une famille est le plus sûr moyen de les confiner dans une marginalité et une représentation qui, au mieux, amusent la société.*

P.9 *En cas de divorce de ses parents, l'enfant doit être protégé de la trop fréquente mise en cause des compétences parentales de son parent homosexuel. Ce véritable déni de parentalité risquerait de le priver durablement de ses liens avec celui-là.*

P.10 *Lorsque nos enfants sont nés dans un contexte homosexuel, le partenaire homosexuel est souvent un co-parent. Il a souhaité la venue de l'enfant au monde et est prêt à engager sa responsabilité pour entretenir cet enfant, lui transmettre ses biens, l'éduquer et assumer l'autorité parentale avec l'autre parent. Cette personne a un rôle parental évident sans en avoir le statut juridique. Nous cherchons un cadre institutionnel pour le lien parent-enfant. La notion de couple indissolublement lié par le* *mariage n'est plus la norme. Le couple est provisoire. Les familles se décomposent et se recomposent. C'est le lien parent-enfant qui est pérenne, intemporel et indissoluble. Les parents ne sont-ils pas ceux qui ont voulu donner la vie et s'engager à conduire un petit d'homme à l'âge adulte? Nous fondons la notion de parent sur l'acte qui consiste à reconnaître un enfant comme le sien et à s'engager vis-à-vis de lui, devant autrui, dans un lien indéfectible. En ce sens, les familles homoparentales sont composées comme les autres de parents qui donnent la vie à des enfants, les aiment et les élèvent. Si ces familles contemporaines interrogent la société, les enfants qui en sont issus n'en ont pas moins besoin d'un cadre institutionnel qui leur fait actuellement défaut.*

P.11 *Pour cela, il faut tenir compte de trois types de filiation qui coexistent (et souvent se superposent) dans les familles, qu'elles soient composées, décomposées ou recomposées. Une filiation biologique, une filiation légale/généalogique et une filiation sociale/domestique (co-parent, beau-parent). Un enfant peut être inscrit dans une filiation légale et être élevé par des parents «sociaux» qui partagent le lieu de vie des enfants dont ils prennent soin, et dont certains ne sont pas leurs parents biologiques.*

P.12 *Reconnaître un statut distinct à ces trois filiations permettrait à tous les enfants d'avoir accès à leurs origines (filiation biologique), d'avoir une place dans la chaîne des générations (filiation légale), d'être élevés par tous les parents (filiation sociale). Cela permettrait aux enfants de bénéficier d'un «plus»: l'autorité parentale partagée de manière consensuelle par plus de deux personnes.*

P.13 *Il n'y a, hélas, aujourd'hui pas de place légale pour la pluriparentalité. Pourquoi ne veut-on connaître qu'une filiation? Pourquoi s'interdit-on de créer les concepts nécessaires pour penser les situations familiales où des enfants sont élevés par des parents qui ne sont pas ceux que la loi désigne?*

P.14 *Gays et lesbiennes, nous souhaitons élever nos enfants dans des conditions de développement harmonieux, en contribuant ainsi au devenir de la société. Même si nos structures familiales sortent de l'ordinaire - mais en quoi menacent-elles l'équilibre de l'ensemble? — nous croyons que la société a tout intérêt à nous aider à assumer nos responsabilités envers nos enfants.*

Le Monde, 12 December 1997

Suggested answer:

Part 1: From the beginning down to the end of the second paragraph, the narrators are stating their position: they are speaking as members of *l'Association des parents et futurs parents gays et lesbiennes (APGL)* and will be defending the views of this organisation against those expressed by two people in an earlier issue of *Le Monde*: Serge Bakchine, a neuropsychologist and Irène Théry, a sociologist.

Part 2: From the beginning of the third to the end of the penultimate paragraph, the narrators defend their position against the views of Irène Théry and Serge Bakchine. In the course of this defence, we, the readers, become fully acquainted with the views of the opposition. This section is an excellent example of the **dialectical** structure of argumentative discourse.

Part 3: The final paragraph marks a return to the form of direct, personal address that we saw in the first paragraph. The speakers are once more expressing the desire to bring up children. At the same time however, by summarising Part 2 - such unconventional families do not constitute a threat to the social order as the opposition claims - they expand on the initial position. The text ends with a general comment on society.

2.2. Further features of the argumentative text

2.2.1 Presence of the speaker

   a) The use of pronouns

      The argumentative text is frequently characterised by a particular use of the pronouns *nous* and *on* (the latter also often meaning 'we'). These pronouns can be employed to establish a complicity with the reader: they become a means of assimilating the reader, of drawing her/him towards accepting the point of view of the speaker.

   b) The use of modality

      By **modality** is meant the devices whereby the speaker is making clear her/his position on a subject rather than hiding behind neutral statements (see also Chapter 4 on Tense cohesion). Devices conveying modality include:

      (i)   Verbs and impersonal expressions conveying notions such as probability, impossibility, etc. with *devoir, pouvoir, croire, il se peut que, il est probable que*, etc.

      (ii) Adverbs such as *vraiment, jamais, mieux, pire*.

      (iii) Explicit, evaluative adjectives such as *stupide, écœurant, merveilleux, édifiant*.

2.2.2 Lexical organisation

Argumentative discourse is frequently characterised by the use of lexical fields that relate to the two sides of the argument. In many of J.J. Rousseau's texts for example, the lexical field of nature is opposed to that of civilisation. Opposition can also occur **within** lexical fields.

2.2.3 Connectors

Another characteristic feature of this type of discourse is the frequent use of connectors, in particular causal (*parce que, afin de,* etc.) and adversative/concessive connectors (*mais, cependant,* etc.).

2.2.4 Additional rhetorical devices

The following rhetorical devices may also appear in argumentative discourse:
   a) An accumulation of adjectives, especially those that express a criticism
   b) The use of superlatives
   c) Rhetorical questions (which do not expect an answer from the addressee)
   d) Repetition
   e) Metaphor
   f) The use of parallelism, such as *ni tout à fait ceci, ni tout à fait cela,* or expressions such as *non… mais…, soit que… soit que…*

Worked example:

Now look again at the article by Dubreuil and Grad in *Le Monde*. Can you find one example of each of the four features of the argumentative text (presence of the speaker, lexical fields, connectors and other rhetorical devices)?

Possible answers:

1. Presence of the speaker

This article illustrates the way a newspaper can publish an exchange of readers' views. This article, published in *Le Monde,* is an answer to a comment, also published in *Le Monde,* made by two readers about an article itself originally published in *Le Monde*! The presence of the speaker is thus made explicit, with:
   a) The use of the first person plural *nous.* The article is a personal address to readers. A sense of immediacy and of direct involvement is thereby conveyed. Note that in the use of pronouns:
      • most of the *nous* represent the authors of the article, i.e. the speaker: *nous souhaitons* (P.1), *nous nous en réjouissons* (P.3), *nous contestons* (P.6),

nous ne demandons (P.6), *nous cherchons* (P.10), *nous fondons* (P.10); except for *nos enfants* in P.10 (an attempt to involve the reader!), *gay et lesbiennes, nous*... and all the *nous/nos* of the last paragraph, which stand for the whole of the gay community.

- *on,* as usual, has a variety of referents:
  - *on n'en aime pas moins:* 'universal' on (P.5)
  - *on y trouvera:* the reader/addressee (P.6)
  - *peut-on refuser:* the authorities (P.7)
  - *on a déjà vu dans le passé:* the public (the observers) including the reader and the authors (P.7)
  - *pourquoi ne veut-on pas connaître:* the authorities (P.13)
  - *pourquoi s'interdit-on:* the authorities (P.13)
- the interrogative pronoun *qui* – which poses existence but not identity appears in Paragraph 7 (*Qui peut décider de la compétence...*) and has the value of an indefinite pronoun
- impersonal *il* also appears once in the same paragraph (*Faudrait-il instituer...*)

b) The use of devices conveying modality such as the verbs *contester* (P.6), *croire* (last paragraph) and *souhaiter* (first and last paragraphs), and the interjection *hélas* (penultimate paragraph).

The authors express in turn regret, anger and recommendations, and even make threats, but they also show their desire to contribute positively to society: *nous souhaitons... en contribuant ainsi au devenir de la société,* the fact that they are not a 'danger': *mais en quoi menacent-elles [les structures familiales homoparentales] l'équilibre de l'ensemble?*

The text ends on a note of advice mixed with a veiled threat: *... nous croyons que la société a tout intérêt à nous aider à assumer nos responsabilités envers nos enfants.* Note here again the clever use of *nos,* referring to the children of homoparental families but also by extension to the children of the whole of society.

c) The use of the conditional to contest the truth value of someone else's words, e.g. *Serge Bakchine avance ensuite qu'il **n'existerait pas** de travaux scientifiques...* (P.6). This is countered by an example of such a 'scientific work': *L'APLG a publié un Petit guide...* The conditional is also used to express a hypothesis of what might happen in the future if something is not done now:... ***risquerait** de le priver durablement...* (P.9). Finally it is used to express a happy hypothesis, i.e. what would be a happy outcome if...: *Reconnaître un statut distinct à ces trois filiations **permettrait...*** (P.12).

d) The expression of a moralising stance with the cultural allusion *On a déjà vu dans le passé les méfaits d'un tel tri...* (P.7) and an allusion to the duties of society towards all minorities: *la société se doit d'assurer aux homosexuels...* (P.8) and *La société a tout intérêt à nous aider...* (P.14) See also the use of quotes in 4. Additional rhetorical devices.

2. Lexical fields and opposition

This concerns for instance the opposition within the lexical field of 'family', between 'traditional family' (parents male and female) and 'non-traditional family' (both parents the same sex). Further oppositions are brought into play, such as 'responsibility' vs 'irresponsibility' (lexical field of moral state), 'healthy or harmonious child development' vs 'unhealthy or disturbed child development' (lexical field of child development), 'approval of scientific establishment' vs 'disapproval of scientific establishment' (lexical field of scientific establishment), etc.

3. Connectors

A variety of connectors are used at key points (e.g. at the beginning and end of paragraphs) in the article. For instance:

    (i)   concessive:
- *certes* (P.3)
- *mais si... alors...* (P.3)
- *si une partie... d'autres...* (P.3)
- *même si* (last paragraph)

    (ii) adversative
- *mais* (last paragraph)

    (iii) temporal
- *enfin* (P.3)
- *ensuite* (P.6)
- *lorsque* (P.10)

(Note that *enfin* and *ensuite* can be used to establish a chronology of events, as they are here, in a list of arguments)

    (iv) additive
- *et* (P.6)

(which begins a sentence).

4. Additional rhetorical devices

The most striking rhetorical device is the use of rhetorical questions. Paragraph 7 for instance is composed almost entirely of such questions, as is the penultimate paragraph. Paragraph 5 also contains two rhetorical questions, but here the narrators then give the answers.

Further devices:

- The use of semi-legal vocabulary to create the impression of authority, e.g. *un enfant peut être **inscrit dans une filiation légale*** (P.11); *un **cadre institutionnel** pour le lien parent-enfant* (P.10); and psychological jargon, with ***négation de l'Autre*** (P.5).

- Allusion to what the French law allows or not, with an explicit or implicit comparison with what happens elsewhere (in other countries) to show that the present situation is not a kind of 'natural order' but the result of the law of a certain country, at a certain time, e.g. *... la procréation médicalement assistée (PMA) **aujourd'hui pratiquée à l'étranger*** (P.3); *Le **droit français** ne permettant pas aux couples de personnes de même sexe d'adopter* (P.3).

- The use of the present tense, to stress today's state of affairs, e.g. *Les familles gays et lesbiennes... sont une réalité* (P.2); *Le temps est révolu où...* (P.2); *Le couple est provisoire* (P.10); *Les familles se décomposent et se recomposent* (P.10).

- The use of universal *on* + present tense to give a statement a value of universal truth e.g. *Pour aimer autrement, on n'en aime pas moins un autre que soi* in P.5 (one could also note here the slight obsolescence of the turn of phrase, which makes the statement sound more like a maxim).

- The use of quotes to create a distance between the reported speech and the opinion of the reporter: e.g. *«personnes qui n'assument pas leur finitude»* (P.3); *«régression biologique»* (P.3); *«fantasme d'auto-engendrement»* (P.5); quotes are also used in one instance to isolate a word which does not belong to the same register as the rest of the article and thus clashes: *Cela permettrait aux enfants de bénéficier d'un «plus»* (P.12); and in two others to introduce neologisms: *«parenter»* in P.7 (based on *enfanter*) and *«sexuellement corrects»* in P.3 (based on *politiquement correct*).

Production exercises:

1. You are a barrister trying to convince the jury of the innocence of your client who is accused of murdering her husband. Write a short speech in her defence taking on board the arguments of the prosecution.
2. Write a short speech persuading your audience of the need for a motorway just outside their town. You must take into account the views of the ecologists, etc. who oppose such a development.

CHAPTER 10

REGISTER AND GENRE

INTRODUCTION

Like cultural assumptions and presuppositions, **register** plays a key role in the production of textual coherence. By the term register is meant a variety of language related to the degree of formality. This degree of formality is determined by the circumstances in which language is used, i.e. by its social function and context. It is manifested principally in the choice of vocabulary and of syntax.

Register could be:
  a) standard, as in many newspaper articles
  b) formal, as in official documents
  c) informal, as in conversation and some letter-writing.

Sub-categories include the colloquial register and the vulgar register.

Finally, note that the term register is also used to describe different fields of discourse such as the legal register, the scientific register, etc.

The classificaction of texts into **genres** is dependent on the text register, as well as on the subject matter and stylistic form. These components create a field of expectation in the reader/listener, establishing an implicit contract between author and reader or speaker and interlocutor.

1. Notion of register

Together with cohesive devices, register is what helps define a passage of discourse as a text and what gives it its coherence. The notion of register has several characteristics:

— it is influenced by the **meaning** or **subject matter** of an oral or written utterance
— it is concerned with the **representation of experience** and includes interpersonal relationships as well as personal attitudes: the speaker's opinion and motives. As such, it reflects social (age of the speaker, social status…), expressive and communicative features
— it is finally determined by the **mode of delivery** chosen by the speaker to deliver her/his message in a specific situation. The message can for instance be given in a narrative, didactic, directional, persuasive, or even poetic mode.

If we take as an anecdotal example the banal situation of going to the cinema with a friend, various modes of delivery may be chosen. Consider the following examples:

a) *Son ami vint le voir à l'improviste et lui intima de le suivre sur-le-champ jusqu'au cinéma le plus proche à quelques mètres de là. Ils partirent aussitôt.*
(narrative mode)

b) *Il te faut me suivre immédiatement jusqu'au cinéma le plus proche, déclara son ami. Il est indispensable que tu voies ce film dont je t'ai parlé.*
(persuasive mode)

c) *Ecoute bien, je vais t'expliquer, voilà ce que tu vas faire: va jusqu'au carrefour puis tourne à droite au deuxième feu. Tu arriveras au cinéma à quelques centaines de mètres d'ici.*
(directional mode)

d) *Lorsque le soir tombera et que la lune pointera dans le ciel, je souhaiterais vivement que tu puisses m'accompagner au cinéma le plus proche et là nous nous délecterons de ce que nous avons toujours rêvé de voir ensemble mais qu'hélas jusqu'ici le destin ne nous avait pas permis de faire.*
('poetic' style)

Register can vary at the lexical (use of vocabulary) as well as the syntactic (sentence formation) level with a **greater or lesser degree of formality** depending on the situational context (*environnement de l'élocution*). The choice of the text's syntax and terminology will depend on the specific relationship with the addressee as well as the social context. A lecturer, for instance, will talk of different topics with a different choice of vocabulary and syntactic constructions when she talks to her colleagues in the staffroom, when she gives a tutorial to a student in her office, when she delivers a paper at a conference or when she is addressing her 3-year-old son at home. The situation in which the lecturer finds herself will determine the degree of formality or informality she adopts.

Certain **contexts** such as a political speech to the nation, a sociological study in a newspaper, a philosophy lecture, a literary article or a technical report, will dictate a more formal register and are likely to contain an important degree of technical and abstract, sometimes rare, vocabulary, specific to their subject matter. At the syntactic level, they will show formal uses of grammatical forms (subjunctive imperfect, rhetorical questions with complex inversion, etc.) and longer sentences with subordinate clauses.

An **informal level of register** may in turn include slang, argotic, idiosyncratic or popular expressions (*J'en ai ras le bol!*), indiscriminate use of new words (neologisms), careless grammatical constructions, elliptical forms (*T'as vu* instead of *Tu as vu* or *Chais pas* for *Je ne sais pas, y a* for *il y a*, etc.), interjections and hesitations (*Génial!, euh…*), unfinished sentences (*C'est pas le genre de film que j'aime. Je m'attendais à aut'chose un petit peu … euh! d'un petit peu plus… mais enfin c'est un film policier, il fallait s'y attendre.*) or truncated words such as *resto, ado* (apocope) and a general manner of speech which concentrates upon personal feelings and expressions such as in this dialogue.

> — *Salut Kamel!*
> — *Salut. Ça va?*
> — *Ça va. T'es tout seul?*
> — *Ouais, me répond-il. Mais j'attends les autres. On va aller faire du vélo jusqu' à chez les paysans. Tu veux venir?*
> — *Avec quoi? J'ai pas de braque.*
> — *Ah, t'as pas de braque? fait-il surpris.*
> *Et aussitôt:*
> — *T'en veux un?*
> — *Comment, j'en veux un? T'en as un à me refiler?*
> — *Te casse pas la tête. Je vais finir de réparer cette putain de roue et on va aller t'en trouver un, de vélo.*
>
> Azouz Begag, *Le Gone du Chaâba*

This register is predominant in speech but is also used to a greater or lesser extent in informal letter writing, news articles and literature, for realistic effect or reasons of audience reception.

Note that certain situations (such as teenage letters to friends) are more likely to rely on a high degree of informal syntactic and lexical forms. Some 20th century literary texts, such as women's texts of the 70s or *Beur* literature of the 80s, use the impact of familiar register against the backdrop of classical literary conventions, to assert a different type of reality and the social identity of their protagonists. However, a great number of texts use a **standard level of register** – that is a more neutral language accessible to a majority of people – and most often include a **mixture of several registers**.

2. Notion of genre

The subject matter, the presence of the speaker and the mode of delivery which define the register are likely to vary according to the specific genre of the text. However the concept of genre contains in itself some degree of indeterminacy since the boundaries between different types of texts are not fixed and tend to overlap. Genres of texts also have their sub-genres: a literary text for instance will have different characteristics if it is a novel, a poem or a theatre play.

Broadly speaking, one can nevertheless assert that different types of texts or genres will tend to favour certain types of register. For instance:

• A literary genre will favour a narrative mode: its aim is generally to tell a story, or to recount an experience in a fictional mode. Although the mode of delivery may vary – it can be explicitly autobiographical or not – a literary genre tends to use more figures of speech, especially metaphors and similes (see Chapter 6) than a non-literary genre. The degree of formality at the syntactic level, especially in the choice of tense and aspect (see Chapter 4, Tense cohesion), may denote an historical evolution: 20th century texts are likely to favour the use of the present and perfect as opposed to the past historic favoured in 19th century texts. Compare for instance Zola's or Balzac's way of writing with that of Camus or Duras.

> *Il y avait quinze jours que Laurent ne pouvait approcher de Thérèse. Alors il sentit combien cette femme lui était devenue nécessaire: l'habitude de la volupté lui avait créé des appétits nouveaux, d'une exigence aiguë. Il n'éprouvait aucun malaise dans les embrassements de sa maîtresse, il quêtait ces embrassements avec une obstination d'animal affamé.*

Emile Zola, *Thérèse Raquin*

> *Il s'allonge près d'elle, il s'appuie sur sa main libre, il la regarde. Il ne l'a jamais vue d'aussi près. Il ne l'a jamais vue dans une lumière aussi intense. Elle écoute toujours le bruit. Elle ferme les yeux, elle veut les fermer, ses paupières frémissent sous l'effort de le vouloir.*

Marguerite Duras, *L'Amour*

- Sociological, psychological, historical, economic and scientific texts will mostly be recognisable by their subject-matter, reflected in the choice of a specialized vocabulary, and in the use of syntactical devices such as the indefinite third person pronoun, that serve to strengthen the 'truth effect'.

See for instance this example of literary theory, relating aptly here to the concept of literary genres:

> *Les genres littéraires ne sont pas des êtres en soi: ils constituent, à chaque époque, une sorte de code implicite à travers lequel, et grâce auquel les œuvres du passé et les œuvres nouvelles peuvent être reçues et classées par les lecteurs. C'est par rapport à des modèles, à «des horizons d'attente», à toute une géographie variable, que les textes littéraires sont produits puis reçus, qu'ils satisfassent cette attente ou qu'ils la transgressent et la forcent à se renouveler.*

P. Lejeune, *Le Pacte autobiographique*

Worked examples:

1. Analyse the degree of formality of this text:

> *Au retour des vacances de Noël, la prof a décidé qu'en géographie on parlerait de la Corse, tout un dossier là-dessus. Ça me gonfle et en vérité, j'en ai rien à faire de sa Corse! Je sais que c'est «son pays», c'est elle qui nous l'a dit, mais ça ne m'intéresse pas, c'est tout! Y a qu'elle qui se fait plaisir dans l'histoire. Je suis sûre que les autres aussi, ils s'en foutent, mais ils ne disent rien. La dernière fois, comme je faisais encore le pitre, elle m'a dit:*
> *— Alors, Samia, ça ne t'intéresse pas ce que l'on fait aujourd'hui?*
> *— Non, ça ne m'intéresse pas!*
> *Si la Corse elle est comme elle, alors vraiment je préfère rien savoir! Et les châtaignes, je suis sûre que je trouverais les mêmes au marché. Sa Corse, elle doit être triste; elle nous fait colorier des paysages en gris avec des vieilles sur des ânes, toutes habillées en noir, comme elle. Bonjour la Corse! Je préfère encore ma cité.*
>
> Soraya Nini, *Ils disent que je suis une beurette*

Suggested answers:

Many lexical and syntactic features mark the text as belonging to a familiar/informal register. The manner of speech relies on a monologue: that of a schoolgirl who relates her irritation with her teacher. The presence of the first person narrator is reinforced **at the lexical level** by the high degree of the narrator's expression of personal feelings, such as:

- *ça me gonfle* or *ça ne m'intéresse pas, c'est tout* (irritation)
- *j'en ai rien à faire de sa Corse* or *vraiment je préfère rien savoir* (assertion of personal choice)
- *Sa Corse, elle doit être triste* (judgement, opinion)

Similarly one finds a high incidence of familiar/slang expressions:

- *Ça **me gonfle***
- *Y a qu'elle qui **se fait plaisir** dans l'histoire*
- *...les autres aussi ils **s'en foutent**...*

Such a familiar way of speaking is very revealing of the age of the narrator: that of a young schoolgirl.

At the syntactic level, the use of exclamations also reveals the presence of the speaker in e.g. *alors vraiment je préfère rien savoir*! or *Bonjour la Corse*!. The abundance of juxtaposed clauses and the absence of connectors are also congruent with the spontaneous speech of a young person. The use of the present as the basic tense of the passage for the relaying of personal feelings, as opposed to a limited use of the perfect tense (*la prof a décidé... c'est elle qui nous l'a dit...*) which carries the narrative line, is also a sign of the highly marked presence of the speaker.

The use of elliptical grammatical forms such as ***j'en** ai rien à faire de sa Corse* (instead of ***je n'en** ai rien à faire*) or ***Y a** qu'elle qui se fait plaisir (for **Il n'y a** qu'elle...*) or *je préfère rien savoir* (for *je préfère **ne** rien savoir*); the use of clause ellipsis in *qu'en géographie on parlerait de la Corse, [**qu'il y aurait**] tout un dossier là-dessus* contrasts with the repeated use of coreferents in the following dislocated constructions (which are typical of the informal spoken register):

— *Je suis sûre que <u>les autres</u> aussi, **ils** s'en foutent*
— *Et <u>les châtaignes</u>, je suis sûre que je trouverais **les mêmes** au marché*
— *Si <u>la Corse</u> **elle** est comme elle* or *<u>Sa Corse</u>, **elle** doit être triste.*

All these characteristics indicate use of a familiar register, more typical of speech than of a written text. However, as the narrative mode of *Ils disent que je suis une beurette* reveals, these characteristics are also those of a literary sub-genre, that of diary-writing. Its high degree of informality contributes to the realistic effect of the narrative.

2. Compare and contrast the beginnings of these two daily newspaper articles about the vote on a new immigration law at the National Assembly.

IMMIGRATION: LA GAUCHE INVENTE LA PARTICIPATION SANS SOUTIEN

1. Le vote définitif du projet de loi relatif à l'entrée et au séjour des étrangers et au droit d'asile, acquis hier soir par un vote à main levée (donc expéditif, pour éviter de souligner les divisions au sein de la gauche), est intervenu à l'Assemblée dans un contexte de forte mobilisation des sans-papiers, qui **5.** occupent plusieurs églises et orchestrent des manifestations pour empêcher les reconduites à la frontière. Ce texte ouvre une crise politique majeure au sein de la majorité « plurielle » sur la question fondamentale de l'immigration, où l'on a inventé une nouvelle forme d'alliance: la participation sans le soutien! Et ce en dépit des propos minimalistes de Jean-Marc Ayrault, le **10.** président du groupe PS, pour lequel les Verts « *font l'apprentissage du pouvoir* ».

En réalité, les cinq députés Verts sur six (à l'exception d'André Aschieri, des Alpes-Maritimes) qui voulaient voter contre le texte, après avoir refusé de participer au vote lors des deux premières lectures, réclament la **15.** régularisation de tous les sans-papiers, et l'abrogation des lois Pasqua-Debré, comme les élus communistes. Ces derniers, qui jugent ce projet « *mi-chèvre, mi-chou* », selon la formule de leur président de groupe, Alain Bocquet, voulaient pour la plupart s'abstenir, et la droite RPR-UDF voter contre.

Avant l'ouverture des débats, le premier ministre, tenant un discours plus **20.** droitier qu'à son habitude, a solennellement pris la défense du ministre de l'Intérieur, Jean-Pierre Chevènement, cible des attaques d'une partie de la gauche, mais aussi des cinéastes et des évêques. Lors de la séance des questions au gouvernement, Lionel Jospin a fustigé les « *non responsables, ceux qui incitent spectaculairement* » les étrangers en situation irrégulière, « *sur les lieux* **25.** *mêmes du départ, à ne pas partir* ». Sans les nommer, Lionel Jospin a clairement désapprouvé l'attitude des députés Verts et communistes refondateurs qui ont participé aux manifestations de soutien aux sans-papiers. Les députés PS lui ont fait une ovation, debout, tandis qu'aucun député PC n'a applaudi.

30. Jean-Pierre Chevènement n'est à l'évidence pas parvenu, selon son souhait, à faire adopter une législation consensuelle et durable. [...]

Le Figaro, 9 April 1998

IMMIGRATION: LA LOI PASSE MALGRÉ LES VERTS ET LE PC

1. Le débat s'annonçait houleux, il n'a été que somnifère. Hier, la troisième et dernière lecture du projet sur l'immigration à l'Assemblée nationale a été à l'image des précédents: un hémicycle certes mieux rempli, mais une droite toujours logorrhéique, et une gauche qu'il a fallu encore rameuter **5.** pour qu'elle participe au vote. Malgré cette mini péripétie, la loi Chevènement a été vite adoptée, à mains levées, par les socialistes, avec l'abstention des communistes. Six députés de la majorité, cinq verts et un PCF (Patrick Braouezec), ont inauguré l'ère de la contradiction en votant contre, avec l'UDF et le RPR. Mais, d'après Alain Bocquet, président du **10.** groupe communiste, «*la contradiction, c'est la vie*».

«**Idée de nation**». Si le ministre de l'Intérieur s'est senti déstabilisé par les remous de la gauche plurielle, il n'en a rien laissé paraître. Il a servi aux députés un discours bourré de métaphores jardinières et républicaines. Le projet, qualifié comme toujours de «*ferme et digne*» a ainsi écopé du nom **15.** floral de RESEDA (relatif à l'entrée et au séjour des étrangers et au droit d'asile). A ceux qui, à gauche, le trouvent trop répressif, le ministre a lancé que «*prétendre faire vivre les droits de l'homme hors de leur contexte, c'est prétendre faire pousser des violettes dans le désert*». Pour expliquer la nécessité des frontières, que personne n'a jamais contestées à l'Assemblée, **20.** le ministre a évoqué «la bête qui prospère lorsque les forces du progrès laissent en jachère l'idée de nation». Mais les rôles étaient distribués d'avance, et l'agriculture n'a pas convaincu les terres réfractaires, de droite ou de gauche. [...]

Libération, 9 April 1998

a) Examine the subject-matter of these two texts: to what extent do they indicate the respective newspapers' socio-political positions?

b) Compare and contrast the ways these texts are written in order to define their register.

Suggested answers:

a) Subject matter of the two newspaper articles

As *Le Figaro's* main heading makes clear, *Immigration: la gauche invente la participation sans soutien* stresses the new type of alliance invented by the left as *sans soutien*, and as the last sentence of the article (from *Jean-Pierre Chevènement... durable*) indicates, such an invention is doomed to failure.

The *Libération* heading, *Immigration: la loi passe malgré les verts et le PC*, on the contrary emphasises the positive outcome of the vote and does not question the value of the law as such.

Both articles agree on the swiftness of the vote by a show of hands, but while *Le Figaro* stresses the political impact of the bill which is perceived as starting a major political crisis, *Libération* refers to the debate on the bill as a *somnifère* non-event. The opposition to the bill, rather than being the sign of a crisis for *Libération*, marks the inauguration of *l'ère de la contradiction*, a phrase immediately supported by the quotation *La contradiction, c'est la vie* to give it a positive overtone.

Finally, while *Le Figaro* relates the support of the Prime Minister, Lionel Jospin, to right-wing views, and his own antagonism to left-wing positions, *Libération* concentrates on the position of the left-wing MPs who find the bill repressive, and on the unconvincing performance of the Home Secretary Jean-Pierre Chevènement.

The examination of the subject matter of these two texts, while stressing a fairly standard topic for a journalistic genre, shows the political bias of each newspaper.

b) Register

Both articles adopt a factual mode to narrate the events, and both generally rely on standard French with well-formed sentences, 'correct' use of grammar and a choice of vocabulary fairly standard for their subject matter.

Indeed, in *Le Figaro* we find:

- **A standard level of French:** the article contains a few long but simply structured sentences (lines 1-6, 12-16) and, on the whole, with the possible exception of *fustigé* (line 23), a level of vocabulary accessible to a majority of readers.
- **Examples of a more informal register:** the recourse to colloquial expressions like *juger le projet «mi-chèvre mi-chou»* (lines 16-17) or to common media

phrases: *au sein de la majorité «plurielle»* (lines 6-7), together with instances of unusual/'incorrect' use of vocabulary, a kind of liberty not uncommon in journalistic writing. The term *droitier* for instance (line 20), meaning 'from the right' (as opposed to its usual meaning, 'someone who is right-handed'), gives the text a more informal style.

In *Libération* we find:

- A **greater variety of registers:** *Libération* also relies on a standard level of French to relate the vote on the new law, but it also uses a greater variety of features belonging to other registers, with the mention of more elaborate words and expressions: from the more formal *logorrhéique* on line 4 (*logorrhée: flux de paroles inutiles; besoin irrésistible, morbide de parler*) to the occasional informal terms *rameuter* on line 4 (*rameuter: lit. ramener les chiens en meute, en arrêtant ceux qui sont écartés*) or *bourré de* on line 13.

- Use of **figures of speech:** the text exploits the use of figures of speech to a much greater extent. As if mimicking the contents of the Home Secretary's discourse, described as *bourré de métaphores*, the text is itself filled with metaphors!
  − *Le débat s'annonçait* **houleux**, *il a été* **somnifère** (1)
  − *les* **remous** *de la gauche plurielle* (12)
  − *Il a* **servi** *aux députés un discours bourré de métaphores* (12-13).

- A **mode of delivery which relies on irony:** beside the particular chosen emphasis of the subject matter, we note that metaphors are deliberately used to inscribe the narrator's critical distance. They serve to ironically dismiss J-P. Chevènement's intervention in the debate, as shown in the expression: *Il a servi un discours bourré de métaphores jardinières et républicaines* (12-13). The metaphorical reference to the restaurant in *servir*, added to the absurd, ironic association of the two adjectives *jardinières et républicaines*, together with the judgemental meaning of *écoper* on line 14 (*écoper: fam, recevoir quelque chose de désagréable*) to qualify the incongruous name of RESEDA given by the minister (an acronym used to refer to the right of asylum of foreigners and which, as a word, is usually the name of a flower!) discredit the impact of his speech. Continuing with the agricultural metaphor in *l'agriculture n'a pas convaincu les terres réfractaires, de droite et de gauche* (22-23), the text mimics further the minister's speech and enhances the derisive tone of the piece.

249

- **Use of syntax to express semantic oppositions and contrasting states:** the subject matter of the *Libération* article, which sees the debate as the beginning of *l'ère de la contradiction* (8), is inscribed syntactically in the sentence formation and in the use of cohesive devices:
  - by the juxtaposition of independent clauses expressing lexical opposition: *Le débat s'annonçait houleux, il n'a été que somnifère* (1), i.e. **mais/en fait,** *il n'a été que*... or between a main and subordinate clause: *Si le ministre de l'Intérieur s'est senti déstabilisé par les remous de la gauche plurielle, il n'en a rien laissé paraître* (11-12)
  - by the use of adversative connectors: *Un hémicycle **certes** mieux rempli, **mais** une droite toujours logorrhéique* (3-4); ***Malgré** cette mini-péripétie...* (5).

3. What is the genre and register of this extract?

> *On imagine mal aujourd'hui, dans ce monde dominé par la culture populaire – ou plutôt par la* popular culture, *car l'anglais fait entendre, me semble-t-il, moins le mot «peuple» qu'une certaine complaisance américaine envers la bêtise –, dans ce monde d'écrans et de* zapping, *de* sex hard *ou siliconé, où les seules sensations fortes se repaissent de meurtres et de procès théâtralisés jusqu'à la dissolution, on imagine mal, donc, la délicatesse que revêt la force d'esprit d'un homme prenant la parole dans – pour et contre – la culture, pour affirmer que la culture existe et nous fait vivre, certes, mais à la seule condition qu'on ne cesse de la déchiffrer, c'est-à-dire de la critiquer pour la déplacer sans fin.*
>
> J. Kristeva, *Sens et non-sens de la révolte*

Suggested answer:

The subject matter of this short extract from Julia Kristeva's *Sens et non-sens de la révolte* deals with the importance of the concept of culture envisaged as an entity which, in order to be understood, needs to remain, according to the text, the object of constant criticism.

The mode of delivery is mostly analytical, reflecting upon the state of contemporary social attitudes in relation to the concept of culture. The noticeable critical tone in relation to today's world, detectable in the reference to *une certaine complaisance américaine envers la bêtise* or in the reference to *ce monde d'écrans* creates an effect of distanciation in the reader.

The lexical register is mostly standard French. Its sophistication or more formal tone comes from its readiness to include matter-of-fact English-based terms, such as 'popular culture', 'zapping', 'sex hard' – though themselves stressed by the use of a different font – thus giving the text a contemporary tone through the emphasis on American culture. Apart from the metaphorical use of *se repaissent*, whose negative connotation reinforces the critical stance against today's media habits, the vocabulary remains standard and matter-of-fact.

The formality of the text is however strongly marked at the syntactic level. The whole paragraph consists of a single sentence characterised by numerous expressions used to accurately define the text's subject matter. Today's world is first defined as *dominé par la culture populaire* – a term itself redefined in the following brackets with the reference to the English expression of 'popular culture' – and secondly as *ce monde d'écrans et de* zapping…, also further explained by another clause introduced by the connector *où* (*où les seules sensations fortes se repaissent…*). However, the repetition of *ce monde* and especially of the main clause *on imagine mal* in the second half of the text ensures that the structure of the sentence remains present in the reader's mind.

Finally the positive reference to culture is elaborately specified with the use of connectors: *certes, mais, c'est-à-dire*, which reinforce the argumentative nature of the paragraph.

The presence of the speaker in the text (*me semble-t-il*) introduces a personal note to the mode of delivery. The criticism of today's world dominated by popular culture, the media and American influence can be discerned in the use of the accumulative terms: 'zapping', 'sex hard' *ou siliconé* or in the emphasis of *les seules sensations fortes*, both terms *seules* and *fortes* reinforcing each other. It is also evident in the use of imagery, used to qualify the strong emotions provoked by this media world, with the metaphorical *repaissent* whose connotations stress the compulsive need to feed on catastrophic news. This criticism of contemporary society is semantically opposed to another lexical field, that of the valorisation of culture described as essential to life: *la culture… existe et nous fait vivre…*

This text, whose subject matter deals with the relevance of culture in contemporary life, and which is imbued with a strong critical stance, belongs to a **sociological** genre. Its standard use of vocabulary signals however that this text is aimed at the popularisation of the object of study examined: it is in fact an extract from the lectures that the French theorist and psychoanalyst Julia Kristeva originally aimed at her students.

ASSIGNMENTS

1. *La Femme gelée*

a) Analyse the degree of formality of this text.

b) Is this literary extract typical of its genre? How does it compare with the extract from *Ils disent que je suis une beurette* studied earlier in this chapter?

Ils sont enfin à côté de nous, les garçons, prenant les notes du même commentaire sur Phèdre. *Pas plus brillants que nous, pas supérieurs. Plus frondeurs, certains, mais avant que le cours commence, pour épater la galerie, pas en face du maître de conférences qu'ils clameraient que ce type-là ils lui chient à la gueule. Toujours prêts comme ils disent à foutre le bordel, au restau, à la cafétéria, devant les portes des amphis, mais bien sages à l'intérieur, un de mes étonnements. Pourtant j'en avais vu des blablateurs de première dans mon café, et des agités sur leur scooter, des péteux en réalité, je ne pensais pas en trouver à la fac, naïveté. Au cours de philo où officie un assistant blond qui jette un regard dominateur sur l'assemblée avant de parler de la Personne et du Temps, mes voisins se tiennent cois, le stylo avide, un sérieux à couper au couteau, pas une question. Même silence en histoire, aucune voix mâle, de celles qui braillent dans le couloir, n'interrompt le soliloque triomphant de Froinu, ça ne les gêne pas plus que les filles d'être traités de demeurés par le prof. A moins qu'ils n'aient peur de se faire remarquer, examen first. Pour le conformisme et la passivité, l'égalité des sexes était parfaite à la fac.*

Annie Ernaux, *La Femme gelée*

2. *Onze Etudes sur la poésie moderne*

Read this extract and analyse which aspects of the text's register help to define it as an example of literary criticism.

> *Voici définie, avec insistance et force, une éthique de la mobilité: mais plus poétiquement importantes et neuves les rêveries en lesquelles cette morale s'enracine. Georges Mounin a par exemple remarqué, dans son beau livre, le goût de Char pour les fleuves et pour les eaux courantes, l'écoulement capricieux de la rivière nous est en effet ici la merveilleuse image d'un temps fluide et transparent. Chaque seconde nous y apporte une eau nouvelle, une fraîcheur que nul encore n'a savourée: « Quand on a mission d'éveiller, on commence par faire sa toilette dans la rivière. Le premier enchantement comme le premier saisissement sont pour soi ». Ce qui enchante ici c'est l'éternelle reprise de la véhémence, c'est une infinie variété de mouvement et de murmure que Char évoque avec le bonheur d'un grand poète baroque. [...]*

Jean-Pierre Richard, *Onze Etudes sur la poésie moderne*

3. Rewrite the text of Annie Ernaux's *La Femme gelée* in Exercise 1 in a more formal register.

Production exercise:

Driving back from university you have been involved in an accident: a bus suddenly cut across your path at a crossroads just outside the university.

Write one or more of the following texts:

- a report for the local paper
- a letter to your best friend to relate the accident
- a report for your insurance company
- a warning to your friends or other students.

In each case, relate the choice of register (vocabulary, syntax, etc.) to the context.

SUGGESTED ANSWERS TO ASSIGNMENTS

1. *La Femme gelée*

a) Degree of formality

As with the Nini's extract, the Ernaux text possesses a high degree of informal language.

At the **lexical** level, the choice of vocabulary varies:

- from familiar, with:
  - colloquial expressions: *être traités en demeurés* or *braillent dans les couloirs*
  - truncated words: *au restau* or *les amphis* (apocope)
  - neologisms: *des blablateurs de première* (with ellipsis: *de première classe*) or *des péteux*
  - use of foreign words: *examen first*
- to vulgar, with: *ils lui chient à la gueule* or *foutre le bordel*.

At the **syntactic** level, the text disregards accepted sentence constructions for formal written French, with:

- redundancy of coreferents (with the use of dislocated constructions): <u>*Ils*</u> *sont enfin à côté de nous,* **les garçons** *or ils clameraient que* **ce type-là** *ils* <u>*lui*</u> *chient à la gueule*

- use of ellipsis, especially of the main verb, which creates the agrammatical sentence construction: *Pas plus brillants que nous, pas supérieurs. Plus frondeurs, certains,…* or *Toujours prêts comme ils disent à foutre le bordel…*

- erroneous relative clause construction: *pas en face du maître de conférences qu'ils [à propos duquel ils] clameraient que ce type là ils lui chient à la gueule,* or subordinate clauses treated as independent clauses: *A moins qu'ils n'aient peur de se faire remarquer…*

- disregard of punctuation: *je ne pensais pas en trouver à la fac, naïveté* (there should be a semi-colon after *fac*).

All these features indicate a careless, spontaneous way of expressing oneself in speech.

b) As with the Soraya Nini's extract, this one is at odds with conventional prose writing and strongly recalls speech. It uses a colloquial/slang vocabulary and idiosyncratic expressions, but which reflect the age of the narrator, a young adult, as opposed to the child narrator of the first text. Its informality also relies more on syntactic features: ellipsis of key words, redundancy of coreferents (dislocated constructions), and is more disrespectful of sentence constructions and of punctuation. As with the Nini extract, it is strongly autobiographical, but its deliberately careless style of writing is a strategy for depicting a current of consciousness and for reinforcing the sense of immediacy.

2. Onze Etudes...

It is mostly the subject matter which identifies this text as belonging to literary criticism. It concentrates on the characteristics of René Char's poetry: its thematic content – rivers and flowing waters – linked to an ethic of mobility, its identification with baroque poetry and its anticipated effect on the reader: *ce qui enchante*...

The expository mode of delivery reinforces the subject matter with the use of literary quotations (*Quand on a mission d'éveiller*...), and the reference to other critical works (*Georges Mounin a par exemple remarqué*...) supports the literary explanation of Char's poetry.

The presence of the speaker, visible in the *nous* of *Chaque seconde nous y apporte*..., with the allusion to the reader's expected appreciation, clearly involves the reader in the text.

While the lexical level remains standard French, the literary nature of the subject matter is reinforced by the use of terms such as *mais plus poétiquement importantes, merveilleuse image, fraîcheur que nul n'a encore savourée, le premier enchantement, ce qui enchante, l'éternelle reprise de la véhémence*, etc.

At the syntactic level, the text is clearly and logically but simply structured. The progression of the text is carefully carried out by a variety of linking expressions, most often connectors. From the expository link, *Voici définie... une éthique*, the text develops through the contrastive *mais* which, after a colon, hides a verbal ellipsis:

> *mais plus poétiquement importantes et neuves [sont] les*
> *rêveries en lesquelles cette morale s'enracine...*

hence the stylistic effect emphasizing the term *rêveries*.

The explanatory linking expression in *Georges Mounin a **par exemple** remarqué*... conveys the subject matter of the previous sentence: the content of Char's poetic rêverie. The reinforcing adverbial expression *en effet* underlines the importance of flowing waters in Char's poetry mentioned just earlier. The temporal expression *chaque seconde* invites the reader to share the experience. The quotation introduced by *Quand*... reinforces the meaning of the previous statement by linking Char's reference to fresh and clear water to the awakening role of this same water. The final sentence, introduced by the presentative *ce qui... c'est* summarises the impact of Char's poetry on the reader. Such varied use of structural tools is consistent with texts of literary criticism, through the use of presentative forms to express emphasis.

3. Example of possible answer:

Les garçons sont enfin à côté de nous, prenant les notes du même commentaire sur Phèdre. Ils ne sont toutefois pas plus brillants que nous ou même supérieurs. Certains sont plus frondeurs mais uniquement avant que le cours ne commence et ceci pour impressionner tout le monde. Ils ne le sont pas cependant en face du maître de conférences, même s'ils clament à son propos qu'il les laisse indifférents. Ils sont toujours prêts, si on les en croit, à semer le désordre au restaurant, à la cafétéria ou devant les portes des amphithéâtres, mais ils sont bien sages à l'intérieur, ce qui d'ailleurs constitue un de mes étonnements. J'avais pourtant vu bien des séducteurs invétérés dans le café de mon enfance! Je ne pensais pas en trouver à la faculté. Que de naïveté de ma part! Mes voisins se tiennent cois, le stylo avide, avec un sérieux impressionnant pendant le cours de philo où officie un assistant blond qui jette un regard dominateur sur l'assemblée avant de parler de la Personne et du Temps. Il n'y a pas une question. C'est le même silence en histoire, où aucune voix mâle parmi celles qui hurlent d'habitude dans le couloir n'interrompt le soliloque triomphant de Froinu. Le fait d'être traités en simples d'esprit par le professeur ne les gêne pas plus que les filles, à moins qu'ils n'aient peur de se faire remarquer, l'examen passant avant tout. L'égalité des sexes était parfaite à la faculté en ce qui concerne le conformisme et la passivité.

CHAPTER 11

ANALYSIS OF TITLES

Titles or headlines always play a significant role in the production of meaning in a text. They function in two ways:

a) Titles refer outside the text to an extra-linguistic reality and/or to other texts.

b) Titles acquire additional meaning when read in the light of their immediate context, that is, in relationship to the opening lines or paragraphs of the text that follows. Their function may be manipulatory in that they give rise to a set of anticipations or reader expectations.

1. Headlines

a) *Assemblée et Sénat: Le retour des ténors*

Balladur, Pasqua, Rocard et Badinter au Parlement

Assemblée et Sénat : le retour des ténors

Bernard Debré (RPR) battu par un socialiste dans la législative d'Indre-et-Loire. Le PS renforce sa position au Palais du Luxembourg.

Le renouvellement d'un tiers du Sénat et quatre élections législatives partielles ont permis, hier, le retour au Parlement de plusieurs « poids lourds ».

● **Edouard Balladur, Nicolas Sarkozy et Bernard Bosson** ont retrouvé leur siège de députés à Paris, Neuilly et Annecy.

● **En revanche, Bernard Debré** (RPR), ancien ministre de la Coopération, a été battu de 326 voix par Jean-Jacques Filleul (PS) en Indre-et-Loire.

● **Charles Pasqua** a, dans les Hauts-de-Seine, été réélu

au Sénat, où les socialistes Michel Rocard (Yvelines) et Robert Badinter (Hauts-de-Seine) font leur entrée.

● **Les sénatoriales,** qui organisaient le renouvellement de 177 sièges dans 28 départements, ont été marquées par une progression socialiste (+ 8), notamment symbolisée par le gain de trois sièges à Paris, au détriment de la liste RPR-UDF, qui cède en outre un siège au PC.

● **Président du groupe RPR** au Palais du Luxembourg, Josselin de Rohan a jugé les résultats « très signi-

ficatifs » pour son parti, qui gagne deux sièges.

● **L'UDF** est la principale victime du scrutin d'hier, avec la perte de six sièges.

● **Le PC** sauve son groupe, avec quinze élus.

● **René Monory,** président de la Haute Assemblée, réélu dans la Vienne avec Jean-Pierre Raffarin, ministre des PME, estime que « *le fait qu'il y a des ténors qui veulent venir comme Rocard, comme Badinter, cela veut dire que le Sénat a maintenant pris une certaine dimension* ».

(Pages 6 à 10)

Le Figaro, 25 September 1995

– Comment on the typography of the title and subtitles.
– What lexical devices are used to catch the attention of the reader?
– Comment on the construction of the reference in the title and subtitles: how much are we supposed to know? Which coreference devices are used, and which thematic order becomes apparent?
– Comment on the presence (or absence) of the speaker.

Analysis of title and subtitles

As is often the case in newspaper articles, a subtitle comes first, followed by the main title, then possibly a second subtitle.

Typography

Here, it is typical of that of a newspaper article: the size of the letters corresponds to the order of the perceived importance of the information given.

(i)   The first subtitle is in large letters, underlined: names of well-known politicians are given, two right-wing, two left-wing (but we do not know what has happened to them).

(ii) The main title is in larger, bold, letters: the most important piece of news is that the above politicians have been (re-)elected.

(iii) The second subtitle is in bold italics: names of minor politicians can be given now, even if it means announcing a defeat for the political side supported by the newspaper.

Examination of style, through the use of lexical devices

The aim of press titles is to catch the attention of the reader. Several devices are used to achieve this aim:

(i)   Few determiners

In the main title, we have two proper nouns, without a determiner: *Assemblée* and *Sénat* (an illustration of the 'telegraphic' style favoured in press titles), linked by an additive connector, the conjunction of co-ordination *et,* showing the list of two elements to be 'complete' and representing the whole of the *Parlement* of the first subtitle. The colon announces an explanation. This is an extremely common journalistic device[1].

(ii) Few parts of speech

There are a lot of proper nouns, which are all characters or institutions known by the reader and therefore needing no further introduction.

There are no adjectives, no pronouns, no adverbs, but two adverbials of place: the two known institutions. This again announces the factual nature of the article that follows.

(iii) Sentences without a verb, but with verbal nouns instead

They are typical of announcements: *le retour des ténors* instead of *les ténors reviennent* corresponds to the *arrivée du vol AF 630* in airports instead of *Le vol AF 630 va arriver/vient d'arriver*.

(iv) Relationships between clauses, sentences and paragraphs

Co-ordination is only occurring between nouns, not between sentences. The sentences happen to be very short, and there is no subordination either.

- The first subtitle is a complete list with commas and a conjunction of coordination, *et*, before the last item; the adverb of place comes last, unstressed. The four nouns are in thematic position.

- For the main title, it is the reverse: the adverbial of place is the theme (*Assemblée* and *Sénat*), followed by a colon announcing an explanation: *le retour des ténors* (see above), which is a lexical anaphor of the four nouns mentioned in the first subtitle.

- In the second subtitle, we have two short sentences: one without a verb but which can be interpreted as passive with elision of the auxiliary, the other with a verb in the narrative present: the second subtitle expands on the main information of the article.

(v) Verbs

These reappear in the third and fourth sentences, which form the second subtitle:

- there is one sentence seemingly without a verb, but we can consider it as a passive form with elision of the auxiliary: *[est] battu.*

- we can also note the use of the passive to express failure: *Bernard Debré... battu...* and active for success: *Le PS renforce sa position.*

This may seem odd in a newspaper known for its right-wing bias. However, quite apart from the connotations attached to the very words 'passive' and 'active', we have to consider the theme and the focus of the sentence, in other words what is given greater or lesser importance. Indeed, we could consider the effects produced by turning the passive into active:

Ex: *Un socialiste bat Bernard Debré dans la...*

The attention of the reader would be drawn to the word *socialiste* and to the fact that the socialist is victorious (*bat*).

Referential cohesion
- **Determiners**

  They establish the existence and/or identity of items, appear mainly in the second subtitle (now that the reader has reached this stage, the journalist can relax a little!):

  – *un socialiste*: his name is not given, perhaps so as to lessen his importance (the indefinite article poses existence, as opposed to identity);

  – *la législative* (identified by the expansion of the noun phrase *d'Indre-et-Loire*);

– *le PS*: a proper noun – although an acronym – and therefore a unique referent, assumed to be known by the reader;

– *sa position* (= that of the PS);

– *au Palais du Luxembourg*: proper noun, i.e. a unique referent, known by the reader as the seat of the *Sénat*.

– *Bernard Debré* and *RPR*: RPR is an acronym (*Rassemblement pour la République*) which does not need further introduction for a French reader. It appears between brackets after the proper noun *Bernard Debré*. This is the equivalent of an apposition, and helps to identify the lesser known *Bernard Debré*. (see Chapter 2, Section 1, NB(2)).

The title is intended for an average politically educated French reader, who does not need an introduction to the main institutions of his/her country or its main politicians, and at the same time does not need to know details of every person involved in the election results.

• **Construction of the coreference**

In an article on election results like this one, even the title is likely to have to mention the same things more than once (name of party each time the name of a person is mentioned, and name of chamber to which (re-)elected). In order to avoid tedious repetitions, a useful device is **lexical anaphora**, which has the advantage over pronominal anaphora that it should be unambiguous: one name equals another. Another is **metonymy**, where one relies on the powers of interpretation of a politically educated readership. These two devices are used to the full here. Coreference is thus expressed in the following ways:

– *Parlement* ⟶ *Assemblée Nationale* & *Sénat* (lexical development of *Parlement*);

– *Balladur, Pasqua, Rocard, Badinter* ⟶ *les ténors*, a lexical anaphora of the four names, which is also a hackneyed metaphor (the figurative use of *ténors* suggests the following:
– the Parliament is an Opera House;
– the tenors have a strong, powerful voice)

– *Rocard, Badinter* ⟶ *le PS* (metonymy).

There are two further lexical anaphoras:

– *la législative d'Indre-et-Loire* refers by metonymy to a by-election for the *Assemblée*;

– ...*au Palais du Luxembourg*: refers directly, as a synonym, to the *Sénat*.

A thematic order is also apparent:

– *Balladur, Pasqua, Rocard et Badinter* are four members of the Parliament

– *Assemblée* and *Sénat* are the two components of the French Parliament
– *les ténors* is a lexical anaphora (see above) coreferential with the four names quoted in the first subtitle
– *le retour des ténors* alludes to the fact that these four men have been members of the Parliament at a certain time – in one of the two chambers – have left it, and are today back in it, following the results of recent elections, the subject of the article.

In the second subtitle, the thematic order is reinforced:
– the first sentence refers to a result pertaining to the *Assemblée*;
– the second sentence refers to a result pertaining to the *Sénat*.

The thematic order is also respected in the three titles. Indeed:
– *Balladur; député de Paris; Assemblée; législative*
– *Pasqua; réélu au Sénat*
– *Rocard; élu au Sénat*   }   *Sénat; Palais du Luxembourg.*
– *Badinter; élu au Sénat*

Presence of the speaker

There is no explicit presence of the speaker in this headline: no evaluative or emotive terms, and the only pronoun used is that of the third person. The article attempts to be as factual and objective as possible.

Conclusion

The title gives a feeling of coherence and objectivity through a balance between the *Assemblée* and the *Sénat*.

Cohesion is also respected, although there is not much leeway for going wrong with this type of press title: the first four sentences announce and summarise the tenor of the article, which is about the overall results of:

— legislative by-elections;
— general senatorial elections.

Footnote:
For instance, in *Les Echos* of 21 September 1995, there are no fewer than twelve titles on the same model on the first page:

- 'Budget 1996: la transition avant les réformes possibles'
- 'Recettes: épargnants, entreprises et consommateurs mis à contribution'
- 'Dépenses: progression limitée à 1,8%, mais par rapport au collectif de juin'
- 'Sécurité sociale: Alain Juppé promet le retour à l'équilibre en 1997'
- 'Réactions politiques et syndicales: de l'expectative à la vive critique'
- 'La relance au Japon: 140 milliards de dollars'
- 'Télécoms: ATT éclaté en trois sociétés'
- 'La Société Générale: toujours en forme'
- 'Monnaie unique: Bonn met l'Italie hors-jeu'
- 'Buba: nette baisse des déficits publics allemands en 1995'
- 'SNCF: la tension sociale s'accentue chez les cheminots'
- 'Manutention portuaire: l'acte II de la réforme.'

Most of the time, the colon is followed by a sentence without a verb (there are only three exceptions in the examples above).

b) *Le chant des coucous*

Le chant des coucous

PERSONNE ne peut prétendre que la situation politique soit bonne. Sauf à se boucher les oreilles, fermer les yeux et taire ses observations. Examinez les sondages : ils indiquent, pour le moins, un désenchantement. Ecoutez les rumeurs de la ville : elle bruisse de mille suppositions toutes alarmistes.

PAR MICHEL SCHIFRES

Tel est le microcosme, comme dirait M. Barre : à l'image des coucous suisses, il vient régulièrement caqueter, pour amplifier ce qu'il croit sentir de l'opinion. M. Juppé et les siens auraient tort de s'en alarmer : pour peu que le balancier prenne la direction inverse, ces gens-là chanteront aussi vigoureusement l'air du triomphe qu'ils entonnent, ces temps-ci, celui de la déception. C'est ainsi : il faut l'accepter, à moins de renoncer à la politique et à ses intrigues.

Le calendrier lui-même ne favorise pas la tâche du gouvernement. Voilà les grands d'Espagne de retour sur la scène : MM. Balladur, Pasqua, Sarkozy, Léotard, Rocard, Badinter et d'autres, viennent d'être élus, qui au Sénat, qui à l'Assemblée. Les uns et les autres ont trop de talent, trop d'idées et trop d'originalité pour rester muets. Ils ont besoin également de se manifester. Quoi de plus facile alors que de critiquer, plus ou moins vivement, la politique gouvernementale ? Une situation monétaire grave – la France n'y est pour rien –, des experts réservés, un rapport alarmant, autant d'éléments qui permettent, sans grand mal, de faire entendre sa différence.

M. Juppé peut invoquer, avec raison, la nouveauté de son gouvernement : ce n'est pas en quelques mois qu'une politique porte ses fruits. Le premier ministre n'a d'ailleurs jamais caché que le redressement et le renouveau qu'il proposait exigeaient trois bonnes années. D'autant que la situation économique reste très difficile – voyez le poids de la dette – et que les résultats encourageants, comme la lente diminution du chômage, sont occultés par d'autres polémiques, telle celle sur l'ampleur de la réduction des déficits. Marier l'espérance née de la victoire de M. Chirac au credo de M. Mitterrand – « laissez du temps au temps » – n'est pas aisé. Il y a toujours de l'impatience dans les démocraties et de l'injustice dans tout jugement politique.

Au-delà des ronchonnements de l'opinion ; au-delà des grognements de circonstance de dirigeants patronaux et syndicaux ; au-delà de quelques maladresses ministérielles, il reste des réformes à mener et des débats à ouvrir. Celui sur les retraites et leurs différences entre les secteurs privé et public en est un. Il est essentiel. C'est un des exemples où la réflexion ne doit pas vaciller devant les conservatismes et où, comme lors de la campagne présidentielle, l'apport de tous à la discussion est nécessaire. M. Juppé, juge-t-on, a de la ténacité, du pragmatisme et le goût de l'innovation. C'est sa tâche, redoutable, de le prouver au quotidien.

Le Figaro, 25 September 1995

– Does the title sound plausible for a leading article in *Le Figaro*? Why?

– What exactly is *Le chant des coucous*? When do we find out?

– Comment on the typography.

– Which coreference devices are used?

– Show how lexical cohesion is expressed in the text in relation to the title.

Analysis of title

The leading article, a column to the left of the front page, bears a prominent signature (here that of Michel Schifres).

The daily *Le Figaro* addresses a readership interested in social, political and cultural issues. Even if they are also interested in wild life, these readers would normally turn to another medium to satisfy their quest!

Unlike other press titles, this one does not actually summarise the contents of the article, in the sense that it is not possible to guess which *chant* and which *coucous* are being talked about before reading what follows. In fact, we have to get to line 11, which begins the second paragraph, to understand:

> *Tel est le microcosme, comme dirait M. Barre: à l'image*
> *des coucous suisses, il vient régulièrement caqueter, pour*
> *amplifier ce qu'il croit sentir de l'opinion.*

The title could also be seen as a metaphor of nature, thus contrasting with the political arena. Again the reader only finds out that it is about Swiss cuckoo clocks instead when reading on.

The typography is characteristic of leading articles (as opposed to other, albeit main articles, on the front page): the title is in large italics, but not bold; it is the name of the author which is in bold, suggesting its importance. The title is meant to catch the attention of the reader – by suggesting a pun, an image, etc. – without giving too much away.

The determiners, with the presence of two definite articles – *le chant des* (= *de les*) *coucous* – suggest that the two terms are ultimately **identifiable** by the reader, which helps to catch his/her interest. This is done at the beginning of the second paragraph: *à l'image des* **coucous** *suisses, il vient régulièrement* **caqueter**. *Le chant des coucous* is the sound emitted by Swiss cuckoo clocks, and here it is the sound emitted by the opinion polls and public rumours, which form a *microcosme*, a term often used by Raymond Barre. Like the Swiss cuckoo, it comes back at regular intervals.

Lexical cohesion is shown by the verbs used in the text to refer to the *chant* of the title. They include *caqueter, amplifier, chanteront, entonnent*. The *coucou* has the connotation of something that comes back at regular intervals, and is referred to in the text by the word *balancier*.

That is as far as coreference goes here, between the text and the title, except that *les sondages* and *les rumeurs de la ville* are *le microcosme*, itself the *coucou*.

271

2. Advertisement

Londres, New York: même les taxis n'en savent pas autant que nous.

LONDRES, NEW YORK : MÊME LES TAXIS N'EN SAVENT PAS AUTANT QUE NOUS.

Londres, New York. Deux villes. Deux mondes. Qui changent, bougent, évoluent sans cesse, mais ont au moins un point commun : ne pas se livrer au premier venu. Pourquoi vous contenter de les visiter quand vous pouvez les découvrir ?

Découvrir le musée du cricket, la maison de Charles Dickens ou les boutiques de cashmere à Londres, découvrir la tombe d'Ulysses Grant, les boîtes de nuit et les restaurants branchés à New York. En un mot : tout ce qui fait leur Bien Vivre.

GUIDE GAULTMILLAU LONDRES OU NEW YORK. 125 F.

GAULT·MILLAU
Les Toqués du Bien Vivre.

BON DE COMMANDE : Pour recevoir les guides GAULTMILLAU Londres et/ou New York, complétez, détachez et retournez ce bon de commande avec votre règlement à : Boutique GAULTMILLAU - 61, av. Hoche - 75411 Paris cedex 08.
OUI, je profite de votre offre pour acquérir les guides LONDRES et/ou NEW YORK au prix de 125F chacun.
Je joins un chèque bancaire ou postal à l'ordre de GAULTMILLAU.

...... guide(s) LONDRES à 125F. soit ...... F.   ...... guide(s) NEW YORK à 125F. soit ...... F.   Soit un total de ..... F.

Nom : .... Prénom : .... Adresse : ....
.... Code postal : .... Ville : ....
Offre valable uniquement en France métropolitaine - Pour des envois vers l'étranger, nous consulter.

Le Point, No 1206, 28 October 1995

– Show how the typography and the punctuation construct the main sentence used in the advertisement as a title.
– Examine the first part of the message (*Londres, New York*) and identify the lexical devices used to arouse the interest of the reader.

– Which set expression do you find in the title? What effect does it have on the reader in the context of the sentence?

– Comment on the interaction between the visual and the linguistic message.

– Which word indicates the presence of the speaker in the title?

– Which stylistic figure can you identify in the expression *les taxis n'en savent pas autant que nous* ?

This text constitutes the major element of a one-page advert about *GaultMillau* guides which appeared throughout autumn 1995 on a weekly basis in the magazine *Le Point* and less regularly in *L'Express*.

Le Point and *L'Express* are two rival news magazines which emphasise a marked preoccupation with international as well as national news items in the areas of society, politics and culture. The nature of these periodicals also suggests a sustained yet direct use of language which remains linguistically in touch with the realities of modern life.

Analysis of title

For the purpose of this study, the elements of cohesion and coherence will be studied together, though we will note that the first part of the title is mostly relevant in terms of cohesion whereas the second part will mainly draw on notions of coherence.

Visual layout and typography

As so often in French advertising, the main title is in fact a whole sentence, contrary to the usual notion of a title as often seen in books and articles, which has no verb or full-stop. The effect of using a full sentence is to immediately draw the reader into the topic. The titular status of the sentence used is given by its strategic position at the centre right of the page and by the use of typography as a major syntactic tool (here enlarged bold characters).

Lexical devices and punctuation

The first part of the title, terminated by a colon, is short, punctual, made up of two words: *Londres* and *New York*. The names of the major Western capitals are internationally recognisable and as such echo the nature of the magazines already mentioned above. The lexical juxtaposition of the two proper nouns, shown at the syntactic level by the presence of a comma, also reflects the directness of style often used in these publications.

The lexical (here the juxtaposition of proper names) and punctuation (here the comma) devices heighten the dramatic impact and arouse the reader's curiosity as to the nature of the message. A solution to the enigma is announced by the presence of the colon which ends the first section of the title, since such a punctuation mark can syntactically be used to signal the beginning of an expository text.

Tenses and ellipsis

The second element of the titular clause is longer and reveals a series of ambiguities which establish the title as an enigmatic whole. The use of a present with *savent* gives the title a flavour of universal truth against which the enigma of the text can be supported.

The title is centred around an enigma with the presence of the set expression *en savoir*. As in all set expressions of this kind, *en savoir* invites the reader to wonder what the advert is about.

Interaction between the visual and the linguistic message – presence of the speaker

There is another enigma at the level of the presence of the speaker with the unexplained presence of the pronoun *nous* which ends the titular message (who does *nous* refer to?) and gives the message its discursive register. The title alone does not provide an explanation of what the pronoun refers to within its linguistic encoding. As very often in press advertising there is an interaction between the picture and the linguistic message, and the reader can only make out what the linguistic message is about by glancing at the nearby pictures – here the picture of the front covers of two tourist guides situated immediately on the left of the title. A foreign reader is more likely to do this at an early stage, thus reducing straight away the ambiguity of the title[1].

If however we consider the linguistic message only, this *nous* represents a missing semantic link which deprives the message of the possibility of a clear interpretation. Furthermore the metonymic use of *taxis* – when in fact what are referred to are the taxi-drivers – however common nowadays, reinforces, though to a lesser degree, the enigmatic value of the text.

The presence of the speaker seems apparent in the message with the *nous*, contrasted with the generality of the definite article *les* in *les taxis*; it establishes a field of opposition evident in the other lexical coreferents used in the title.

The lexical field of knowledge suggested by the verb *savoir*, and reinforced by the superlative value of the adverb *même*, as well as in the comparative presence of *autant que*, gives:

– on the one hand, increased importance to the knowledge to be acquired, while the nature of this knowledge is not revealed and

– on the other hand, renewed emphasis to the *nous*, the favoured recipient of this knowledge (against the *taxis*), while the nature of this *nous* remains unclear.

Through this series of oppositions and ambiguities inscribed in the coherence of the discourse by the use of its lexical coreferents, the title - in spite of the presence of a colon which seems to promise an explanation at the end of the first part - retains its enigma. The reader needs to glance at the visual element or read on in order to make sense or ascertain the meaning of the message: an enticing technique often used in advertising.

Conclusion

The complexity of the title in fact echoes that of the main text. The title announces:

– an equally enigmatic discursive explanatory text. It is only at its very end that one discovers what the advert is about, with what could possibly have been the real title: *Guide GaultMillau: Londres ou New York 125F*

– a lexical field linked to travelling (the taxis) and to the tourist activity of discovering famous cities. The verb *découvrir*, repeated twice in a short text and mentioned in relation to this discovery, echoes what the reader has already practiced in order to make sense of the title

– a message where the speaker is present. The presence of the *nous*, which gives the title a personal touch, is relayed later in the main text by an instance of direct speech: *Pourquoi vous contenter de les visiter quand vous pouvez les découvrir.*

These aspects of cohesion and coherence of the main text could be developed further.

Footnote:

[1]Paradoxically also, a French reader is more likely to be confused by the visual display of the two guides since the name *GaultMillau* recalls that of well-known restaurant guides in France. This is an example of the fact that extra-linguistic knowledge can sometimes hinder rather than help the understanding of a message.

3. Literary text

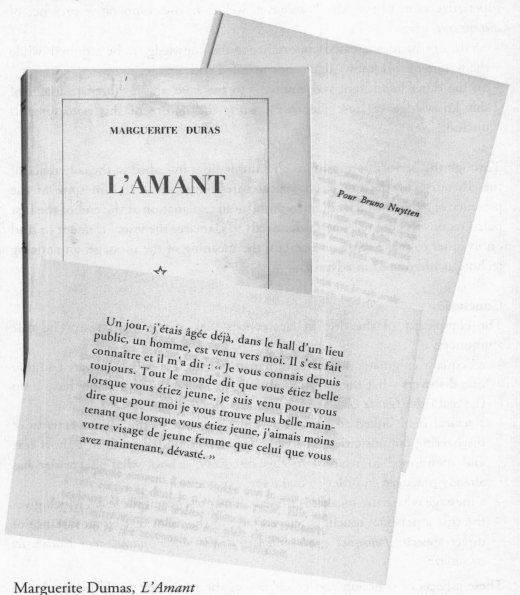

MARGUERITE DURAS

L'AMANT

Pour Bruno Nuytten

Un jour, j'étais âgée déjà, dans le hall d'un lieu public, un homme, est venu vers moi. Il s'est fait connaître et il m'a dit : « Je vous connais depuis toujours. Tout le monde dit que vous étiez belle lorsque vous étiez jeune, je suis venu pour vous dire que pour moi je vous trouve plus belle maintenant que lorsque vous étiez jeune, j'aimais moins votre visage de jeune femme que celui que vous avez maintenant, dévasté. »

Marguerite Dumas, *L'Amant*

– Looking at the title alone, what type of book does it suggest? In other words, does the title make you think of any particular genre or type of literature?
– Does the title remind you of other works of Marguerite Duras? If so, how does this affect your expectations of how the story might unfold?

– Do you think that the title sows the seeds of a story? If so, how do you predict the story might unfold? To help you answer these questions you may like to consider the following:

a) What types of relationships or general patterns will be established between the principal characters? Will someone be helping or hindering somebody else? (see Chapter 9 on Textual schemata)

b) do you anticipate a hero/villain scenario? (see narrative models in Chapter 9, Textual schemata).

– Do you read the dedication as a separate entity outside the novel or do you in some way associate the name *Bruno Nuytten* with the lover of the title?

– Can you establish lexical cohesion between the title and the dedication? If so, how?

– Which words or utterances in the first paragraph reinforce the concept of the lover and of love? Can you group them into lexical fields?

– Are there any unexpected associations in the first paragraph that qualify and enrich the meaning of the title?

– Apart from the construction of lexical fields, what other cohesive devices are employed in the first paragraph?

Analysis of title

The text of Marguerite Duras entitled *L'Amant* is a contemporary novel first published in 1963. A product of what is termed the *avant-garde*, this work calls into question the conventional means whereby cohesion and coherence are achieved in a text: the reader is assigned, for example, a much greater role than is customary in the production of meaning.

Outline

The title will be studied in isolation and then in relationship to its immediate context. The immediate context will be defined as:

1) the dedication

Because of the nature of the title – the absence of any individual identification – the reader is inevitably led to make links with the dedication: is the lover *Bruno Nuytten?* is the text partly autobiographical?

2) the opening paragraph

The absence of any individual chapter headings ensures that the focus remains on the main title. This title acquires both a density and specificity of meaning as the text unfolds.

The title *L'Amant* on the cover page

The title consists of a noun, *Amant*, preceded by the definite article, *L'*. It refers to both a person (male) and an activity or function (loving). The choice of the definite article *l'* instead of the indefinite *un* highlights the stereotype, the generic, as opposed to the individual. The reader's background knowledge is being elicited: it is cultural associations or connotations which are responsible for the title's initial coherence. These associations or background knowledge are of two kinds:

– They relate to a knowledge of genre or text type. The title *L'Amant* evokes a particular type of popular romantic literature (in England we might think of Mills and Boon). Appearing on the title page, it awakens a number of expectations: the reader anticipates a particular type of story or distribution of narrative roles.

– Secondly, the title *L'Amant* may encourage the reader to make associations with other texts of the same author that possess similar titles (*L'Amour, L'Amante anglaise, L'Amant de la Chine du Nord*). This establishment of intertextual links may lead the reader to reassess an interpretation based solely on the conventional love-story and to anticipate a possible subversion of the traditional and of the stereotype.

The title and the dedication

The positioning of the dedication: *A Bruno Nuytten* – you cannot fail to see it – together with the choice of a male name raises questions such as: is there a link between the title and the dedication? Is the dedication part of the text? More specifically, can we establish lexical cohesion in the shared notion of masculinity, or in the shared notion of the foreign connoted by the name *Nuytten*, the foreign or strange being for Duras an essential attribute of love? These questions remain open and the cohesion, if indeed it does exist, remains extremely loose.

The title and the opening paragraph

The opening paragraph of a text establishes the fictive parameters. Internal networks of meaning are set up (text reference as opposed to situation reference) and the associations of the title become more specific.

• Lexical cohesion

a) lexical fields

We begin by extracting those lexical items that have a semantic link with the title. We then group them into lexical fields:

Beauty
Vous étiez belle
je vous trouve plus belle maintenant

Physical appearance
j'aimais moins votre visage de
jeune femme que celui que vous a
avez maintenant, dévasté

Age
j'étais âgée déjà
lorsque vous étiez jeune

Relationship
il s'est fait connaître
je vous connais depuis toujours

The construction of these lexical fields represents an undermining of the stereotypical associations of the title. Instead of associating the values of love and beauty with youth and physical blossoming, the narrator links them with age and physical destruction. The traditional concept of romantic love is thus being called into question.

b) repetition

A key device in the establishment of cohesion is the repetition of words and phrases within the opening paragraph that have a close semantic or syntactic link with the title. For example, the same verbs are used in the 3rd person narrative and in the 1st person direct speech:

un homme est venu (line 2)	and	*je suis venu* (line 5)
il s'est fait connaître (lines 2-3)	and	*je vous connais* (line 3)

The text presents the symbolic interplay between the self and the Other that characterises the Durassian concept of love, a concept that is based on an essential fluidity or instability of identity: subject and object positions (see Chapter 9, Textual schemata) are constantly switched round – the same character may appear at one point in the narrative as *je* and at another as *il* or *elle*.

The direct speech is itself characterised by an abundant use of repetition:

> *Tout le monde dit que vous étiez belle lorsque vous*
> *étiez jeune, je suis venu pour vous dire que pour moi*
> *je vous trouve plus belle maintenant que lorsque*
> *vous étiez jeune...*

The effect is of a litany or chant; it can be said that the text moves at this point into the temporal dimension of the sacred: the reader is once more being alerted to the unconventional, non-realistic presentation of love and the lover.

c) opposites

A common cohesive device is the use of two words or phrases that are opposite in meaning. In the opening paragraph a contrast is made between *tout le monde* and *je*, between singular and plural, or society and the individual:

> *Tout le monde dit que vous étiez belle lorsque vous étiez*
> *jeune, je suis venu...*

Once again the effect is to highlight the notion of unconventionality or of difference, thereby reinforcing the meaning of the title.

• Coreference and contrast

a) determiners

Here we shall be examining the function, in relation to the title, of the indefinite article *un*, which appears in the opening sentence:

> *Un jour, j'étais âgée déjà, dans le hall d'un lieu public,*
> **un** *homme est venu vers moi.*

An enigma is immediately posed: we ask ourselves 'who is this man?'. The context however inevitably leads us to make an anaphoric association (i.e. to refer backwards) with the title *L'Amant*. Is this the same man? The element of uncertainty that is being introduced at this point reinforces the theme of instability of identity that we have already mentioned.

b) personal pronouns

Pronouns play a key role in producing cohesion within the passage. The *il* of the second line (**il** *s'est fait connaître*) refers back to *un homme* (*un homme est venu vers moi*) and the pronoun is repeated with insistence in the same line (**il** *s'est fait connaître et* **il** *m'a dit*). It is also evident from the direct speech which ensues that *je* and *il* are one and the same person. By the time we reach the end of the first paragraph, we have a clearer idea as to the possible identity of the lover of the title, a number of referential anchors having been laid within the text.

c) comparative reference or contrast

Cohesive links between phrases or utterances are also established through a striking use of comparatives:

> *je vous trouve* **plus** *belle maintenant* **que** *lorsque vous*
> *étiez jeune, j'aimais* **moins** *votre visage de jeune femme*
> **que** *celui que vous avez maintenant, dévasté.*

The conventional association between youth and beauty is thereby being challenged and a more revolutionary concept of love (and the lover) is being posited.

Conclusion

Our examination of the title and of its immediate context has brought to the fore a number of devices, in particular those relating to lexical and referential cohesion. Although less tightly knit than in conventional realist narrative, these devices are nevertheless essential to the production of meaning. At the same time, however, we must not forget the role of external factors such as genre and background cultural knowledge (intertextuality) in our interpretation of titles (see Chapters 8 and 10).

ASSIGNMENTS

1. *Quand l'assiette se met au vert* (*Libération*, 6-7 April 1996)

Quand l'assiette se met au vert

Les Français n'ont pas attendu les craintes suscitées par la maladie de la vache folle pour s'assurer que la viande n'était pas indispensable à chaque repas. Mais de là à faire bonne chère devant une assiette tout en légumes et céréales... **Page 20**

Analyse the cohesion and coherence of the title and the text that follows. Show how the coherence of the message depends on the visual layout of the advert, but also (and mainly) on the reader's extra-linguistic knowledge.

A few questions to consider:

1. What does the title evoke at first reading?
2. What does the illustration add to the possible interpretation(s) of the title?
3. How does the first sentence of the text clarify *se mettre au vert*?
4. What is the meaning of *l'assiette*? Why the definite article?
5. What is the peculiarity of the second sentence in the text? What is its effect?
6. Consider that second sentence and:
   – Suggest possible semantically equivalent expressions for *faire... céréales...*
   – Suggest possible ways to complete the second sentence (after *céréales...*).

2. *Chine: une diva est de retour* (*Le Monde*, 10 April 1996)

Chine : une diva est de retour

« *LES GRANDES puissances sont comme les divas : leur retour sur scène, comme leur sortie, ne peuvent se concevoir sans quelques crises.* » Cette remarque de Fareed Zakaria, le directeur de la revue américaine *Foreign Affairs*, s'applique particulièrement bien aujourd'hui au cas de la Chine. Ce pays, dont la France accueille à partir du 9 avril le premier ministre, Li Peng, connaît, depuis le début des années 80, un développement économique spectaculaire. L'empire du Milieu tend ainsi à retrouver, dans le théâtre mondial, son rôle de grande puissance. On ne peut guère imaginer que ce retour se fasse sans quelques crises, à l'intérieur du pays comme sur la scène mondiale.

Engagées à partir de 1979, les réformes mises en œuvre à l'initiative de Deng Xiaoping ont provoqué un véritable décollage du pays. Il est certes difficile aujourd'hui de qualifier l'économie chinoise. Les dirigeants parlent d'« *une économie socialiste de marché* ». Il s'agit en réalité d'un système « en fusion », mélange complexe d'une organisation centralisée, planifiée, politisée à la soviétique et de capitalisme sauvage. Mais un fait ne peut être contesté : jamais, depuis les débuts de la révolution industrielle, un pays aussi peuplé (1,2 milliard d'habitants) n'avait connu pendant une période aussi longue (seize ans) une croissance aussi forte (une moyenne de 10 % par an). Des grandes cités complètement nouvelles émergeant au milieu de rizières, des capitales engorgées, une consommation d'énergie en plein boom, un poids croissant dans le commerce mondial : même si les chiffres doivent être observés avec prudence, les signes de ce décollage sont désormais visibles pour tous.

Officiellement, l'administration du plan de Pékin estime que la production totale chinoise (son PIB) aurait été multipliée par dix en quinze ans, atteignant 4 400 milliards de yuans (un yuan vaut 0,60 franc) en 1994, l'équivalent d'un gros tiers du PIB français. Selon les méthodes de calcul retenues, certains experts occidentaux affirment qu'avec une telle activité la Chine se place au neuvième rang dans le monde.

Erik Izraelewicz

Lire la suite page 15, nos informations page 2 et un point de vue page 14

Analyse the cohesion and coherence of this title.

A few questions to consider:

1. Which word poses a problem of interpretation in the title?

2. What is the most obvious interpretation of the title?

3. Why is this implausible?

4. What is the effect produced?

5. When and how is the reader enlightened?

6. What is peculiar about this first sentence?

7. How should the title be interpreted, from the point of view of its syntax, in the light of what we now know?

3. *Laffont fait sa rentrée...* (*Le Point,* No 1205, 21 October 1995)

Analyse the cohesion and coherence of the title of this advertisement. Show how the coherence of the message depends largely on both the reader's extra-linguistic knowledge and on the visual layout of the advertisement.

A few questions to consider:

1. Which word is likely to carry the most enigmatic meaning when looking at the title only?
2. Which set expression do you find in the title and what extra-linguistic knowledge does it refer to?
3. On what figure linked to the set expression does the message rely?
4. What punctuation do you find in the title and which meaning does it give to the message?
5. To what extent may the typography used in the title echo and reinforce the extra-linguistic knowledge of the set expression?
6. What is the significance of the tense used?

Laffont fait sa rentrée...

Dans ce livre, peut-être le plus secret de son œuvre, Alphonse Boudard raconte celle qui fut si proche et si lointaine -sa mère- et évoque, en très grand écrivain, le monde disparu de sa jeunesse.

Alphonse Boudard Mourir d'enfance ROMAN

Robert Laffont

270 pages - 119 F

Jean Carrière Achigan ROMAN

Robert Laffont

224 pages - 119 F

Ce superbe roman de Jean Carrière est celui d'une quête universelle : la découverte de soi. Un soir d'hiver, au fin fond des Cévennes, on découvre un homme amnésique et mutique, il a juste un tatouage à la place du cœur.

1955 : Libertade, écrivain célèbre, éventre sa femme et se mure dans le silence. 1995 : son psychanalyste raconte l'affaire à un éditeur. Après *Le Bonheur du manchot*, un nouveau Chabrol inattendu, et attachant.

Jean-Pierre Chabrol Les aveux du silence ROMAN

Robert Laffont

324 pages - 129 F

Michel Field Contes cruels pour Anaëlle RÉCIT

Robert Laffont

216 pages - 119 F

Michel Field raconte à sa fille ce qui s'est passé dans le monde en ce jour ordinaire, si extraordinaire, qui fut celui de sa naissance, et explore aussi ses souvenirs d'un fils devenu père. Quinze "contes" d'un très bel écrivain.

L'auteur de *Ségou* avait toujours rêvé d'adapter à l'univers caraïbe *Les Hauts de Hurlevent*, d'Emily Brontë. En voici une libre variation, pleine de violence et de sensualité, et d'une extraordinaire force d'envoûtement.

Maryse Condé La migration des cœurs ROMAN

Robert Laffont

352 pages - 129 F

Christian Combaz Franz ROMAN

Robert Laffont

496 pages - 149 F

Autour de Franz, être singulier qui étonne par ses dons et sait prédire l'avenir, gravitent toutes les passions : une immense fresque qui marque le grand retour au romanesque de Christian Combaz.

Des livres Robert Laffont

4. *NRJ* radio station advertisement (*Le journal du dimanche*, 24 September 1995)

Show how the coherence of the title is established and decide on the function of the visual layout for the understanding of the message.

A few questions to consider:

1. Which main word is likely to carry an enigmatic meaning for a number of unaware readers?

2. In reference to which other main word of the title can the enigmatic meaning of the title be resolved?

3. Identify the verbs and nouns of the titular message. Identify their register and say to what extent this also contributes to the enigmatic value of the message.

4. What is the function of the verbal expression *creuser l'écart* and of *plus encore* in the title?

5. How can the reader finally dispel the uncertainties of the title?

5. *Désert*

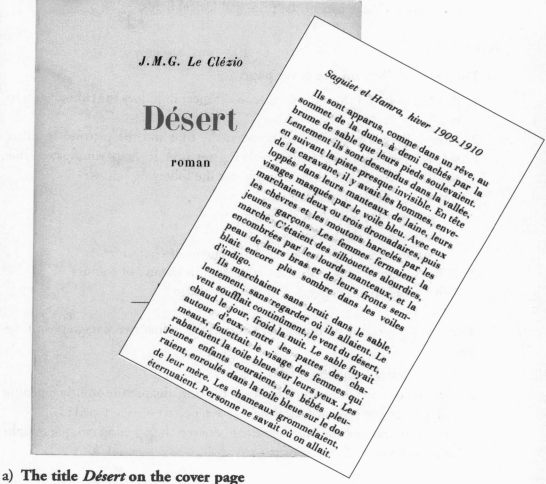

J.M.G. Le Clézio

Désert

roman

Saguiet el Hamra, hiver 1909-1910

Ils sont apparus, comme dans un rêve, au sommet de la dune, à demi cachés par la brume de sable que leurs pieds soulevaient. Lentement ils sont descendus dans la vallée, en suivant la piste presque invisible. En tête de la caravane, il y avait les hommes, enveloppés dans leurs manteaux de laine, leurs visages masqués par le voile bleu. Avec eux marchaient deux ou trois dromadaires, puis les chèvres et les moutons harcelés par les jeunes garçons. Les femmes fermaient la marche. C'étaient des silhouettes alourdies, encombrées par les lourds manteaux, et la peau de leurs bras et de leurs fronts semblait encore plus sombre dans les voiles d'indigo.

Ils marchaient sans bruit dans le sable, lentement, sans regarder où ils allaient. Le vent soufflait continûment, le vent du désert, chaud le jour, froid la nuit. Le sable fuyait autour d'eux, entre les pattes des chameaux, fouettait le visage des femmes qui rabattaient la toile bleue sur leurs yeux. Les jeunes enfants couraient, les bébés pleuraient, enroulés dans la toile bleue sur le dos de leur mère. Les chameaux grommelaient, éternuaient. Personne ne savait où on allait.

a) The title *Désert* on the cover page

1. What does the title mean for you? What does it denote?
2. Why is the article (*le* or *un*) omitted? What is the effect of this omission?
3. Does the title remind you of any other text?
4. If you are already familiar with other texts of Le Clézio, what associations does the title immediately awaken? Does it have a positive or a negative value?
5. Does the title suggest a particular story-line to you?

b) The title and its immediate context

1. Can you establish a cohesive link between the main title and the reference (in italics) preceding the main text: *Saguiet el Hamra, hiver 1909-1910*? What potential meaning of the title is being actualised here?

2. Can you establish lexical cohesion between the title and the first two paragraphs? Make lists of the principal lexical fields.

6. *La Terre*

a) **The title *La Terre* on the cover page:**

1. Read in isolation from the picture, what meanings does the title suggest to you?
2. How is cohesion established between the title and the picture? In other words, what semantic fields are being set up? To help you answer this question, it may be helpful to consider the following points:
   – the use of colour and line
   – the size and position of the cross
   – the nature of the buildings
   – gestures, facial expressions and movement of characters.
3. What semantic oppositions are suggested in the use of colour?
4. What story-line is suggested in the cover page?

b) **The cover page and its immediate context** (the first two paragraphs of the text):

1. How is lexical cohesion established?
2. How is cohesion established between the title, the picture and the opening two paragraphs? What lexical fields are repeated or developed?
3. How is narrative coherence achieved between the opening two paragraphs and the lay-out of the cover page?

PREMIÈRE PARTIE

I

JEAN, ce matin-là, un semoir de toile bleue noué sur le ventre, en tenait la poche ouverte de la main gauche, et de la droite, tous les trois pas, il y prenait une poignée de blé, que d'un geste, à la volée, il jetait. Ses gros souliers trouaient et emportaient la terre grasse, dans le balancement cadencé de son corps; tandis que, à chaque jet, au milieu de la semence blonde toujours volante, on voyait luire les deux galons rouges d'une veste d'ordonnance, qu'il achevait d'user. Seul, en avant, il marchait, l'air grandi; et, derrière, pour enfouir le grain, une herse roulait lentement, attelée de deux chevaux, qu'un charretier poussait à longs coups de fouet réguliers, claquant au-dessus de leurs oreilles.

La parcelle de terre, d'une cinquantaine d'ares à peine, au lieu dit des Cornailles, était si peu importante, que M. Hourdequin, le maître de la Borderie, n'avait pas voulu y envoyer le semoir mécanique, occupé ailleurs. Jean, qui remontait la pièce du midi au nord, avait justement devant lui, à deux kilomètres, les bâtiments de la ferme. Arrivé au bout du sillon, il leva les yeux, regarda sans voir, en soufflant une minute.

7. Find the titles

1. Headlines

a) Suggest a title for the following text from *Le Monde,* of which we have already seen an extract in Chapter 6.

Avec la crise de la vache folle qui agite et inquiète l'Europe, l'agriculture moderne vient de montrer son vrai visage. Celui d'un productivisme forcené qui a transformé les campagnes en usines sans toit et les animaux d'élevage en machines à fabriquer de la viande et du lait. Au lendemain de la deuxième guerre, l'impératif du tonnage était une religion chez les paysans, investis d'une belle mission: nourrir les populations affaiblies par six années de conflit et de privations. Deux coups de baguette magique ont sonné l'heure des métamorphoses: la machine, qui a soudain rendu inutile la force musculaire du bœuf et du cheval; la chimie, qui a permis l'accroissement spectaculaire des rendements, apportant au Vieux Continent une sécurité alimentaire durable payée au prix d'un brutal exode rural et d'un bouleversement des méthodes traditionnelles. L'apparition d'excédents laitiers et céréaliers n'a pas enrayé l'engrenage qui venait de se faire jour: dans un contexte d'économie ouverte, de guerre commerciale et de course - folle, elle aussi - aux subventions, l'agriculture a vu ses marges de profit, et donc de manœuvre, diminuer. La solution est devenue la même pour tous: s'endetter, investir, produire toujours plus au coût le plus bas en intensifiant les cultures, en augmentant la taille des élevages.

Une agriculture monstrueuse est née. Une agriculture contre nature. On a retourné des prairies pour planter du blé et du maïs, au risque d'abîmer les sols et de polluer l'eau souterraine. On a construit de véritables cathédrales de métal et de ciment pour l'engraissement des veaux, vaches, cochons, couvées. Les étables sont devenues des forceries; les élevages porcins, des ateliers à mille truies; les poules de basse-cour, les passagers involontaires d'immenses vaisseaux éclairés jour et nuit à l'ampoule électrique (pour favoriser la ponte), gavées d'antibiotiques et autres bonnes choses. Sous couvert de rentabilité, d'économies d'échelle, de «seuils minimum d'activité», qui conduisent à concentrer les élevages en même temps que leur alimentation, le système est à son tour devenu fou, ou plutôt absurde à force de logique marchande poussée toujours plus loin.

b) Suggest a title and a subtitle for the following text from *Libération*:

> *Des dizaines de milliers d'Européens vont devoir effectuer de nouvelles analyses pour contrôler leur séropositivité: la firme américaine Abbott a en effet reconnu le manque de fiabilité de son test de dépistage du sida commercialisé depuis septembre 1995. Une nouvelle inquiétante mais qui ne devrait pas concerner la France, où l'on utilise deux tests consécutifs de marques différentes pour le dépistage de la maladie. Reste une incertitude pour les transfusions de sang, où l'on n'effectue qu'un seul dépistage pour les donneurs.*

2. Advertisements

Which product or type of product is advertised in the two advertisements shown as a) and b) on the following two pages? Specify which elements of cohesion or coherence have helped you to decide on your answer.

a) *Comme vous pouvez le constater, ce paysage est rempli de canalisations de...*

"COMME VOUS POUVEZ LE CONSTATER, CE PAYSAGE EST REMPLI DE CANALISATIONS DE   ."

Pourquoi les Français préfèrent   ?

Ami lecteur bonjour, j'ai concocté à votre intention un petit problème de logique que je soumets à votre réflexion.

Problème : "sachant que le Français aime se laver à l'eau chaude, qu'il ne rechigne pas à rester des heures sous sa douche, qu'il aime la bonne chère, la gastronomie sous toutes ses formes, qu'il aime aussi vivre au chaud l'hiver et sachant que rien ne ressemble plus à une canalisation

qu'une autre canalisation   , comment le Français a-t-il fait pour conserver à son territoire cette incomparable variété de paysages que le monde entier lui envie?"

Réponse : "les paysages français sont préservés parce que les canalisations   sont souterraines, et c'est tant mieux pour la nature et les touristes qui la fréquentent".

POUR PLUS DE RENSEIGNEMENTS, APPELER LE N°Vert **05 16 3000**
APPEL GRATUIT
DU LUNDI AU VENDREDI, DE 9 H À 18 H.

, LE CHOIX DE LA QUALITÉ.

b) *Jour après jour de...*

Jour après Jour de

Parce que la forme se construit jour après jour.

Pour contribuer au bien-être et à l'équilibre de votre corps,   a mis au point un   révolutionnaire. Savamment dosé en vitamines et oligo-éléments, enrichi de fibres bifidogènes, il vous apporte forme et vitalité et vous offre sa saveur en plus de ses bienfaits. Du jamais vu dans l'   !

L'ESSENTIEL EST DANS

3. Literary texts

a) **Passage 1:** what title would you suggest for the following text?

> Jetez-moi dans la mer... car je sais que
> c'est moi qui attire sur vous cette grande
> tempête.
> Jonas, I, 12.

Gilbert Jonas, artiste peintre, croyait en son étoile. Il ne croyait d'ailleurs qu'en elle, bien qu'il se sentît du respect, et même une sorte d'admiration, devant la religion des autres. Sa propre foi, pourtant, n'était pas sans vertus, puisqu'elle consistait à admettre, de façon obscure, qu'il obtiendrait beaucoup sans jamais rien mériter. Aussi, lorsque, aux environs de sa trente-cinquième année, une dizaine de critiques se disputèrent soudain la gloire d'avoir découvert son talent, il n'en montra point de surprise. Mais sa sérénité, attribuée par certains à la suffisance, s'expliquait très bien, au contraire, par une confiante modestie. Jonas rendait justice à son étoile plutôt qu'à ses mérites.

Il se montra un peu plus étonné lorsqu'un marchand de tableaux lui proposa une mensualité qui le délivrait de tout souci. En vain, l'architecte Rateau, qui depuis le lycée aimait Jonas et son étoile, lui représenta-t-il que cette mensualité lui donnerait une vie à peine décente et que le marchand n'y perdrait rien. « Tout de même », disait Jonas. Rateau, qui réussissait, mais à la force du poignet, dans tout ce qu'il entreprenait, gourmandait son ami. « Quoi, tout de même ? Il faut discuter. » Rien n'y fit. Jonas en lui-même remerciait son étoile. « Ce sera comme vous voudrez », dit-il au marchand. Et il abandonna les fonctions qu'il occupait dans la maison d'éditions paternelle, pour se consacrer tout entier à la peinture. « Ça, disait-il, c'est une chance ! »

b) **Passage 2:** can you find a title to this prose poem?

> *Un beau matin, chez un peuple fort doux, un homme et une femme superbes criaient sur la place publique: « Mes amis, je veux qu'elle soit reine! » Elle riait et tremblait. Il parlait aux amis de révélation, d'épreuve terminée. Ils se pâmaient l'un contre l'autre.*
>
> *En effet, ils furent rois toute une matinée, où les tentures carminées se relevèrent sur les maisons, et toute l'après-midi, où ils s'avancèrent du côté des jardins de palmes.*

SUGGESTED ANSWERS TO ASSIGNMENTS

1. *Quand l'assiette se met au vert*

1. At first reading, the title evokes something to do with eating (*assiette*) and perhaps the countryside (*se mettre au vert*).

2. We see a vegetable (a pimento), so perhaps the article is about eating vegetables or being a vegetarian, rather than literally 'going to the countryside to get some rest'.

3. *la maladie de la vache folle*, a major source of preoccupation in 1996, is mentioned: *se mettre au vert* now appears as a cross between – literally – 'eating vegetables' and 'moving towards a healthier lifestyle'.

4. *l'assiette* here does not mean literally 'the plate', but rather what one puts on one's plate, i.e. it is a reference to meals in general (see Metonymy in Chapter 6, Lexical fields).

5. The second sentence is unfinished: it ends with suspension marks and has no verb. The reader is invited to finish it. The stucture *de là à…* suggests that one should not go too far in that direction (i.e. eating vegetables only/ being a vegetarian).

6. – Semantic equivalent expressions for *faire… céréales…*: *ne manger que des légumes/devenir végétarien/abandonner complètement la viande…*
   – Possible ways to complete the second sentence (after *céréales*) may include: *c'est demander trop, il ne faut pas exagérer…*

2. *Chine: une diva est de retour*

1. A word which poses a problem of interpretation in the title is *diva*. We know (or we can find out from a dictionary) that *une diva* is *une cantatrice en renom*, a well-known opera singer. It is also a rather old-fashioned word. The mystery is deepened by the use of the indefinite article, which poses existence, but not identity.

2. Most obvious interpretation of the title: that a well-known opera singer has made her come-back in China.

3. Articles on the front page of a newspaper normally refer to important, well-known facts and situations, or very topical ones. Opera singing in China is for the *cognoscenti*, not the average *Le Monde* reader.

4. The effect produced is that it is an enigma. The reader is intrigued and wants to find out more about what could be so important about this opera singer.

5. The reader is enlightened when reading the first sentence of the first paragraph containing a simile: *Les grandes puissances sont* **comme** *les divas*.

6. It is a quote, made by someone about *les grandes puissances* generally, but which the author of the article thought was particularly appropriate for China.

7. We have an interesting example of lexical cataphora, whereby the defined element, *Chine*, a proper noun, is in thematic position, followed by its referent, *une diva*. In other words, *La Chine est une diva, et cette diva est de retour.*

3. *Laffont fait sa rentrée...*

1. The proper noun *Laffont*.

2. *Faire sa rentrée*, which commonly refers to 'going back to school' in a French context.

3. A metaphor. The message relies on the metaphor of the return to school mentioned in Answer 2: an expression usually applied to schoolchildren. The publisher Laffont, like schoolchildren at the beginning of the academic year, starts the autumn season with a series of new books.

4. The suspension marks echo to some degree the reader's hesitation in the meaning to be given to the title and, as such, they incite the reader to read on or to look at the visual layout.

5. The typography used in the title echoes and reinforces the extra-linguistic knowledge of the set expression by the use of italics which, for a French reader, may recall early school experiences of writing.

6. The present tense in *fait sa rentrée* contributes to the immediacy of the message and the sense of excitement experienced at the beginning of the school year.

Brief summary of analysis:

The proper noun *Laffont* suggests an enigma which remains unexplained at first reading, especially for a foreign reader. The meaning of the message is to some extent linked to the understanding of the lexical set expression *faire sa rentrée*, used as a metaphorical figure. On the one hand it gives the title a sense of relevance, since the advert was published in an October issue of *Le Point*, a time when the expression is more likely to be used widely in the French context of returning to school. On the other hand the set expression insists on the aspect of novelty offered by the books advertised by the *Laffont* publishing house. The meaning of the title can however only be ascertained by looking at the visual layout – title and visual display being tightly linked by the common use of the white and blue colours and by looking at the subheading which concludes the advert: *Des livres Robert Lafont*. We find the same enticing device in this titular message as in the main study on adverts analysed previously at greater length.

4. *NRJ* radio station advert (*Le journal du dimanche*, 24 September 1995)

1. The acronym *NRJ*, which incidentally connotes positively the word 'energy' – *énergie* – a connotative meaning more likely to be noticed however when spoken.

2. The enigmatic meaning of the title can be resolved by linking it to the name *Europe 1*, a more widely known radio station.

3. *creuse l'écart, cibles, comptent:* the register is scientific (statistics). These expressions create gaps in the message: we do not know what *creuser l'écart* and *cibles* refer to.

4. The verbal expression *creuse l'écart* emphasizes the sense of difference between the two radio stations, *NRJ* and *Europe 1*. This meaning is reinforced by the use of *plus encore* in the second half of the title, which introduces the specific reference to *NRJ's* targetted public, and as such triggers further the reader's curiosity, enticing her/him to look at the diagrams that follow.

5. The reader can finally dispel the uncertainties of the title by looking at the visual layout: *cibles* refers to social categories of listeners and *creuser l'écart* refers to the audience ratings of the two radio stations.

5. *Désert*

a) **Study of the title**

1. The title refers both to a place and to the quality of being deserted.

2. The omission of the article encourages a symbolic reading of the text: the reader is led to interpret the book on more than one level.

3. The title is particularly rich in literary and mythical associations. It could, for example, remind us of the Bible, of the work of A. Camus or L. Gaspar or of adventure stories centred on the theme of the desert island.

4. The title suggests the image of empty space or nothingness (*le vide*), a central theme of Le Clézio. Empty space is seen as positive, the ideal relationship between people and their environment.

5. It is unlikely to suggest a specific story-line. However the desert (and being

deserted) is often associated with dramatic events, with a confrontation or battle with elemental forces. A scenario human vs cosmic is thus anticipated.

b) **The title and its immediate context**

1. An anaphoric link is established. The two paragraphs on the next page, referring back to *désert*, anchor the story in a specific geographic (and historic) reality. The spatial connotations of the title are being actualised when the reader has access to these two paragraphs.

2. Cohesion can be established in two areas:
   - The title as denoting a concrete visual reality. The key lexical fields that emerge here are those of the sand (*au sommet de la dune, la brume de sable, la piste,* etc.), the wind and dryness.
   - The title as denoting the quality of being deserted. The lexical fields that are developed here are: silence, emptiness and disorientation (*personne ne savait où on allait*).

6. *La Terre*

a) **Study of the title and the cover**

1. Meanings suggested by the title: the earth, the countryside, land, soil on the concrete level, or earth as opposed to heaven on the abstract level.

2. Suggested semantic fields:

   a) countryside
      This is evoked both in the choice of title and in the visual objects (and their layout) that make the picture. The buildings seem immersed in a natural setting, dominated by the vegetation.

   b) peasant
      This is evoked in the figure in the right foreground whose gestures and physical appearance suggest the semes of work, simplicity and poverty conventionally associated with the peasantry. When read in the light of the picture, the title acquires more specific connotations, suggesting not only a place but also an action – that of tilling the soil.

   c) authority of the Church
      This is evoked by the size of the cross on the left handside that clearly dominates the whole picture. The figure of the peasant appears swamped, almost crushed in comparison. The choice of the colour black also suggests that the authority is negative, associated perhaps with the semes of repression, of unhappiness and of death.

d) work

The focus of the picture is on the peasant engaged in work. There is a marked absence of any objects or gestures that might suggest leisure or fun, a world beyond the bare necessities of life.

e) starkness

This atmosphere is conveyed in the use of colour – black and white – and the absence of any object or activity that does not relate to the essentials of life: work, food and shelter.

f) solitude

This is evoked in the presence of a single figure. There is no suggestion of any human communication or interaction.

3. The use of colour as opposed to black and white may suggest the passionate vs the drab and habitual, or new life (green) vs death, or optimism vs pessimism.

4. The story-line suggested is that of peasants shown as the subject of a quest to till the soil and make a living. The opponents (starkness, poverty and the church) are evoked as a strong power in determining the life of the people, not necessarily in a positive sense (cf. the black cross).

b) **The cover page and its immediate context** (the first two paragraphs of the text)

1. Lexical cohesion is established:
   – by the use of repetition: *La terre grasse, la parcelle de terre*
   – by the use of lexical anaphora: *la pièce du midi* and *la parcelle de terre*
   – by the use of the grouping of terms that possess a common denominator, e.g. sowing: *un semoir, une poignée de blé, la semence blonde, pour enfouir le grain, le semoir mécanique; une herse attelée de deux chevaux, un charretier poussait..., au bout du sillon.*

2. The lexical fields which are developed are: countryside, peasant, work, starkness or simplicity, solitude, authority (cf. the cross in the picture, the master in the text).

3. Similar positions are set up with positive and negative connotations: conflict suggested between life of individual peasant and some higher authority – *le maître de la Borderie*. The colour green of the title on the cover page, read in association with the act of sowing in the first two paragraphs, suggests a positive goal to the peasant's quest: the renewal of life, hope, spring.

7. Find the titles

1. Headlines
a) The title is:

Une agriculture contre nature

b) The title and subtitle are:

Sida: l'angoisse du test défectueux
Le test Abbott suspendu dans plusieurs pays européens

2. Advertisements

a) ***Comme vous pouvez le constater, ce paysage est rempli de canalisations*** ... from *Télérama*, no 2773, 5 June 1996

The following advertisement concerns *Le gaz naturel*.
Elements of cohesion and coherence which help decide on what the advertisement is about:
— The main element is a parallel established between the **lexical fields** of environment (*canalisations, paysages, préserver, No. vert*...) and that of French everyday living (*se laver à l'eau chaude, aime la bonne chair, aime aussi vivre au chaud l'hiver*). The relationship between the two fields constructs the need for the advertised product.
— **Lexical reiteration:** *le Français* (insists on generality, truth value of argumentation) and *sachant que* (insists on the logical value of argument and need for the product).

a) *Comme vous pouvez le constater, ce paysage est rempli de canalisations de . . .*

Gaz de France

"COMME VOUS POUVEZ LE CONSTATER, CE PAYSAGE EST REMPLI DE CANALISATIONS DE GAZ NATUREL."

Pourquoi les Français préfèrent le gaz naturel ?

Ami lecteur bonjour, j'ai concocté à votre intention un petit problème de logique que je soumets à votre réflexion.

Problème : "sachant que le Français aime se laver à l'eau chaude, qu'il ne rechigne pas à rester des heures sous sa douche, qu'il aime la bonne chère, la gastronomie sous toutes ses formes, qu'il aime aussi vivre au chaud l'hiver et sachant que rien ne ressemble plus à une canalisation de gaz naturel qu'une autre canalisation de gaz naturel, comment le Français a-t-il fait pour conserver à son territoire cette incomparable variété de paysages que le monde entier lui envie?"

Réponse : "les paysages français sont préservés parce que les canalisations de gaz naturel sont souterraines, et c'est tant mieux pour la nature et les touristes qui la fréquentent".

POUR PLUS DE RENSEIGNEMENTS, APPELER LE N° Vert 05 16 3000
DU LUNDI AU VENDREDI, DE 9 H À 18 H.

GAZ DE FRANCE, LE CHOIX DE LA QUALITÉ.

b) ***Jour après jour de...*** from *Questions de Femme*, no 3, June 1996

Elements of cohesion and coherence which help decide on the product are:

– **Lexical reiteration:** cf. *jour après jour* has the status of a title. Its repetition stresses the importance of taking the product every day; this is reinforced by the meaning of *se construit*.

- **Lexical fields:** parallel and interaction between the two fields of physical well-being *(forme, bien-être, équilibre, corps, vitalité, bienfaits...)*, which stress the effect of the product, and the medical/scientific field *(vitamines, oligo-éléments, fibres bifidogènes...)*, which defines the content of the product.
  A nominal keyword, *saveur*, suggests the lexical field of food.
- **Importance of logical connectors:** *parce que, pour* which reinforce the interaction between the two lexical fields.
- **Presence of the speaker:** expressed in the *vous (il **vous** apporte, il **vous** offre, **votre** corps)* which stresses the benefit drawn from the product.

3. Literary texts

a) The actual title is *Jonas ou l'artiste au travail* from A. Camus's collection of stories *L'Exil et le Royaume*. Any title relating to *Jonas* or to the artist would be acceptable. If, however, a title from a completely different area has been chosen, reasons should be given to justify the choice.

b) The actual title is *Royauté* from Rimbaud's *Illuminations*. Any title relating to the field of royalty or to that of the spiritual (or religious) or to the festive would be acceptable. If a title has been chosen from a completely different area from those suggested above, the choice should be justified.

CHAPTER 12

FURTHER TEXTS FOR ANALYSIS

1. Articles

1.1. Comment on this *éditorial*, paying particular attention to the use of register and to the presence of the speaker.

NOUVELLE FRONTIÈRE

Peut-être. De l'eau a peut-être coulé sur Mars récemment.

L'indispensable prudence qui doit accompagner les découvertes de la sonde orbitale *Mars Global Surveyor* n'empêche pas le frisson. Peu importe si le précieux liquide s'est épanché à la surface de la planère rouge il y a un million d'années ou bien plus tard. S'il s'agit vraiment d'eau ou d'un mélange boueux. L'essentiel est que les spectaculaires prises de vues de la Nasa semblent démontrer que notre voisine n'est pas une planète morte. On se doutait que ses entrailles abritaient de l'eau glacée. Les données publiées hier donnent désormais à penser que de mystérieux mouvements peuvent la propulser à l'air – ténu – libre. Impossible de regarder du même œil la « planète aux canaux ». Les images envoyées par la sonde sont émouvantes par la familiarité qu'elles évoquent au Terrien moyen. On s'imagine arpenter ses dunes dorées modelées par l'érosion, s'abriter à l'ombre de profondes vallées ou même gravir vaillamment ses monts enneigés. La morphologie du paysage martien assure que l'eau y a autrefois coulé en abondance. Sa survie partielle raviverait la question lancinante de la présence d'une forme de vie sur Mars. L'eau est le bouillon primitif d'où surgit cette forme de complexité qu'on nomme « vie ». Sur ce point, rien n'a encore été trouvé. La découverte de microbactéries dans des météorites d'origine martienne reste contestée. Par sa puissance d'évocation symbolique, l'événement ragaillardit les apôtres d'une exploration audacieuse du système solaire. Elle tombe à pic pour une Nasa secouée après le lamentable échec de la sonde *Mars Polar Lander*. En faisant miroiter une nouvelle frontière, un ressort auquel les Américains sont toujours sensibles, la Nasa pourrait clore le cycle pénible des budgets tassés et des ambitions racornies. Il y a vingt-huit ans que l'Homme n'a pas posé le pied ailleurs que sur son globe natal. Or l'incroyable variété du système solaire – Jupiter est entouré de deux satellites aussi différents que la volcanique Io et la glacée Europe – plaide en faveur de cette aventure. D'autant que les astronomes ne cessent de découvrir d'autres systèmes planétaires dans notre Galaxie.

Eric Dupin, *Libération*, 23 June 2000

1.2. Comment on the following article, paying attention to:
 a) the use of lexical fields and the choice of tenses
 b) the presence of the speaker.
To what extent is the humour of the text reliant upon cultural assumptions?

LES DEUX GÉNÉRAUX

La vieillesse est un naufrage, certes, mais plus ou moins. En attestent les témoignages des généraux Jacques Massu et Marcel Bigeard, appelés à réagir, dans *le Monde* de jeudi, aux accusations portées contre eux par Louisette Ighilahriz qui, née en Kabylie, eut vingt ans dans les Aurès et survécut miraculeusement à trois mois de torture, en 1957, à Alger. Le dossier est accablant, les faits sont plus que crédibles – avérés.

Massu, 92 ans, était alors commandant militaire du département d'Alger. Depuis 1971 qu'il signa *la vraie bataille d'Alger*, il ne nie pas que la torture s'y pratiqua. Avec un peu plus de recul du temps, il concède aujourd'hui qu' « on aurait pu faire autrement ». En sa roideur militaire, Massu se prépare doucement à mourir. En vis-à-vis, dans la même page, Marcel Bigeard ne s'y résout pas.

Lui était colonel, alors. Sous Giscard président, il sera en 1976 secrétaire d'Etat (auprès du ministre de la Défense), imposant là sa faconde de soudard, assez appréciée, aux zincs des Ducon-Lajoie, où « les p'tits gars » de Bigeard firent sa gloire autant que son parachutage sur Diên Biên Phû. Un quart de siècle plus tard, c'est une épave qui s'exprime pour tout nier en bloc (« *Tout est faux, c'est une manœuvre* »). Ce fond ne surprend pas; la forme, si, à travers l'emploi pathétique de la troisième personne d'un singulier personnage, mi-révolté, mi-pleurnichard, qui rétorque à son intervieweuse: «Vous êtes en train de mettre un coup au cœur d'un homme de quatre-vingt-quatre ans. (...) Mais dites-vous bien que le vieux, il est battant, et qu'il sait mordre encore. »

On n'en doute pas, si toutefois son dentier veut bien adhérer à sa proposition. A l'attention de Florence Beaugé du *Monde* qui l'interroge pourtant sans gégène, le cacochyme général ose ce mot, qui appartient au registre du chantage sentimental: «Il y a de quoi se flinguer.» Mot terrible, en vérité. Mot terrible dans sa vérité. A le lire, on voit mieux pourquoi, dans les geôles où l'on torture ou pas, sont confisqués au prisonnier ceinture et lacets, et tous autres objets susceptibles de lui permettre d'en finir.

Pierre Marcelle, *Libération,* 23 June 2000

1.3. Analyse the following text, paying particular attention to:

a) the use of headlines

b) the visual element

c) the use of proper nouns and of cultural assumptions.

M. Jospin dans la tourmente des réformes

● Le gouvernement renonce à sa réforme de l'administration fiscale et recule sur l'enseignement professionnel ● « Mortifié », le ministre des finances souhaite démissionner ● Lionel Jospin lance la négociation sur l'avenir des retraites ● Il propose aux fonctionnaires de cotiser plus longtemps

LIONEL JOSPIN devait annoncer, mardi 21 mars à 17 heures, le détail de sa réforme des retraites. Retardé à plusieurs reprises, le dispositif du premier ministre vise d'abord à consolider le système de répartition. Créé en 1998, le fonds de réserve des retraites, qui ne devait accueillir en 2000 qu'à peine plus de 20 milliards de francs, sera abondé de plus de 500 milliards d'ici 2020 grâce à des recettes nouvelles en provenance notamment des dividendes des entreprises publiques.

Le volet le plus attendu et le plus risqué de cette réforme concerne la fonction publique. M. Jospin devrait proposer l'ouverture de négociations, destinées à aligner la durée de cotisations dans le secteur public (37,5 ans) sur celle qui prévaut depuis 1993 dans le privé (40 ans). Cette proposition serait contrebalancée, pour les fonctionnaires, par l'intégration des primes dans le calcul des pensions. Le plan Jospin comprend également un volet important consacré aux personnes âgées, avec l'annonce de la refonte complète de la prestation dépendance.

A la demande du premier ministre, qui s'exprimera mercredi matin sur RTL, Christian Sautter a annoncé, lundi soir, le retrait « *dans un souci de responsabilité et*

● Le plan Jospin sur les retraites. p. 8
● L'abandon de la réforme de l'administration fiscale. Récit. p. 9
● Le recul de Claude Allègre sur les LEP. p. 12
● Quelles matières enseigner à l'école ? p. 18

d'apaisement » de la reforme de Bercy, compte tenu « *de l'opposition persistante des organisations syndicales* ». « *Mortifié* », le ministre des finances souhaite démissionner. Dans l'éducation nationale, le climat reste également tendu, même si le ministre, Claude Allègre, est apparu « *ouvert* » et « *cooperatif* » aux syndicats de l'enseignement professionnel, qu'il a reçus lundi. Les représentants des professeurs ont annoncé que le ministre était prêt à renoncer à sa réforme des lycées professionnels. Deux manifestations sont maintenues mardi et vendredi.

Le Monde, 22 March 2000

1.4. Analyse the following text. What is the role of the quotation marks? How do you interpret the cartoon?

Quinquennat : Chirac change d'avis

● Le chef de l'Etat annonce à la télévision son ralliement à la réduction du mandat présidentiel ● Le 14 juillet 1999, il tenait le quinquennat pour une « erreur » ● La réforme serait soumise aux Français par référendum en octobre ● M. Chirac refuse toute limitation à deux mandats

« *LE PRÉSIDENT* de la République est élu pour cinq ans au suffrage universel direct » : ainsi est rédigé le projet de loi constitutionnelle que Jacques Chirac devait présenter aux Français, lundi soir 5 juin, au cours d'un entretien télévisé avec Patrick Poivre d'Arvor et Claude Sérillon. Le chef de l'Etat devait expliquer pourquoi il s'est résolu à la réduction de la durée du mandat présidentiel, pourquoi il s'est converti à un quinquennat qu'il a longtemps combattu – « *très réservé* » sur ce sujet le 14 juillet 1997, il le considérait comme une « *erreur* » le 14 juillet 1999 – et pourquoi il a décidé d'aller vite. La réforme pourrait être définitivement votée, par référendum, en octobre. Dans l'article 6 de la Constitution, le mot « *cinq* » remplacera alors le mot « *sept* ».

Lorsqu'il avait relancé l'idée du quinquennat, Valéry Giscard d'Estaing avait proposé de le limiter à deux mandats. M. Chirac et Lionel Jospin préfèrent le quinquennat sans limitation. Le président de la République, converti à la réduction du mandat présidentiel, ne se l'appliquera pas à lui-même. Le quinquennat concernera donc le prochain président. M. Chirac s'est aussi rallié au calendrier proposé par le premier ministre. Transmis dès lundi matin au Conseil d'Etat, le projet sera examiné à partir du 13 juin par l'Assemblée nationale et

EXPLIQUEZ-NOUS, PARCE QU'ON A UN PEU DE MAL À COMPRENDRE !

C'EST POURTANT SIMPLE !

pourrait l'être les 29 et 30 juin par le Sénat. Si tout se passe comme prévu, les Français pourraient se prononcer par référendum le 8 octobre, une des dates envisagées pour l'instant. M. Chirac devait cependant laisser ouverte la voie d'un vote par le Congrès, ce qui supposerait l'approbation de trois cinquièmes des députés et des sénateurs. Le chef de l'Etat devait aussi expliquer pourquoi le quinquennat, à son avis, ne modifiera pas les institutions de la Ve République. Cet avis n'est pas partagé par tous les dirigeants des partis politiques.

Lire pages 6 et 7

Le Monde, 6 June 2000

1.5. Analyse this text, paying particular attention to anglicisms and 'trendy' vocabulary. What are the cultural assumptions underlying the text?

AUJOURD'HUI-STYLES

Au rendez-vous de la fripe « millésimée »

À Paris, la rue Tiquetonne abrite des boutiques spécialisées dans le kitsch et le vêtement ancien garanti d'origine. Du pull de ski étriqué des « années Killy » aux jeans d'avant-guerre

ENTRE la rue Saint-Denis et la rue Etienne-Marcel, les vestiges de l'ancien ventre de Paris ont complètement disparu. Dans ce quartier du 2ᵉ arrondissement, semi-piéton depuis 1991, les boucheries désaffectées et les anciens entrepôts de grossistes de la rue Tiquetonne ont cédé la place depuis quatre ans aux boutiques de vêtements, aux bars et aux restaurants à la mode. « *C'est un quartier populaire-branché. La clientèle est variée, moins "ghetto" que dans le Marais* », se réjouit Mickaël Sillas, qui a ouvert au mois de juin 1998 Le Lézard, un café-terrasse installé au début de rue, à l'angle de la rue Etienne-Marcel, en face du Café, autre institution dans l'air du temps.

Côté mode, la rue Tiquetonne est l'un des passages obligés des amateurs de seconde main et de vintage, ces vêtements millésimés rigoureusement sélectionnés par les collectionneurs. « *La fripe, c'est la deuxième vie du vêtement, le désir de pas être dépendant d'une marque en particulier* », explique Stéphanie Audoin, directrice de M'zelle Margalette, bureau de presse spécialisé dans le vieux vêtement, jamais porté ou d'occasion, qui a quitté le 2ᵉ arrondissement pour la rue Tiquetonne.

« MARCEL » METALLICA

Les rédactrices de mode lui empruntent de tout, comme récemment des « Marcel » Metallica ou AC/DC, remis au goût du jour par Jeremy Scott. Installé au croisement de la rue Etienne-Marcel depuis 1995, Killwatch a doublé sa surface de vente en septembre 98 pour devenir un megastore de la seconde main de 600 mètres carrés.

Si la fripe des années 70 et la mode Deschiens ont fait leur temps, on porte aujourd'hui des Adidas sans âge avec une nuisette grand-mère ou un vieux trench Burberry's. Bernard Graf, PDG de liwatch et de la chaîne de vêtements au kilo Kiloshop, fait ses choix parmi 2 000 tonnes de linge entassés dans ses entrepôts de 5 000 m² situés à Rouen. Fort du succès de Didier Ludot, il inaugurera prochainement, dans la boutique de la rue Tiquetonne, un espace de pièces griffées, avec les imprimés d'Emilio Pucci ou les vieux Dior des années 60.

« *En 1999, l'engouement pour le vêtement de travail sous toutes ses formes va se poursuivre. On recherche de l'aisance et des coupures sages* », explique-t-il. Si certains traquent déjà les panoplies de chasse des années 50, d'autres se réapproprient sous complexe les symboles de l'univers carcéral américain, comme la chemise en chambray bleu marquée d'un

matricule. Très bien cotées aussi, la chemise de bowling brodée ou l'hawaïenne des années 50 peuvent se négocier 4 000 francs.

Au rayon des jeans, des modèles Levis s'acquièrent encore à 15 000 francs mais la marque des pionniers américains fait moins d'émules, après les sommets atteints lors de la vente à Drouot de 1992, où une veste en jean de 1937 s'est vendue... 43 000 francs. Aujourd'hui, les *fashion victims* traquent plutôt les jeans japonais, fabriqués sur des métiers à tisser traditionnels et siglés d'un liséré rouge.

Rue Tiquetonne, on en trouve chez Kult et Preppy Clothing, comme le Evisu vendu 1 500 francs dans un sac d'aspirateur. Avec une dizaine d'autres boutiques (du coiffeur-piercer-tatoueur à l'agence de voyages-épicerie mexicaine), ils se sont installés dans l'espace de deux ans dans un tron-

çon de rue longtemps déserté, situé entre la rue Saint-Denis et la rue Dussoubs. Des clins d'œil pour adolescents attardés, plus qu'une luxueuse panoplie griffée.

« *Le vintage, c'est une alternative aux uniformes Zara. On recherche l'ambiance de films et de séries cultes* », explique Nordine, ancien vendeur des Puces à la tête de la boutique Kult. Les jeunes consommateurs retrouvent des images de l'enfance, entre un tee-shirt publicitaire en coton de l'amicale laïque de Larmor Plage, le pull de ski étriqué des années Killy ou la chemise Dragon de Bruce Lee.

Au fil des arrivages, on peut dénicher un blouson en polyester étriqué tout droit sorti d'un épisode de *Starsky et Hutch* ou la montre de *Kojak*, une massive Pulsar en plaqué or à 4 000 francs. La demande se porte aussi sur les baskets au cuir raidi après quinze ans au fond d'une boîte. Au

« *Mon créneau, c'est l'achat impulsif d'objets complètement inutiles* », explique le propriétaire de la boutique PVC, ci-dessus.

Preppy Clothing, ci-contre, propose des clins d'œil pour adolescents attardés.

En bas à droite, la propriétaire suédoise de Chez Maman met l'accent sur le design des années 50 à 70.

moment où les marques exploitent le créneau vintage et rééditent leurs modèles phares, comme le jean Calvin Klein porté par Brooke Shield en 1978 ou les Country Adidas de 1978 – en rupture de stock dans de nombreux coloris un mois après leur sortie –, on vient chercher les authentiques.

Mais les Français se convertissent avec modération à ce culte du vêtement à histoire, alors que les sites Internet d'échange de sneakers éculées et les revues spécialisées affluent au Japon. Les prix flambent. Vendue 890 francs à son lancement en 1995, la paire d'Air Max de Nike s'est négociée jusqu'à 4 000 francs en France et 12 000 francs en boutique à Tokyo. Des Nike au logo calligraphié en arabe sont même cotées 17 000 francs. « *L'Asie représente 90 % du marché du vintage* », estime Bernard Graf, qui reconnaît

que la crise a sérieusement égratigné le business des collectionneurs du pays du Soleil-Levant.

La boutique Chez Maman se charge du mobilier qui complète cet univers vestimentaire. Là encore, les séries donnent le ton, de la chaise du *Prisonnier* à la chaîne hi-fi en plastique blanc de *2001 : l'Odyssée de l'espace*. Pièce la plus chère : un bar américain garni de zèbre récupéré dans un vieux pub du Bronx.

La propriétaire suédoise de l'enseigne met l'accent sur le design scandinave des années 50 à 70 avec un téléphone Cobra Ericson de 1954 ou un trône vert gazon de Verner Panton. A côté, Le Dénicheur excelle dans l'accessoire de mauvais goût. Presque tout est à vendre, dans ce lieu de restauration rapide, où talons-aiguilles en vernis noir et baromètre en coquillages peints sont accrochés au mur.

« *L'endroit le plus kitsch après chez ta mère* », précise un écriteau que tient un nain de jardin installé en vitrine. Plus kitsch encore, PVC (le Pays des vedettes célèbres), ouvert en avril 1998 regorge d'objets laids inspirés de « *l'utopie du tout-plastique ou des photos de Pierre et Gilles* », explique Julien Brunois, qui a lancé la marque en 1993. « *Mon créneau, c'est l'achat impulsif d'objets complètement inutiles* », précise le styliste. On trouve pêle-mêle des Aliens gonflables, une lampe en forme de fox-terrier ou une Vierge « *made in Lourdes* » en plastique phosphorescent.

Anne-Laure Quilleriet

Anne-Laure Quilleriet, *Le Monde*, 2 January 1999

315

1.6. Analyse the model of argumentation, register and genre of this text.

Les lettres, discipline plus cruciale que jamais *par Alain Viala*

CHAQUE moment de démocratisation de l'école a été un temps de conflits et de débats, en particulier sur l'enseignement des lettres. Depuis une décennie, le débat est plus nécessaire que jamais ; depuis quelque temps, il s'anime davantage : tant mieux. Mais pour qu'il soit fructueux, encore faut-il qu'il traite des vraies questions. Il y a quelques semaines, il s'embourbait dans des rumeurs. Elles sont dissipées, personne ne peut plus prétendre que les nouveaux programmes de lycée ont supprimé la dissertation, encore moins qu'ils sacrifient la littérature, quand au contraire ils la vivifient. Maintenant, les questions de fond peuvent reprendre la place centrale, qu'elles ont depuis des années dans les préoccupations de milliers de collègues des collèges et des lycées.

« *Le français est une discipline cruciale* » : je l'écrivais il y a cinq ans face à un projet de « *bi-disciplinarité* » pour les professeurs de collège, je le redis plus fort aujourd'hui. Les lettres – car ce qui est vrai du français l'est aussi, pour l'essentiel, des langues anciennes – sont *cruciales* parce qu'elles sont au croisement de trois enjeux majeurs : la langue, la littérature et la culture. Par la langue, elles mettent en jeu le lieu même de la pensée ; par la littérature, la sensibilité, les attitudes face à l'existence et le rapport à la culture ; et par celle-ci, l'esprit critique et la conscience historique.

L'identité de cette discipline est inséparable des fondements de notre identité culturelle, tant collective qu'individuelle. On ne peut donc dissocier ses trois exigences ; aussi le vrai débat consiste-t-il à rechercher le meilleur équilibre entre elles.

Mais l'enseignement du français est menacé par des dogmatismes qui aboutissent fatalement à scinder les trois enjeux. Non seulement ils peuvent stériliser la réflexion en vaines polémiques, mais il font aussi, pire, des ravages en pratique dans l'esprit des élèves. Pour s'en convaincre, il suffit de considérer par exemple le sort fait, dans les séries technologiques du lycée, à l'enseignement d'« *expression* » à finalité professionnelle : sous prétexte

d'utilité, il ne relève pas du cours de français. Ainsi ces élèves, qui ont tant besoin d'améliorer leur maîtrise de la langue et de la culture, sont induits à regarder celui-ci comme un alibi décoratif.

Mais il faut aussi voir que, dans une symétrie remarquable, la dissertation littéraire sur œuvres imposées a suscité un rejet de la part des bacheliers : au fil des ans, la proportion de candidats qui choisissent ce sujet a dégringolé, jusqu'à 1,5 % en 1999 dans les séries technologiques. Même en série littéraire, elle atteint à peine 10 %. Qui voudrait tuer la littérature et la dissertation n'a qu'à laisser cet étouffement s'achever.

La visée utilitaire, dans le premier cas, nie la valeur esthétique, mais un discours esthétique imposé, dans le second, n'a pas de prise. Ainsi, le dogme utilitariste et son symétrique, l'esthétisme, sont des Charybde et Scylla pour l'enseignement littéraire. Et les autres exercices du bac de français, ballottés entre ces deux écueils, ont dérivé vers le technicisme : le sens s'y perd dans le jargon creux, la démarche critique dans l'ânonnement, et la réflexion personnelle dans le psittacisme.

Il était urgent de sortir de ce cercle vicieux, de proposer d'autres' démarches. La démocratisation de l'école est aujourd'hui un défi historique. Le lycée n'est plus, comme il y a une génération, réservé à une minorité, et si nombre d'élèves n'ont pas reçu la culture littéraire par héritage familial, elle n'est pas non plus immédiate pour les autres : la vraie démocratisation exige donc de la donner à tous. Mais la répétition d'un petit nombre d'exercices formels sur un petit nombre de textes n'y suffira jamais : il y faut aussi des lectures d'œuvres plus nombreuses.

De même, la formation d'une culture active, gage d'autonomie, demande que la lecture soit sans cesse réinvestie dans l'écriture, pour nourrir le jugement – qui est le but de la dissertation – mais aussi l'invention. Enfin, une maîtrise effective de la langue exige d'associer la réflexion sur l'expression personnelle à l'observation des modèles.

Ces propositions structurent les nouveaux programmes. Elles appellent une démarche fondée sur des perspectives croisées, des lectures plurielles, et une approche critique de l'histoire littéraire – que les précédents programmes avaient désertée – qui fasse dialoguer le présent et le passé. Enfin et surtout, elles rendent aux professeurs le pouvoir de choisir, au sein d'un cadre commun, les œuvres qui nourriront le mieux la réflexion de leurs élèves ; ce faisant, elles leur

> ## Hugo a cloué au pilori de l'humour ceux qui estiment que les normes importent plus que les hommes : renvoyons-y les dogmatismes, et gardons l'œil fixé sur le pari de l'Ecole pour tous

rendent la confiance qui leur est due et l'autorité essentielle en matière d'enseignement.

Le débat s'éveille désormais à l'université ; tant mieux, car la recherche est la condition de toute rénovation. Le conflit éclate, à propos du Capes, entre l'espace des savoirs et celui de l'utilité pédagogique, qui hante les IUFM (instituts universitaires de formation des maîtres). Il est évident que les connaissances fondamentales doivent être premières. Mais il est clair aussi que la question est plus complexe.

Les lettres sont menacées par une conception restrictive de leur domaine (*cf.* Philippe Hamon dans votre page « Débats », *Le Monde* du 16 mars), et il serait néfaste de borner leur rôle à la préparation des concours. Mais, pour ne parler que de celle-ci, elle a tout à gagner à être d'abord renforcée à l'université : en développant des lectures plus nombreuses, en affirmant la maîtrise de la langue comme une priorité majeure, en ouvrant la réflexion culturelle sur l'histoire et la philosophie et, pour l'orientation professionnelle, l'histoire de la discipline. Du coup, le concours s'articulerait mieux au futur métier : par les épreuves de langue et de dissertation à l'écrit, et, à l'oral, par l'analyse de textes et par la réflexion sur l'enseignement des lettres, mais aussi par l'attention enfin portée à la capacité d'exposer et de dialo-

guer, qui est indispensable à l'exercice du métier d'enseignant.

Or la filière littéraire a aujourd'hui une chance de se donner une identité forte. A la charnière du lycée et de l'université, la terminale L change. La littérature en était absente ; grâce aux efforts de quelques-uns, elle y a conquis sa place ; d'abord réduite à la portion congrue de deux heures hebdomadaires, je vois qu'à force d'obstination elle en aura le double désormais. Preuve, si besoin était, que l'avenir des lettres réside d'abord dans la force des propositions que nous élaborerons. A leur mesure, elles influent aussi sur l'autre question-clef, celle des moyens indispensables.

Le Groupe technique disciplinaire a toujours tenu le débat ouvert, pour rédiger des projets comme pour les amender. Si ce débat s'englue dans le passionnel, il sera vain ; s'il est passionné mais lucide, il sera plus riche d'idées fortes. Hugo a cloué au pilori de l'humour, dans sa préface de *Cromwell*, ceux qui estiment que les normes importent plus que les hommes : renvoyons-y les dogmatismes, et gardons l'œil fixé sur le pari de l'école pour tous. L'enjeu essentiel des lettres, « *ce sont hommes* », le rôle de leur enseignement, c'est de donner les fondements de la pensée et de l'identité. A une époque où l'univers des discours change, elles sont cruciales plus que jamais.

Alain Viala est professeur de littérature française aux universités de Paris-III - Sorbonne nouvelle et d'Oxford, président du Groupe technique disciplinaire lettres.

Alain Viala, *Le Monde,* 22 March 2000

2. Literary and other texts

2.1. Conduct a full analysis of this text, paying particular attention to cohesive features (coreferents, connectors...) and to the notions of register and genre.

La chute des étoiles.

Pourquoi scrutons-nous avec une curiosité malsaine les liaisons, les ruptures, les deuils de ceux qu'on appelle les stars? C'est que ces êtres hors du commun à qui il suffit d'apparaître pour être et que l'on reconnaît même si on ne les connaît pas, ces êtres qu'aucun tabou, aucun excès ne retient ne sont vénérés que pour être ensuite ramenés au niveau commun. Condensant sur eux la plus vaste quantité de désir social, ils devraient avoir pour fonction de nous soustraire à l'empire de la monotonie; mais ils ne le perturbent que pour mieux le confirmer. Et la presse du cœur n'existe peut-être que pour rassurer ses lecteurs, les certifier dans l'idée que princes, vedettes de cinéma et du show-biz sont les incarnations ambivalentes du bonheur, d'un idéal qu'ils peinent à réaliser. De là notre délectation amère de les voir frappés des mêmes maux que nous.

Ces *happy few* censés sublimer notre destin, nous arracher à nos soucis ridicules, à nos malheurs insignifiants nous prouvent qu'aucune caste ou classe supérieure ne connaît la béatitude, seul apanage des dieux, disait déjà Aristote, alors que «les hommes sont heureux autant qu'un mortel peut l'être». Et qu'enfin une secrétaire peut avoir la vie tumultueuse et agitée d'une princesse et une princesse mener l'existence rangée et popote d'une ménagère. C'est cela le processus démocratique: les orgies et les excès sardanapalesques des anciens monarques sont désormais accessibles au tout-venant. A travers les indiscrétions des médias, nous vérifions avec soulagement et tristesse que ces gens-là ne sont pas d'une autre essence que nous: en quoi ces mêmes médias constituent aussi des *machines à freiner l'envie* et remplissent derrière leur futilité un rôle essentiel. Dans son panthéon clinquant, la star échappe peut-être à l'anonymat mais elle succombe tout comme nous au désarroi, à la solitude, à l'âge (la disparition progressive de la beauté chez les actrices somptueuses est une figure de rhétorique obligée dans une certaine presse qui la consigne avec un sadisme navré). Nous élisons les stars comme les hommes politiques et les gommons avec la même indifférence, la même versatilité. Notre appétit de ragots, de détails n'a pas sa source, comme on l'a dit, dans l'aliénation ou la dépossession. Le culte de la célébrité puise directement et contradictoirement dans les progrès de l'égalisation démocratique.

Pascal Bruckner, *L'Euphorie perpétuelle*

2.2. Study this text, paying particular attention to:

a) lexical fields

b) cultural assumptions

c) register and genre.

La lecture comme construction

On ne perçoit pas l'omniprésent. Rien de plus commun que l'expérience de la lecture, et rien de plus ignoré. Lire: cela va tellement de soi qu'il semble, à première vue, qu'il n'y ait rien à en dire.

Dans les études sur la littérature, on a parfois – rarement – envisagé le problème de la lecture, de deux points de vue très différents: l'un prend en compte les lecteurs, dans leur diversité historique ou sociale, collective ou individuelle; l'autre, l'image du lecteur, telle qu'elle se trouve représentée dans certains textes: le lecteur comme personnage, ou encore comme 'narrataire'. Mais il reste un domaine inexploré, celui de la logique de la lecture, qui n'est pas représentée dans le texte et qui pourtant est antérieure à la différence individuelle.

Il existe plusieurs types de lecture. Je ne m'arrêterai ici que sur un seul d'entre eux, non le moindre: la lecture des textes de fiction classiques, plus exactement des textes dits représentatifs. C'est cette lecture et elle seule qui s'effectue comme une construction.

Bien que nous ayons cessé de considérer l'art et la littérature comme une imitation, nous avons du mal à nous débarrasser d'une manière de voir, inscrite jusque dans nos habitudes linguistiques, qui consiste à penser le roman en termes de représentation, de transposition d'une réalité – qui lui serait préexistante. Même si elle ne cherche à décrire que le processus de création, cette vision fait déjà problème; elle est franchement déformante si elle se rapporte au texte même. Ce qui existe, d'abord, c'est le texte, et rien que lui; ce n'est qu'en le soumettant à un type particulier de lecture que nous construisons, à partir de lui, un univers imaginaire. Le roman n'imite pas la réalité, il la crée: cette formule des préromantiques n'est pas une seule innovation terminologique; seule la perspective de construction nous permet de comprendre correctement le fonctionnement du texte dit représentatif.

La question de la lecture se rétrécit donc de la manière suivante: comment un texte nous conduit-il à la construction d'un univers imaginaire? Quels sont les aspects du texte qui déterminent la construction que nous produisons lors de la lecture, et de quelle façon?

Tzvetan Todorov, *La Lecture comme construction,* in *Poétique de la prose*

2.3. Analyse this opening passage from Proust, paying particular attention to the use of cohesive devices such as:
   a) use of pronouns
   b) demonstrative determiners
   c) possessives
   d) connectors
   e) similes.

Longtemps je me suis couché de bonne heure. Parfois, à peine ma bougie éteinte, mes yeux se fermaient si vite que je n'avais pas le temps de me dire: «je m'endors». Et, une demi-heure après, la pensée qu'il était temps de chercher le sommeil m'éveillait; je voulais poser le volume que je croyais avoir encore dans les mains et souffler ma lumière; je n'avais pas cessé en dormant de faire des réflexions sur ce que je venais de lire, mais ces réflexions avaient pris un tour un peu particulier; il me semblait que j'étais moi-même ce dont parlait l'ouvrage: une église, un quatuor, la rivalité de François 1er et de Charles-Quint. Cette croyance survivait pendant quelques secondes à mon réveil; elle ne choquait pas ma raison, mais pesait comme des écailles sur mes yeux et les empêchait de se rendre compte que le bougeoir n'était plus allumé. Puis elle commençait à me devenir inintelligible, comme après la métempsycose les pensées d'une existence antérieure; le sujet du livre se détachait de moi, j'étais libre de m'y appliquer ou non; aussitôt je recouvrais la vue et j'étais bien étonné de trouver autour de moi une obscurité, douce et reposante pour mes yeux, mais peut-être plus encore pour mon esprit, à qui elle apparaissait comme une chose sans cause, incompréhensible, comme une chose vraiment obscure. Je me demandais quelle heure il pouvait être; j'entendais le sifflement des trains qui, plus ou moins éloigné, comme le chant d'un oiseau dans une forêt, relevant les distances, me décrivait l'étendue de la campagne déserte où le voyageur se hâte vers la station prochaine; et le petit chemin qu'il suit va être gravé dans son souvenir par l'excitation qu'il doit à des lieux nouveaux, à des actes inaccoutumés, à la causerie récente et aux adieux sous la lampe étrangère qui le suivent encore dans le silence de la nuit, à la douceur prochaine du retour.

Marcel Proust, *Du Côté de chez Swann*

2.4. Study this extract from Marcel Pagnol's *Le Temps des secrets,* paying particular attention to the following features:

a) the relevance of the title in relation to the extract
b) the presence of the narrator and its influence on the narration of events
c) the use of verbal moods and tenses in relation to the objectivity of the text
d) the syntactic cohesion such as the use of connectors and punctuation.

Rewrite this text from the point of view of a neutral observer and analyse to what extent the text has changed its register.

La musette à l'épaule, et mon bâton à la main, je partis tout seul vers les collines enchantées.

Pour aller au «champ des becfigues», je n'avais qu'à traverser le petit plateau des Bellons et à descendre dans le vallon: en remontant le fond de la faille, je pouvais arriver au champ perdu en moins d'une heure. Mais je décidai de faire un détour par les crêtes, en passant sur l'épaule de la Tête-Ronde, dont la noire pinède terminale, au-dessus de trois bandeaux de roche blanche, se dressait dans le ciel du matin.

Le puissant soleil de juillet faisait grésiller les cigales: sur le bord du chemin muletier, des toiles d'araignée brillaient entre les genêts. En montant lentement vers le jas de Baptiste, je posais mes sandales dans mes pas de l'année dernière et le paysage me reconnaissait.

Au tournant de Redouneou, deux alouettes huppées, aussi grosses que des merles, jaillirent d'un térébinthe: j'épaulai mon bâton, je pris mon temps (comme l'oncle Jules), et je criai: 'Pan! Pan!'. Je décidai que j'avais tué la première, mais que j'avais tiré trop bas pour la seconde et j'en fus navré.

La vieille bergerie avait perdu la moitié de son toit; mais contre le mur en ruine, le figuier n'avait pas changé: au-dessus de sa verte couronne, la haute branche morte se dressait toujours, toute noire contre l'azur.

Je serrai le tronc dans mes bras, sous le bourdonnement des abeilles qui suçaient le miel des figues ridées, et je baisai sa peau d'éléphant en murmurant des mots d'amitié.

Puis je suivis la longue 'barre' qui dominait la plaine en pente de la Garette... Sur le bord de l'à-pic, je retrouvai les petits tas de pierres que j'avais construits de mes mains pour attirer les culs-blancs, ou les alouettes des montagnes... C'est au pied de ces perchoirs que nous placions nos pièges l'année précédente, c'est-à-dire au temps jadis...

Lorsque j'arrivai au pied du chapiteau du Taoumé, j'allai m'asseoir sous le grand pin oblique, et je regardai longuement le paysage.

Au loin, très loin, sur ma droite, au-delà de collines plus basses, la mer matinale brillait.

Devant moi, au pied de la chaîne de Marseille-Veyre, nue et blanche comme une sierra, des brumes légères flottaient sur la longue vallée de l'Huveaune…

Enfin, à ma gauche, la haute barre feuilletée du Plan de l'Aigle soutenait l'immense plateau qui montait, par une pente douce, jusqu'à la nuque de Garlaban.

Une brise légère venait de se lever: elle attisa soudain le parfum du thym et des lavandes. Appuyé sur mes mains posées derrière moi, le buste penché en arrière, je respirais, les yeux fermés, l'odeur brûlante de ma patrie, lorsque je sentis sous ma paume, à travers le tapis de ramilles de pin, quelque chose de dur qui n'était pas une pierre. Je grattai le sol, et je mis au jour un piège de laiton, un piège à grives tout noir de rouille: sans doute l'un de ceux que nous avions perdus le jour de l'orage, à la fin des vacances… Je le regardai longuement, aussi ému que l'archéologue qui découvre au fond d'une fouille le miroir éteint d'une reine morte… Il était donc resté là toute une année, sous les petites aiguilles sèches qui étaient tombées lentement sur lui, l'une après l'autre, pendant que les jours tombaient sur moi… Il avait dû se croire perdu à jamais…

Marcel Pagnol, *Le Temps des secrets*

2.5. Analyse this Baudelaire poem, paying particular attention to the use of lexical fields.

L'ennemi

Ma jeunesse ne fut qu'un ténébreux orage,
Traversé çà et là par de brillants soleils;
Le tonnerre et la pluie ont fait un tel ravage,
Qu'il reste en mon jardin bien peu de fruits vermeils.

Voilà que j'ai touché l'automne des idées,
Et qu'il faut employer la pelle et les râteaux
Pour rassembler à neuf les terres inondées,
Où l'eau creuse des trous grands comme des tombeaux.

Et qui sait si les fleurs nouvelles que je rêve
Trouveront dans ce sol lavé comme une grève
Le mystique aliment qui ferait leur vigueur?

– Ô douleur! ô douleur! Le Temps mange la vie,
Et l'obscur Ennemi qui nous ronge le cœur
Du sang que nous perdons croît et se fortifie!

Baudelaire, *L'Ennemi,* in *Les Fleurs du mal*

2.6. Analyse this calligramme by Apollinaire.

La mandoline, l'œillet et le bambou

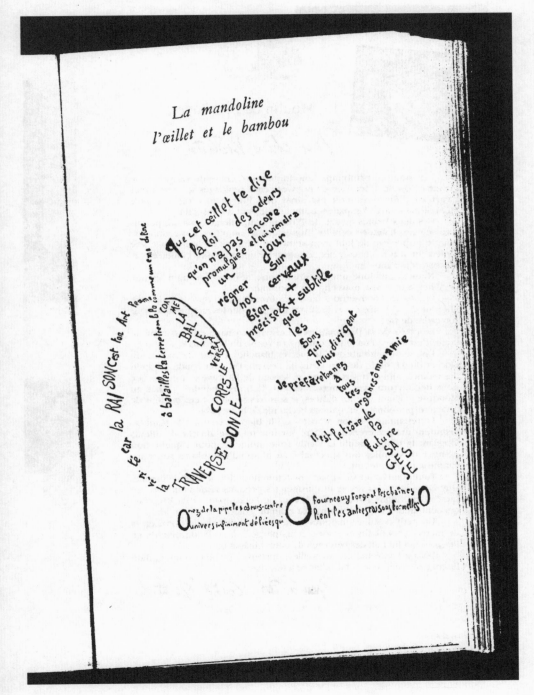

3. Advertisements

3.1a. Analyse the following two advertisements.

LES NIDS D'AMOUR

Le Moulin de l'Abbaye

Ma chère Violette

J'ai, pour ce printemps, une impérieuse envie de terroir et de France profonde. L'occasion de ces week-ends prolongés se prête à mes caprices d'évasion, et c'est ainsi que Pierre m'a rejoint gare Montparnasse, avec l'impatience amoureuse dont il a le secret. Ces deux heures quinze de TGV vers Angoulême nous ont permis d'aplanir nos habituels conflits. Tu sais que je me refuse à la routine du couple et préfère de loin mon statut de fiancée. En bref, ma chère Violette, je n'ai pas encore acquis ta sagesse… mais je sais combien mes inconstances t'amusent !

Nous avions loué une voiture à notre descente du train, et une demi-heure plus tard, nous étions à Brantôme.

Brantôme, l'écrivain des fameuses *Dames Galantes* – la littérature libertine du XVIᵉ siècle – avait autant de goût pour les femmes que pour son cadre de vie !

Le cours de la Dronne enserre ce vieux village en dessinant un cœur, c'est ainsi qu'on le surnomme « La Venise du Périgord ».

Une imposante abbaye de pierres blanches à flanc de rocher, un clocher du XIᵉ siècle (le plus vieux de France). Un pont coudé, le jardin des moines, tout cela sert d'écrin au Moulin de l'Abbaye et c'est ce que nous découvrons avec émerveillement de notre chambre « Château Montrose ». Plutôt que les palaces, je suis très sensible à ces maisons de caractère, personnalisées, qui font le charme de notre pays.

Le restaurant – façon Monet – où le bleu, le jaune et le blanc se disputent ma préférence, s'ouvre sur une terrasse abritée de tilleuls longeant la rivière. Seule la vieille roue moussue, pour laquelle bon nombre de couples ont succombé au plaisir d'une photo souvenir, égrène le temps présent.

Pour que chaque dîner soit une fête renouvelée, le chef de cuisine, Guy Guénégo, a su revoir et cuisiner les produits régionaux avec un sacré talent. Nous avons arrosé le tout de Pécharmant et de Bergerac, qui donnèrent à nos soirées un petit grain de gaieté !

Un petit déjeuner majestueux nous réveillait chaque matin et, la dernière « chocolatine » avalée, nous partions à la découverte de ce Périgord qui fut l'un des berceaux de notre civilisation.

Voilà ma Violette, ces merveilleux instants à peine envolés, et mon Pierre pense déjà que je lui échappe à nouveau…

Bien à toi, Cathy Bedford.

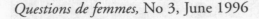

Questions de femmes, No 3, June 1996

3.1b.

De retour dans nos belles régions françaises, Cathy Bedford a débusqué un moulin dans la verte Dordogne.

Le Moulin de l'Abbaye,
24310 Brantôme.
Relais et Châteaux
Tél. : (16) 53 05 80 22.
Fax : (16) 53 05 75 27.
Tarifs
Chambres : de 550 F
à 900 F (« Château
Montrose » : 850 F)
Suites : de 1 000 F
à 1 350 F (possibilité
demi-pension)
Menus : de 220 F
à 450 F.
Carte : de 400 F
à 480 F.
Directeurs :
Bernard
et Yvette Dessum

D.R. Ces pages sont libres de toute publicité et de toute complaisance.

Brantôme
La Venise du Périgord

Questions de femmes 97

3.2. Analyse the following advertisement.

Varilux,® Anti Effet Retard.™
Vous n'aviez jamais vu comme ça.

Dès vos premières lunettes, les verres Varilux Comfort et leur système Anti Effet Retard vous permettront de voir net à toutes les distances, instantanément. Et ceci, avec une seule paire de lunettes.

Varilux Comfort combat les effets retard, ces temps morts qui, avec d'autres verres progressifs, empêchent de faire la mise au point dans l'instant même. Alors, finis les mouvements de tête inconfortables pour trouver l'image nette, et les champs de vision trop limités. De plus, vos verres Varilux sont réalisés sur mesure, en fonction de vos besoins et de votre mode de vie.

Et surtout, vous vous y habituerez très vite, Essilor s'y engage: c'est l'adaptation rapide garantie* Varilux Comfort. Une Carte de Vue vous sera remise par votre Opticien lors de l'achat: elle matérialise cet engagement et prouve l'authenticité de vos verres Varilux.

Alors, n'attendez plus, et demandez conseil à votre Spécialiste.

VARILUX®
UN VERRE ESSILOR

*Adaptation Garantie sous 1 mois maximum: voir modalités dans le Guide d'Utilisation Varilux Comfort remis avec vos verres.

Télérama, No 2449, 21-27 December 1996

3.3. Analyse the following advertisement.

Télérama, No 2630, 10-16 June 2000

GLOSSARY

abstract/concrete nouns (*noms abstraits/concrets*)

Abstract nouns are nouns which refer to qualities, emotions, states, etc., for instance *la beauté, le bonheur, la fatigue*.

Concrete nouns are nouns which refer to entities which can be seen or touched, for instance *une table, un chat*.

acronym (*sigle*)

An acronym is a method of word-formation whereby words are formed from the initial letters of a group of words. For instance *l'ONU* is an acronym which stands for *l'Organisation des Nations Unies*.

actantial narrative schema (*schéma narratif actantiel*)

The actantial narrative model is the name given to a fundamental narrative model elaborated by the French semiotician A.J. Greimas. This schema presents six key narrative functions or roles arranged in three sets of binary opposition: subject/object, sender/receiver, helper/opponent. Together, the six actants and their organisation account for all possible relationships within a story and indeed within the sphere of human action in general:

Sender ——— Object ——→ Receiver

Helper ——→ Subject ←—— Opponent

The role of anti-subject, a variant of the opponent, may also be included within this diagram. These narrative positions may be held by people, places, objects, or abstract ideas.

See under separate headings for definitions of each particular actant.

alliteration, assonance (*allitération, assonance*)

Alliteration, from the Latin *littera* ('letter') is a phonological device which concerns the repetition of the initial **consonant** in two or more words in the same phrase or sentence. For instance:

> *Pour qui sont ces serpents qui sifflent sur vos têtes.*
> (Racine, *Andromaque*)

Assonance, from the Latin *sonare* ('to sound') concerns the repetition of the same **vowel** sound in a phrase or sentence (e.g. *les longs sanglots des violons*).

anaphora, anaphoric reference (*anaphore, référence anaphorique*)

a) In grammar, an anaphora serves to link two utterances, two paragraphs, etc. by using a connecting term referring **back** to some concept already mentioned. For example, in *Marie est entrée dans le jardin.* ***Elle*** *portait une jolie robe à fleurs,* the third person personal pronoun *elle* functions as an anaphora referring back to *Marie.* Anaphora is a key device in the establishment of textual cohesion.

See also **cataphora**.

b) In rhetoric, anaphora is a figure of speech involving repetition of the same word or expression at the beginning of sentences, in order to create a dramatic emphatic effect.

animate/inanimate (*animé / inanimé*)

The term 'animate' refers to human beings and animals, whilst the term 'inanimate' refers to objects, including plants. This distinction is important in French grammar where, for instance, the interrogative pronoun *qui* is reserved for animates and *que* for inanimates. In English, such a difference will apply to relative pronouns, with 'who' reserved for animates and 'which' for inanimates. The distinction is also important semantically, so that for instance nouns and verbs must be paired off (i.e. must collocate) appropriately. For instance, whilst in English you can say 'Paul **agrees** with Mary' as well as 'The adjective **agrees** with the noun', French distinguishes between *Paul* ***est d'accord*** *avec Mary* and *L'adjectif* ***s'accorde*** *avec le nom.* Violation of these rules lead to either nonsense or metaphors.

aphesis, apocope (*aphérèse, apocope*)

With aphesis, the **initial** syllable of a word is omitted, for instance *le bus* for *l'autobus.*

With apocope, the **last** syllable of a word is omitted, for instance *une photo* for *une photographie, un ado* for *un adolescent, un amphi* for *un amphithéâtre.*

apposition (*apposition*)

In a sentence, an apposition is usually a noun phrase appearing between commas, with the same referent as the subject of the sentence. Appositions are usually either identifying, with a proper noun or a noun preceded by a definite article (e.g. *Cet homme, M. Mitterrand, . . .* or *Cet homme, l'ancien président de la République*) or descriptive, with an indefinite (e.g. *Cet homme, un ancien président de la République*).

argumentative text (*texte argumentatif*)

An argumentative text is a text that puts forward and defends a particular point of view. Its overall aim is to persuade the reader to adopt this point of view as opposed to any other. To achieve this aim, a number of rhetorical* procedures are set in place. These may include:

1) the use of a dialectical* structure where both sides of the argument are put
   or/and

2) a progressive development of the argument through, for example, techniques of demonstration and examplification (with the use of logical connectors* such as *en outre, certes, par conséquent*).

An argumentative text can usually be divided into three broad sections, producing a **model of argumentation** (*modèle d'argumentation*):

a) the statement of the narrator's position

b) the justification for this position: this part may contain a presentation of the evidence and an elaboration of the initial standpoint. It may also contain an outline of the arguments for and against.

c) the conclusion: this may include a logical expansion of what has already been said, or it could simply formulate – or restate – the narrator's acceptance or rejection of a particular argument.

aspect (*aspect*)

Applied to verbs, 'aspect' refers to the perspective or point of view from which a story is viewed by the narrator.

> **Grammatical aspect** is determined by the form of the conjugation: either **accomplished** with compound tenses (e.g. *il a mangé*) or **non-accomplished** with simple tenses (e.g. *il mange*).

> **Lexical aspect** – or mode of action – concerns the meaning of the verb, which can be **stative** (e.g. *être, avoir, sembler, connaître*) or dynamic and thus either **perfective**, i.e. the process can be envisaged to its completion (e.g. *arriver, entrer, sortir, trouver*) or **imperfective**, i.e. the process is envisaged in its duration (e.g. *chanter, manger, dormir, chercher*).

asyndeton/polysyndeton (*asyndète/polysyndète*)

Asyndeton describes the marked **absence** of conjunctions in a sentence (e.g. *Il m'a demandé, prié, supplié de le faire à sa place*).

Polysyndeton describes the marked **accumulation** of conjunctions in a sentence (e.g. *Ce chat est jeune et beau et intelligent et il sait tout faire*).

canonical narrative schema (*schéma narratif canonique*)

The canonical narrative schema is the name given to the second of the narrative models devised by the French semiotician A. J. Greimas. Like the actantial narrative schema* (of which it is a development), the canonical narrative schema presents a universal prototype for the structure of narrative. It is composed of three tests: the qualifying test, the decisive test and the glorifying test, which unfold in a logical succession. These tests are preceded by the stage of manipulation or contract.

contract	competence	performance	sanction
	qualifying test	**decisive test**	**glorifying test**
acquisition of a wanting-to-do or a having-to-do	acquisition of a being-able-to-do and/or of a knowing-how-to-do	the primary event where object of value is at stake	action of subject is evaluated: success/failure praise/blame

This narrative macro-structure can be exploited by individual texts in a variety of different ways. Certain stages or tests may be foregrounded, others remain implicit: in adventure stories, for example, the emphasis is on the decisive test, whereas legal discourse is centred more on the stage of sanction.

cataphora, cataphoric reference (*cataphore, référence cataphorique*)

Cataphora denotes a linguistic reference which is forward-looking (as opposed to anaphora*, which is backward-looking), thus creating a kind of 'suspense', or helping to emphasize a particular element of a sentence, often with a dislocated structure (e.g. *Il l'a finalement vendue, sa voiture, Paul*).

clause (*proposition*)

A clause is a syntactic structure comprising a noun phrase (the subject) and a verb phrase (the predicate), hence it is equivalent to a **simple sentence** (e.g. *Le chat boit son lait*).

See also **sentence, phrase**.

coherence, coherent (*cohérence, cohérent*)

In contrast to **cohesion***, coherence is a semantic or even pragmatic concept and refers to the logical consistency of a text. The less cohesion there is in a text, the more coherence depends on inference (see **cultural assumptions, knowledge of the world**).

cohesion, cohesive (*cohesion, cohésif*)

According to Halliday and Hasan (1976), cohesion is a syntactic concept and refers to the various ways sentences are organised to form larger units such as paragraphs, chapters, etc., i.e. texts. Cohesive ties, or links, can be explicit (see for instance **coreference**) or implicit (see **ellipsis**).

collocation (*collocation*)

Collocation refers to the expected co-occurrence of words (e.g. *des éléphants gris* or *roses* but not *des éléphants verts* or *noirs; effacer un mot* but *enlever une tache; battre les œufs* but *faire la mayonnaise; retrousser ses manches, débarrasser la table,* etc.). Ignoring these expected associations leads to either nonsense or metaphors*.

See also **animate/inanimate**.

concrete/abstract nouns
See **abstract nouns**.

connector (*connecteur*)

A connector is a link word (or group of words) that binds two parts of a text together, thus signalling (i.e. rendering explicit) a logical relationship. It constitutes, therefore, a key device in the creation of textual cohesion*.

Connectors may take the form of conjunctions (*puis, mais, quand, avant que*), or set phrases and expressions (*en conséquence, la raison en est que*). According to Halliday and Hasan (1976), there are four main groups of connectors: temporal, causal, adversative and additive.

connotation (*connotation*)

Connotation refers to a procedure whereby a term, in addition to meanings allotted to it in a dictionary (denotative* meanings) acquires additional significance resulting from the context in which it is applied. In this sense, the term *blancheur*, apart from **denoting** a colour, might **connote** *le désir, l'absence, la spiritualité, la pureté, la mort,* etc. depending on the conditions of its application.

context (*contexte*)

Grammatical (or linguistic) context refers to what surrounds a particular word or sentence, paragraph, etc. and contributes to the understanding of that word, sentence, etc., sometimes called the co-text. Third person pronouns (*il, elle, ils, elles*) are typically used in grammatical context. For instance, in *J'ai vu Paul hier. Il avait l'air pressé,* the *il* of the second sentence can only be understood (interpreted) in relation to *Paul,* its coreferent in the previous sentence.

Situational context refers to the immediate environment which prevails when a communication takes place and includes exophoric reference (pointing at the particular object which is mentioned), but also, more remotely, to cultural assumptions and knowledge of the world. For instance, *Je prendrai celles-ci* can only be understood if the person points at particular objects when saying this; *Je suis désolée d'être en retard: la voiture ne voulait pas démarrer,* where *la voiture* will be understood as the car owned or normally used by whoever says *je*.

contrast (*contraste*)

Contrast is expressed through the use of comparative forms as well as words such as *même, autre* and *tel.* For Halliday and Hasan (1976), contrast plays an important role in the establishment of textual cohesion*.

See also **simile**.

coreference (*coréférence*)

Coreference designates the procedure of referring backwards (anaphoric reference*) or forwards (cataphoric reference*) to the **same item** within a text. It is one of the principal methods whereby textual cohesion is established. Coreference can be expressed in the use of reference words such as personal pronouns, demonstratives, possessives, definitive articles and comparative constructions. It can also be expressed in the use of ellipsis* where a structural element is omitted and can only be recovered by referring to an element in the preceding text.

cultural assumptions; knowledge of the world

The terms 'cultural assumptions' or 'knowledge of the world' describe the cultural presuppositions that underly a text and that play a key role in the establishment of coherence. Indeed, without the assumption of a shared knowledge of the world, some texts would be totally meaningless. An example would be the newspaper headline: 'Minister condemns spin-doctoring'. Cultural assumptions, therefore, relate to the procedure of reference **outside the text**, a procedure that – in this case – is culture-bound.

deixis, deictic (*déixis, déictique*)

Deixis refers to the 'here' and 'now' of the speaker. For instance, *Je viendrai te voir ici demain à 8 heures* can only be understood (interpreted) if the addressee shares the time of enunciation with the speaker (the same utterance, found written on a piece of paper in the street would be meaningless to anybody except perhaps Sherlock Holmes!)

denotation (*dénotation*)

Denotation designates the process of referring to the dictionary meanings of a word. It is often opposed to connotation*, which relates to additional meanings resulting from the context in which the word is used. The English word 'rose', for example, **denotes** a flower or the shrub bearing it. In a particular context, however, the word 'rose' might **connote** love or the House of Tudor.

dialectical (*dialectique*)

The term 'dialectical' relates to texts whose primary concern is with the presentation of both sides of an argument, the *pro* and *contra*. This structure characterises argumentative texts*.

discours/récit

According to Benveniste (1966), *discours* concerns the **subjective** mode of utterance and involves both addresser and addressee in the situation of enunciation*. *Récit* is the **objective** mode and concerns the narration of events in the past. Texts often show a mixture of the two modes.

discourse

For Halliday, the term 'discourse' designates a unit of language larger than a sentence and which is firmly rooted in a specific context. There are many different types of discourse such as academic discourse, legal discourse, media discourse, etc. Each discourse type possesses its own characteristic linguistic features. This understanding of the term is generally accepted in discourse analysis.

discourse modes (*modes de discours*)

According to rhetorical theory, texts can be classified by reference to general modes of organisation. These include:
a) the narrative mode
b) the descriptive mode
c) the argumentative mode
d) the expository mode.

ellipsis (*ellipse*)

An ellipsis is the omission of part of an utterance, but which can be understood by the hearer or reader through the context (situational or linguistic). For instance, *Deux s'il vous plaît* will be understood as *Deux croissants s'il vous plaît* if the speaker points at the same time at a tray of croissants (sometimes called exophoric reference). Ellipsis is used as a matter of course in answers to questions. For instance, *Sur la chaise* could be the answer to *Où as-tu mis mon manteau?* (rather than *J'ai mis ton manteau sur la chaise*).

emphasis (*emphase*)

Emphasis can be made to bear on particular parts of an utterance thanks to various syntactic devices such as dislocated constructions (*Sa voiture, il l'a vendue à Michel*) or cleft constructions (*C'est à Michel qu'il a vendu sa voiture*) or use of certain adverbs (*Je vous avais pourtant bien prévenu!*).

enunciation (*énonciation*)

Enunciation is a language (speech) act designating the actual production of discourse. It involves two domains, that of the **enunciator** and that of the **enunciatee**. The enunciator is the implicit sender of the enunciation (or 'communication'), not to be confused with the narrator (for instance the *je* in *La Recherche du temps perdu*, who is a character in the story, or the external third person narrator in *Germinal*). The enunciatee is the implicit receiver of the enunciation, to be distinguished from the narratee, recognizable within the utterance (for example 'The reader will be amazed...'). Hence the author Albert Camus is the enunciator of the novel *L'Etranger*. Camus delegates his voice to a narrating instance, here finding expression in the narrative actant *je*. The enunciatee of *L'Etranger* is the reading public.

The term **addresser** is equivalent to enunciator, and the term **addressee** to enunciatee.

exophora, exophoric reference (*exophore, référence exophorique*)

Exophoric reference normally refers to the immediate situational context in which the discourse is taking place. For instance, *Fermez la porte!* will only be understood if the speaker points at a particular door, or if there is only one door in the immediate surroundings of both speaker and addressee.

Note that some linguists call exophoric reference anything outside the text.

figurative meaning

In semiotics, the term 'figurative' is similar in meaning to the term **concrete** and can be contrasted with the terms **abstract** and **conceptual**. The figurative meaning of a text emerges in the choice and organisation of the lexical fields. For instance, a passage might illustrate the lexical fields of movement (e.g. a description of budding flowers in spring, a baby being born), of sound (birds singing), of colour (trees blossoming). The abstract meaning underlying this particular passage is that of life.

Figurative meaning (*sens figuré*) also refers to words which are semantically or grammatically marked in some way and includes metaphors, similes, puns, slang, etc. (e.g. *Il est beurré* for *Il est saoûl*), where it is opposed to 'proper meaning' (*sens propre*).

figures of speech (*figures de style*)

See separately:
  metaphor
  metonymy
  hyperbole
  simile.

focus (*focus*)

Focus, or linguistic foregrounding, refers to the centre of interest or emphasis of an utterance, i.e. the new and thus important information. Focus is opposed to theme *(thème),* normally of low information value (either because the info has already been given or it is presupposed). For instance, in the answer to the question *Que fait le chat? Il boit son lait, il* is the theme (old information) and *boit son lait* is the focus (new, important information).

free indirect speech (*discours indirect libre*)

This refers to reported speech in which the speech of the character(s) and the words of the narrator are blurred. This device is common in novels, particularly from the 19th century, where the narrator can thus influence the reader. For instance:

> *Il haussait la voix, le ventre en avant, planté carrément sur ses grosses jambes. Et toute sa nature d'homme raisonnable et patient se confessait en phrases claires, qui coulaient abondantes, sans effort. Est-ce que ce n'était pas stupide de croire qu'on pouvait d'un coup changer le monde, mettre les ouvriers à la place des patrons, partager l'argent comme on partage une pomme? Il faudrait des mille ans et des mille ans pour que ça se réalisât peut-être. Alors qu'on lui fichât la paix, avec les miracles!*

> (Emile Zola, *Germinal*)

generic (*générique*)

The term generic refers to **classes** of objects, as opposed to specific entities. For instance, in *Les chats aiment le poisson, chats* is used in its generic sense (all the cats as a species). On the contrary, in *C'est moi qui m'occupe des (de + les) chats de la voisine, chats* is used in its specific sense (specifically the neighbour's cats).

genre (*genre*)

Genre refers to literature as consisting of different types such as poetry, prose and drama, from which further sub-genres can be distinguished (e.g. tragedy and comedy within drama).

hyperbole (*hyperbole*)

Hyperbole is a figure of speech expressing an exaggeration. Its meaning should not be taken literally. It is frequently used to convey intensity of emotion as well as humour and irony. For example: *Ça m'a fait dresser les cheveux sur la tête!* (It made my hair stand on end!)

hyponym (*hyponyme*)

See **superordinates** and **generals**.

hypotaxis (*hypotaxe*)

See **parataxis**.

intertextuality (*intertextualité*)

The term intertextuality is used in this book to refer to the fact that a text does not exist as a self-sufficient whole but is the result of influences from other past or contemporary texts. These influences can remain implicit, and therefore dependent on the reader's discernment and knowledge, or they can be made explicit through the use of quotations or references.

irony (*ironie*)

Irony is a rhetorical device whereby language appears to mean the exact opposite of what the speaker intended to say. Ironical statements should not, therefore, be taken literally. An example would be the utterance 'How clever of him', about someone who has just committed a foolish act. Irony often serves as an oblique form of criticism. It frequently relies for its effect on cultural assumptions* and presuppositions.

knowledge of the world

See **cultural assumptions**.

lexical field (*champ lexical*)

A lexical field is formed by grouping together in a text words or phrases which pertain to the same topic. For instance, in a weather report, we might say that the words 'ice', 'snow', 'blizzard', etc., all relate to the lexical field of 'weather'.

The term 'semantic field' is frequently interchangeable with 'lexical field'. In this book, however, the term 'lexical field' is reserved for the analysis of verbal discourse, and that of 'semantic field' for the study of visual representation.

logical links (*liens logiques*)

See **connectors**.

metaphor (*métaphore*)

The term metaphor designates the procedure whereby a given sentential item is analogically substituted for another, without the presence of a term signalling the process explicitly. A substitute name or descriptive expression is transferred to some person or object to which it is not literally applicable. For instance, the term 'lamb' may be used to describe a child, or 'monster' to evoke the landscape of a city.

metonymy (*métonyme*)

Metonymy designates the procedure whereby a given lexical unit is substituted for another with which it entertains a relationship of contiguity, e.g. cause for effect, container for contained, part for whole, concrete for abstract. Examples are *les planches* for *la scène,* or *du Mozart* for *des œuvres de Mozart.*

mise en abyme

A *mise en abyme* is a structural device whereby part of a text can be seen as mirroring the whole in terms of form and/or content. For example, in Alain Robbe-Grillet's *La Jalousie,* the African novel read by the characters can be read as a *mise en abyme* as far as it mirrors the situation in which the characters find themselves.

modality (*modalité*)

Modality concerns speakers' attitudes towards their utterances (expressing various degrees of possibility, certainty, obligation, necessity, etc.). Modality is thus mainly expressed with the so-called modal verbs (*pouvoir, vouloir, devoir*), but also adverbs such as *peut-être* or *certainement* (called modalizing terms) and verbs moods (indicative, subjunctive, imperative, conditional).

According to Halliday, sentence types include the following modalities: declarative (for statements), interrogative (for questions), exclamative (for exclamations about one's feelings), and imperative (for commands and requests).

models of argumentation (*modèles d'argumentation*)

See **argumentative text.**

moods (*modes*)

Moods affect the verb. In French, there are three impersonal moods (infinitive, participle and gerund) and four personal moods. Amongst the latter, the basic or unmarked mood is the indicative (to express 'facts'). The other personal moods are the subjunctive (to express hypothesis, uncertainty, desirability), the conditional (to express what might happen when certain conditions are fulfilled) and the imperative (to express orders or wishes and desires).

morphology (*morphologie*)

Morphology concerns the form, i.e. the internal composition of words (stems and affixes). For instance, the noun *nationalité* is made up of the adjectival stem *national* and the noun-forming suffix *-ité*, the verb *nationaliser* is made up of the adjectival stem *national* and the verb-forming suffix *-iser*, the adjective *intolérant* is made up of the adjective *tolérant* and the negating prefix *in-*, the verb form *manges* is made up of its stem *mang-* and a suffix, its conjugation ending *-es* (marking the second person singular in the present indicative).

narrator (*narrateur*)

The term narrator denotes the person in a written text or verbal communication to whom the enunciator (author or text producer) has delegated her/his voice. The narrator may be external to the story, using a third person to refer to the characters, or may be internal to the story, using the first person. The *je* in an utterance, therefore, is not identical with the enunciator but a verbal simulacrum of a narrative presence. For instance, the author Albert Camus is the enunciator of the novel *L'Etranger*. Camus delegates his voice to Meursault, who starts his account with the sentence *Aujourd'hui, maman est morte* and who awaits his execution at the end. Meursault is the narrator, the *je* in the story, constructed by the enunciator to take his place.

neologism (*néologisme*)

A neologism is literally a newly invented word, based on a range of morphological processes, such as compounding, affixation and even acronyms*. For instance, *un eurocrate* is a neologism made up of *euro-* (*Europe, européen*) and the suffix *-crate* from the Latin *cratia* ('power', 'rule') as in *démocrate, plutocrate*, etc. but more importantly as in *bureaucrate*. *Le sida* is a neologism based on an acronym (*syndrome immunodéficitaire acquis*).

noun phrase (*syntagme/groupe nominal*)

A noun phrase (also called noun group) is a structure which has a noun as head (main) word, with or without modifiers. For instance, *Paul, le garçon, le gentil garçon, le garçon que je connais bien* or *le garçon d'à côté* are all noun phrases.

object (*objet*)

See **subject**.

parataxis/hypotaxis (*parataxe/hypotaxe*)

Parataxis concerns the systematic linking of clauses with commas (juxtaposition), rather than conjunctions (subordination or coordination).

Hence the connection between clauses has to be inferred. It is more likely to appear in speech than in writing. For instance *J'avais froid, [alors] j'ai mis un tricot*. See also **asyndeton**.

Hypotaxis concerns the systematic linking of clauses with subordinating conjunctions. It is more likely to appear in writing than in speech, and particularly in argumentative texts.

phrase (*syntagme*)

Phrases are sequences of words that are part of a sentence. For instance, in the sentence *Le chat boit son lait dans la cuisine*, there are three phrases: a noun phrase (*le chat*), a verb phrase (*boit son lait*) and a preposiotional phrase (*dans la cuisine*). Note that the last two include themselves a noun phrase: *son lait* and *la cuisine*.

pragmatics (*pragmatique*)

Pragmatics concerns the way utterances should be interpreted, beyond the meanings of the words used (as defined in a dictionary for instance) and therefore involves looking at the context and particular situation of addresser and addressee. It can thus be loosely defined as the study of language **use**. For instance, in the sentence *Ça va être difficile mais on peut toujours essayer, toujours* should be understood in its pragmatic sense as signifying 'although the outcome is not guaranteed, it is probably worth trying'.

prepositional phrase (*syntagme/groupe prépositionnel*)

See **phrase**.

quotations (*citations*)

Quotation is primarily about citing (and attributing) the words of other people to highlight or confirm a particular viewpoint. However, some authors (particularly in the media) often use them to distanciate themselves from what was said by somebody else. Such a pragmatic interpretation of quotations involves cultural assumptions*. For instance:

> *Alors que l'opposition réclame à cor et à cri la publication des 261 noms de « traîtres à la nation » italiens figurant sur les listes du KGB, révélées par les archives de l'ex-agent Mitrokhine, le gouvernement italien a décidé, vendredi 8 octobre, que l'enquête sur cette affaire serait confiée à la justice et que ce serait « commettre un délit de violation du secret de l'instruction » que de révéler ces noms.*

(*Le Monde*, 10-11 October 1999)

Quotations normally appear in writing enclosed in quotation marks or inverted commas.

récit/discours
See *discours.*

reference (*référence*)
See **coreference.**

register (*registre*)
The term 'register' relates to the degree of formality appropriate to different social uses of language. Registers show the various ways of expressing oneself according to a particular situation (e.g. giving a lecture, talking to a friend, writing to a lawyer, etc.) and involve not only vocabulary (e.g. familiar, poetic) but also syntax (e.g. presence of dislocated constructions) and phonetics (e.g. presence of liaisons).

reiteration (*réitération*)
According to the Halliday/Hasan model, reiteration is one of the principal means of establishing lexical cohesion*. By reiteration is meant the restatement of an item in a later part of the discourse. Reiteration includes the following devices:
a) repetition*, i.e. the literal repetition of the same word or phrase
b) the use of synonymy*
c) the use of hyponyms, superordinates and generals*.

repetition (*répétition*)
According to Halliday and others, repetition constitutes an important device in the establishment of lexical cohesion*. By repetition is meant the repeating of the **same** key word or phrase.

rhetoric (*rhétorique*)
Rhetoric is the 'art of speech' as a means of persuasion; today it has become a central concern of stylistics and pragmatics.

Rhetorical questions do not expect an answer, as they either assert something which is already known to the addressee, or the speaker intends to answer the question him/herself, thus persuading the addressee by directly appealing to him/her. They are found mainly in expository or argumentative texts. For instance:

> *Le titre d'un ouvrage n'est jamais tout à fait neutre. Alors ai-je eu raison d'intituler ce volume: « L'Identité de la France »? Le mot m'a*

séduit, mais n'a cessé, des années durant, de me tourmenter.
(Braudel, *L'Identité de la France*)

semantic field (*champ sémantique*)

See **lexical field**.

semantics (*sémantique*)

Semantics is the study of the linguistic **meaning** of words and sentences. Note that the frontiers between semantics and pragmatics* are often blurred.

See also **semiotics** and **pragmatics**.

semiology (*sémiologie*)

See **semiotics**.

semiotics (*sémiotique*)

Semiotics is the theory of signification, that is, of the generation or production of meaning. In contrast to semiology, which studies sign systems and their organization (e.g. traffic codes, sign language), semiotics concerns itself with **how** meaning is produced. In other words, what interests the semiotician is what makes an entity (verbal, visual, aural, etc.) meaningful, how it signifies, and what precedes it on a deeper level to result in the manifestation of meaning.

sentence (*phrase*)

A **simple sentence** (*phrase simple*), like a clause, consists of a noun phrase (the subject) and a verb phrase (the predicate).

A **complex sentence** (*phrase complexe*) comprises two or more clauses, linked together by a conjunction of coordination (e.g. *Il pleut et il fait froid*) or by a conjunction of subordination. In the latter case, the clause introduced by the conjunction of subordination is called the subordinate clause, and is dependent on the main clause (e.g. *Je sortirai quand j'aurai fini mon travail*).

See also **phrase, clause, text, utterance**.

simile (*comparaison*)

A simile is an explicit comparison between two different items that share a common quality. It is most frequently introduced by 'like' or 'as ... as' (*comme* or *aussi ... que*). Phrases such as 'as if', 'resembling', 'suggesting', that introduce descriptions, are termed quasi-similes (Leech and Short, 1981).

See also **metaphor**.

subject and object (*sujet et objet*)

In semiotic metalanguage, the **subject** denotes a narrative function (or actant). In a narrative, the position of the subject may be held by any actor (character) who performs an action. The subject is always defined in relationship to the **object** of value that is being pursued. Indeed, the quest of a subject for an object is seen as the fundamental structure of all human action and of meaning itself.

In syntax, the **subject** is an essential element of the sentence. It is normally a noun phrase or equivalent, including 'impersonal' subjects such as *il* in *il pleut*. Hence the grammatical subject is what the main conjugated verb agrees with, in number and in person (e.g. ***Deux personnes sont arrivées*** but ***Il est arrivé*** *deux personnes*). The **object** is a noun phrase (or equivalent). It is part of the verb group and normally comes after the verb. It can be 'direct' (e.g. *Je lis **le journal*** or 'indirect', i.e. introduced by a preposition (e.g. *Je vais téléphoner **à Paul***).

superordinates, hyponyms and generals

Textual cohesion can be established through the use of superordinates and hyponyms. A superordinate is a term expressing a whole, denoting a class. The part is expressed by a hyponym, a more specific term. For instance, 'Brazil', 'Spain', 'England', etc. are hyponyms of the superordinate 'country'. Similarly, the superordinate 'animal' can have as its hyponyms 'dog', 'elephant', 'cat', etc. Generals are a little vaguer than superordinates and are expressed in words such as 'thing', 'place' or 'stuff'.

synonym (*synonyme*)

A synonym is:

a) a word that has the same dictionary meaning, or is similar in meaning to another word

b) a word which, in the specific context in which it appears, has a similar or related meaning to another one and refers to the same 'object of the world'.

The use of synonymy is a means of establishing lexical cohesion: in the Halliday/Hasan model, it would come under the general heading of reiteration*.

syntax (*syntaxe*)

Syntax concerns the **structure** of sentences, i.e. the way words, phrases and clauses are ordered and put together. For instance, *Regarde la voiture j'ai achetée* violates the syntactic rule whereby in French (unlike in English), relative object pronouns cannot be omitted (——▶*Regarde la voiture **que** j'ai achetée*).

Syntax also contributes to the **meaning** of sentences. For instance, a sentence such as *Le chat a avalé la planche à pain* is not easily understood (interpreted) because the syntactic rule whereby a verb such as *avaler* requires an object which is 'edible' has been violated.

textual coherence (*cohérence textuelle*)
See **coherence**.

textual cohesion (*cohésion textuelle*)
See **cohesion**.

textual schemata (*schémas textuels*)
See:
    actantial narrative schema
    canonical narrative schema
    argumentative text.

theme (*thème*)
See **focus**.

truncated words (*mots tronqués*)
See **apocope**, **aphesis**.

underlying models (*modèles sous-jacents*)
See **textual schemata**.

utterance (*énoncé*)
Whereas a sentence can be defined syntactically (as having a subject and a verb for instance), an utterance is 'language in use' and thus may include segments which cannot be considered as sentences, but which can still make sense and be interpretable by the addressee. For instance, *Mais ce mec, c'est qu'il commence à me... hum!* or *Tant pis* are utterances, not sentences.

verb phrase (*syntagme/groupe verbal*)
In grammar, the verb phrase, or predicate, complements the noun phrase, or subject, to make a sentence, and includes objects and other complements of the verb. For instance, in *Le chat boit son lait*, *Le chat* is the noun phrase subject and *boit son lait* is the verb phrase.

voice (*voix*)

In grammar, 'voice' (like e.g. aspect or mood) affects the verb. There are two main voices in French: active and passive (e.g. active: *Le chat mange la souris*; passive: *La souris est mangée par le chat*).

In stylistics, 'voice' refers to the voice of the narrator, which can exist explicitly in a text or be prominent throughout in first-person narratives such as autobiographical texts. The voice of the narrator can also remain implicit and only be detectable in the narrator's implied judgement or opinion. In Flaubert's *Madame Bovary*, for instance, the use of the *nous* in the opening of the novel: *Nous étions à l'étude, quand le proviseur entra*... occasionally gives way to a more implicit narrating voice, detectable in the use of descriptive details, images or ironic tone. For instance:

> *A la classe de musique, dans les romances qu'elle chantait, il n'était question que de petits anges aux ailes d'or, de madones, de lagunes, de gondoliers, pacifiques compositions qui lui laissaient entrevoir, à travers la niaiserie du style et les imprudences de la note, l'attirante fantasmagorie des réalités sentimantales.*

In the above passage, for example, the stress on the kitsch aspect of the accumulative terms (*petits anges... madones... lagunes... gondoliers*), added to the judgemental reference to *la niaiserie du style*, reveals the implicit voice of the narrator.

CONCISE BIBLIOGRAPHY

Abbadie, Christian, *et al, L'expression française écrite et orale*, Presses Universitaires de Grenoble, 1994

Arrivé, Michel, *et al, La grammaire d'aujourd'hui*, Flammarion, 1986

Boissinot, Alain, *Les textes argumentatifs*, Bertrand-Lacoste, CRPD de Toulouse, 1994

Djian, Henri, and Rousseau, Jean-François, *Le texte argumentatif*, Hachette Livre, 1995

Eluerd, Roland, *Langue et littérature – grammaire, communication, techniques littéraires*, Nathan, 1992

Fairclough, Norman, *Language and Power*, Longman, 1989

Fairclough, Norman, *Critical Discourse Analysis*, Longman, 1995

Genette, *Figures III*, Seuil, 1972

Georgakopoulou, Alexandra, and Goutsos, Dionysis, *Discourse Analysis: an Introduction*, Edinburgh University Press, 1997

Halliday, M.A.K., and Hasan, Ruqaiya, *Cohesion in English*, Longman 1976

Jeandillou, Jean-François, *L'analyse textuelle*, Armand Colin, 1997

L'Huillier, Monique, *Advanced French Grammar*, Cambridge University Press, 1999

Maingueneau, Dominique, *Eléments de linguistique pour le texte littéraire*, Dunod, 1993

Maingueneau, Dominique, *L'énonciation en linguistique française*, Hachette Supérieur, 1994

Martin, Bronwen, *Semiotics and Storytelling*, Philomel,1997

Martin, Bronwen, and Ringham, Felizitas, *Dictionary of Semiotics*, Cassell, 2000

Nunan, David, *Introducing Discourse Analysis*, Penguin, 1993

Perret, Michèle, *L'énonciation en grammaire du texte*, Nathan Université, 1994

Salkie, Raphael, *Text and Discourse Analysis*, Routledge, 1995

Wales, Katie, *A Dictionary of Stylistics*, Longman, 1994

Typesetting by **Mark Files**
9 Sussex Mews, Tunbridge Wells
Kent TN2 5QJ, England
Tel: ++44 (0) 1892 54 89 89   Fax: ++44 (0) 1892 61 88 51
e-mail: el-parido@lineone.net

printed and bound by **EUROPRINT: Ath. E. Petroulakis S.A.**
3km Koropi – Vari Av. 19400, Athens, Greece
Tel: ++30 1 602 22 42-5/602 00 11   Fax: ++30 1 662 39 57
e-mail: info@europrint.gr

for **Philomel Productions Ltd**, Dublin, Republic of Ireland
Contact address: 1 Queen's Gate Place Mews
                London SW7 5BG, England, UK
                Tel: ++44 (0) 20 7581 2303
                Fax: ++44 (0) 20 7589 2264
                e-mail: markphilomel@productnews.co.uk

Book cover design: Paul S. Vlachos
Book design: Sophia Kakkavas

ISBN 1 898685 39 8
2000